Praise for *Surviving the United Nations*

Robert Adolph is the real deal, a Special Forces officer, United Nations security expert, and scholar in the most dangerous countries of the world. His life mattered in a way that those of the famous often don't.

—*Robert Kaplan,* New York Times *multiple best-selling author*

No rose-colored glasses here. Bob Adolph lays bare his unique experiences in pursuit of idealistic humanitarian purposes while in some of the toughest places on the planet. Sometimes his most dangerous opponents were in the very organization of which he was a part. To paraphrase from the book, *Lonesome Dove,* "he survived because he dealt with things as he found them...not as he wished they would be."

—*Peter J. Schoomaker, General, US Army (retired), former Chief of Staff of the US Army*

Bob Adolph has written a dramatic and engaging record of his early years of service with the UN. His recollections of difficult and dangerous assignments in Sierra Leone, Yemen, and Iraq are vividly portrayed. In fact, he nearly paid with his life while trying to convince senior UN management that their security precautions in Baghdad in 2003 were woefully inadequate. These are wrenching yet illuminating examples of working inside the UN system. The devastating suicide bombing attack in Baghdad—killing 22 and wounding over 150—is painfully yet accurately described and places both

the author and his often-startling book in categories by themselves. The very well written concluding chapters are a testament to Bob's refusal to quit until the fight is done.
—*Gregory Starr, former Director of the US State Department's Bureau of Diplomatic Security, Assistant Secretary of State, and UN Under-Secretary General of the Department of Safety and Security*

Colonel Bob Adolph is the epitome of the Special Forces officer: infinitely competent, completely unflappable, and absolutely loyal. For well over two decades he served in the US Army's Special Operations and Military Intelligence communities. Following his retirement from the active military he chose yet another service organization, the United Nations. There he made an indelible mark in several of the globe's most dangerous regions. He evacuated Freetown in Sierra Leone just ahead of invading Revolutionary United Front guerillas; later he consulted successfully on tribal kidnappings in Yemen; still later, he led the UN's security establishment in Iraq at the time of a devastating jihadist suicide bombing attack. His memoir often reads like a cracking good adventure novel. But this is no work of fiction—it is, instead, history.
—*Ben Lawton, Associate Professor, College of Liberal Arts, Purdue University, and co-editor of the book* Revisioning Terrorism: A Humanistic Approach

Bob Adolph served as a military officer with solid training and experience in Special Operations, leading to his designation as one of Robert Kaplan's *"Imperial Grunts"* in Yemen. Extensive academic pursuits round out his intellectual credentials. His UN-Iraq experience, where I first knew him, thrust Bob both under the gun and into the spotlight because of a massive suicide bombing. His actions that day saved many lives, perhaps even my own. He later performed UN Security Advisor duties in Cairo, where I benefited greatly from his guidance. He went on to serve as the UN Chief of the Middle

East and North Africa in New York, where he focused heavily on the Libya crisis. His extraordinarily insightful book is unusually sensitive, brutally candid, and a must-read for anyone striving to understand the United Nations.
—*Paul Johnson, former UN security officer and survivor of the 19 August 2003 Baghdad suicide bombing attack on the Canal Hotel*

In this engrossing tale, Bob Adolph has provided us with a remarkable account of his service with the UN as a senior security advisor in some of the most challenging and dangerous countries in the world. I came to appreciate his resourcefulness, dedication, and decency while heading up the development and humanitarian work of the UN in Yemen. I also witnessed his courageous actions, which saved lives and were crucial to facilitating our mission. Later, following the tragic attack on our premises in Baghdad, he summoned up a different kind of courage by speaking truth to power, taking on a Kafkaesque bureaucracy that sought a scapegoat for reasons of political expediency and to cover up the serious shortcomings of senior UN officials. A larger than life figure, Bob's professionalism, integrity, and commitment to the values and principles of the UN are on display throughout this noteworthy book.
—*James W. Rawley, former UN Assistant Secretary-General*

This is a noteworthy and very personal story of what happened well before, during and after the August 19, 2003 attack on the UN Headquarters in Baghdad, the Canal Hotel. The actual tale is known only to a few, and there is nobody still alive better suited to tell it than Bob Adolph. He provided immediate leadership in the rubble, saving lives and restoring some semblance of order amidst the chaos and confusion in the wake of the suicide bombing that devastated the UN globally. Bob expertly details a critically important chapter in the larger history of the War of Terror via his narrative. A riveting book, Bob's tenacity, vulnerability, and integrity are at turns heartbreaking and inspiring.

—*Christopher Ankersen, Clinical Associate Professor, New York University Center for Global Affairs and editor of the book* Understanding Global Terror

For many years Bob Adolph has been a trusted colleague and friend. As someone who knows him, allow me to inform his readers that he will not surrender until the truth prevails. During the tragic Baghdad bombings, I was his Chief of Desk at UN Headquarters in New York. Bob's reflections of events before, during, and after these attacks are accurate. He regularly communicated warnings to his superiors in both Iraq and New York concerning UN staff vulnerability in Baghdad. Those warnings were ignored. The facts that are finally unveiled in his book are wholly the result of his character: a never-quit nature, professionalism, and ethical standards of conduct. This tragic yet fascinating record of actual events represents his heartfelt attempt to expose the truth to anyone with the eyes to see it. Every UN staff member should read this book.

—*Annette Leijenaar, Head of Peace Operations and Peacebuilding, Institute for Security Studies, Pretoria Office, South Africa*

Finally, a book that captures the devastating effects of the massive jihadist vehicular suicide bomb attack on the UN Headquarters in Baghdad on August 19, 2003. Chief Security Advisor Bob Adolph skillfully details the gripping story behind outrageous institutional failures to exercise its duty of care to protect staff members. As part of the Security Cell in Baghdad leading up to the devastation that left 22 people dead and many more horrifically injured, I witnessed Bob's daily gargantuan struggle to convince management that there was a credible threat to the UN in Baghdad. Expert security advice based on detailed risk assessments were consistently ignored leading to the single worst preventable tragedy in UN history. Just over a month later we faced another attack that finally drove the us out of Iraq. A must read for all who want an insider view of what transpired during the organization's darkest days and a good man fighting to do the right thing. Powerfully argued, full of critically important observations and insights, the author takes you through a tumultuous, and at times painful early career stretching from West Africa to the Middle East and more.

—*Andries Dreyer, former UNICEF Regional Security Officer for the Middle East and North Africa and current Global Director of Security Training for World Vision International*

As a result of years of practical experience in global conflict and defense, Robert Adolph expertly unravels the complexities of the idealistic intentions of the United Nations as well as the dialectical tensions resulting from attempts at their implementation. Through artful narrative, Robert transports readers through the nuances of deep-seated historical conflicts between actors across multiple national boundaries, legal and political systems, linguistic challenges, and vastly differing cultural and organizational assumptions. Readers, both highly informed and desiring to be so, will benefit from the firsthand lessons sorely won through decades of service while grappling with the multi-faceted organization that is the United Nations. Robert's book serves to make deeper meaning of the many conflicts in which the organization is involved and its attempts to fulfill its mission and keep peace. Any academic interested in gaining greater knowledge of how United Nations' field missions in humanitarian, development, political, and peacekeeping operations are actually accomplished will gain significant insight.

—*Elena Tartaglione Steiner, PhD, Center for Strategic Communication, Arizona State University and Steinbeis, Hochschule, Berlin*

Lieutenant Colonel Bob Adolph's unforgettable and brutally frank history provides graphic meaning to the unattributed quote, "You are either at the table or on the menu."
—*William Garrison, Major General, US Army (retired), former Commanding General of the Joint Special Operations Command and the US Army John F. Kennedy Special Warfare Center and School*

A superb, painfully honest and moving account of a life lived amid the great and lesser crises of our time, this book captures not only stunning violence and grim tragedies on multiple continents, but also does a great service by demonstrating what happens when on-the-ground urgency collides with aid bureaucracies. Bob Adolph's first-hand account of UN operations is alternately inspiring, enlightening, and infuriating (the latter when a failed hierarchy grasps about for a scapegoat in Iraq). A former special-operations soldier and globally recognized security expert, the author has given us the best-by-far nuts-and-bolts account of organizations seeking to do good, only to end up mired in a bloodbath. In short, a vital book by a very good man.
—*Ralph Peters*, New York Times *best-selling author of* Beyond Terror and Endless War

In addition to his fascinating tours of duty in Sierra Leone and Yemen, former UN Chief Security Advisor Robert Adolph paints a compelling portrait of the stunning lack of United Nations security in Baghdad following the overthrow of Saddam Hussein. He makes a convincing case that high officials at the UN failed to act on voluminous pressing warnings regarding their vulnerability. The net result, which he portrays in riveting highly personal detail, is the devastating after-effects of a massive jihadist vehicular suicide bombing attack that all but destroyed their headquarters in Baghdad on August 19, 2003.

The attack killed twenty-two and wounded multiples more. This horrendous bombing—and another over a month later—ultimately compelled the UN to withdraw from Iraq. This book is highly recommended for readability, pacing, and detailed narrative description.

—*L. Paul Bremer III, US Ambassador and former Administrator of the Coalition Provisional Authority for Iraq*

I was fortunate to serve on active duty with Lieutenant Colonel Bob Adolph in Special Forces. He is an outstanding US public and international civil servant who dedicated his life first to country and then to humanity on a truly global scale. I was enormously impressed with his candor and detailed descriptions of events that changed the world. An excellent rendition of true stories that the public only rarely sees about how real history is made.

—*Joe E. Kilgore, Colonel, US Army, Special Forces (retired) (PhD)*

A riveting account of the challenges and perils faced by UN personnel all over the globe, where humanitarian and development work are all too often enmeshed in Great Game power-plays and bureaucratic turf battles. Chief Bob Adolph shines a very human light on stories that too often remain in the shadows.

—*Diarmuid O'Donovan, Director of Emergency Measures, Government of Yukon, Canada*

This book is compulsory reading for anyone thinking of serving in, currently serving, or has served in multinational organizations with overseas missions and field offices. The combination of Bob's unique personal snapshots in time in some of the most challenging security locations in the world culminating in his tragic account of the Baghdad bombing of the

Canal Hotel, highlights a UN system where accountability is as nebulous, elusive, and fickle as the peace that it is chartered to achieve. Surviving the United Nations makes for a truly compelling and thought-provoking read.

—*Christian Shorter, former Head of Global Security, World Bank Group*

Bob Adolph was one of the few people I met in Baghdad in the spring of 2003 that unquestionably knew what he was doing. As security chief for the UN mission based out of the Canal Hotel, he adroitly juggled the difficult task of maintaining the UN's autonomy while working with coalition forces and Iraqis. It was my privilege to work with Bob during this period. His performance, along with that of the staff from the World Food Program, was enough to restore your faith in the UN. The suicide bombing attack on the UN Headquarters in Baghdad came on the heels of his multiple warnings to senior UN managers in both Iraq and New York. What followed was the scapegoating of the one man who had "actually" done his best to prevent the attack. Lesser men would have quit, but Bob went on to serve in yet other conflict zones, always doing things right and making it happen. His chronicle is a tale of a remarkable American whose efforts in numerous failed states have made the world a better place.

—*Martin N. Stanton, Colonel, US Army (retired), author of* Somalia on 5$ a Day *and* Road to Baghdad

Chief Security Advisor Bob Adolph provides truly remarkable insights into hazardous UN operations in West Africa and Yemen, as well as the tragic event in Iraq that shocked the entire UN community worldwide in 2003. He possesses a unique and valuable perspective that highlights the good-the bad-and the ugly. Bob provides the reader with blow-by-blow accounts of gunfights, terrorist bombings, kidnappings, emergency evacuations, and so much more. His narrative is a

gripping read and serves as a true testament to the men and women serving in some of the world's most dangerous UN duty stations.
—*Mick Lorentzen, former Director of Regional Operations, UN Department of Safety and Security*

UN Chief Security Advisor Bob Adolph writes with a sense of both honesty and integrity, two of the commonly found characteristics of former soldiers who know the true meaning of humility and professionalism. Having worked with Bob, I know some of what he has scribed first-hand. After reading Surviving the United Nations, I was left with the feeling that he will help some people find a sense of closure, while providing others with a voice. For me, the book illuminates some of the reasons why I became disillusioned with the organization for what it was, as opposed to what I had always hoped it would be. For that alone, I commend him for his painstaking hours of reliving some extraordinarily emotionally charged episodes in his life. Above all, everything that he has written is true! This is something that is sadly lacking in this age of "hero tells all" tales. I only hope this has been a cathartic journey for Bob, as a lesser man would have been broken by some of the disingenuous UN decision makers he so well and loyally served. This book is a "must read" for anyone currently serving or considering a career in international service, humanitarian aid pursuits, or commercial security. The lessons learned on display are invaluable.
—*Richard C. Mitchelson, Executive Chairman, AKE International Ltd.*

On the afternoon of August 19, 2003, a suicide bomber destroyed the UN Headquarters in Baghdad killing twenty-two and wounding over one hundred fifty staff members and visitors. Not only was the office in ruins, but also the UN effort to demonstrate to the world that it could be an effective player in post-war Iraq. The searing events of that day, and the institutional failure of the organization to exercise its duty of care to protect its employees, are ably told by Bob Adolph, who was the UN Security Chief in Baghdad when the attack took place. In describing his service prior to the attack, Bob provides a fascinating account of his experience in Sierra Leone and Yemen, where he demonstrated the bravery and ability which led to his Iraq assignment. This gripping account of Bob's unjust scapegoating and subsequent battle is inspiring proof that one person can make his voice heard, even within a vast organization.

—*Richard Manlove, former UN Principal Security Advisor for Iraq*

Lieutenant Colonel (retired) Bob Adolph is a friend and brother. I knew him when we both served as active duty US Army Special Forces officers. Bob chose a "non-standard" path to say the least. He retired from the Army and began working as a Chief Security Officer for the United Nations. His excellent book details his early years in Sierra Leone and Yemen, and this portion is riveting reading. It also provides the needed background to understand the key section of the book, which examines in detail the UN debacle in Iraq. Bob took on the Herculean task of trying to convince the international mission in Baghdad to develop adequate security. He was unable to do it, and 22 people died, with another 150 plus humanitarian personnel wounded. This is not an effort to show that others were responsible (they were frankly), but a heartfelt attempt to look at a key incident in the tragedy that was Iraq in 2003–2004, in order to make sense of it. He never gave up doing his job. He fought as a soldier, and he struggled in a different way to protect the lives under his care. It is a sad reminder that regardless of one's best efforts; sometimes the bureaucracy "wins." The fact that he continued to serve in other conflict zones in valuable ways is hugely instructive to most civilians (including many in powerful government positions) that sol-

diers come in many "flavors." Bob is a warrior, who truly spent his life protecting those who needed his strong arm. A great read, and a book worthy of a spot on every bookshelf.
—*Steven P. Bucci, Colonel, US Army, Special Forces (retired) (PhD), former Military Assistant to the Secretary of Defense and Deputy Assistant Secretary of Defense*

The monstrous terrorist suicide attack on the UN office in Baghdad in August of 2003 was both a tragic and traumatic event for the world's best-known international organization. Former Chief Security Advisor Bob Adolph is perhaps the only person who could tell this tale in all its gritty and bloody detail. By beginning with detailed descriptions of his earlier UN assignments in both Africa and Yemen, he introduces the reader to the personal and professional challenges of UN service in support of peacekeeping and aid agencies. The narrative of 4 extraordinarily perilous years demands the reader's attention. The security lessons learned are numerous and clearly identified as you leaf through the fast-paced action. The book unintentionally serves to highlight that UN personnel continuously operate in hazardous security environments around the globe. The training value for any agency's security professionals operating in potentially life-threatening environments, and their senior supervisors, is immeasurable! More particularly, officials at all levels of the UN security management system should read this chronicle and then ask themselves: "Is my team prepared to respond if a catastrophic event occurs at my location?" This is a superb book written by a man that intimately knows his subject—because he lived it.
—*Gerald Ganz, former Head of Training and Director of Field Support, UN Department of Safety and Security*

Lieutenant Colonel Bob Adolph's unvarnished first-hand account of his service as a UN Security Advisor is a must-read for security professionals. Serving in many austere, remote environments, this former special operator's observations are not only exciting reading, but also of great value to security trainers, senior managers of international organizations, national governments, humanitarian agencies, or commercial enterprises with employees and operations overseas. Bob's accounts strip away the Hollywood glamor of this work and tell a story as only someone who has lived it can. This is an essential book for anyone who wants to see the world as it really is or that might have to work in one of these high-risk environments. Having had the privilege of serving with Bob during his time in the US Army, I know that the words of this consummate professional will ring true to those that have served in far-off lands and give those that have not a true glimpse of what that world is about.

—*Francisco Pedrozo, Colonel, US Army, Special Forces (retired) and Senior Vice President for Operations, The Ackerman Group, International Security Consultants*

This is a story that has everything that you expect in an action thriller: a page-turner that is impossible to put down. Adventure, heroism, fear, brutality, intrigue, violence, love, and betrayal. However, this tale of deeds and misfortunes are actual events that Ltc Bob Adolph experienced during his lengthy tenure as one of the United Nation's top security officers. Unlike some, he managed to survive to provide this harrowing account regarding several of the darker corners of our world. Those who have been there will be able to relate, and those who have not will pray they never have it happen to them. This book could easily become a standard reference in the libraries of international affairs scholars, UN staff, forward deployed diplomats, soldiers and special operators, humanitarian INGOs, peacekeepers, and international security specialists--essentially, many of those who regularly operate in dangerously amorphous zones of crisis around our planet.

—*Terry P. Cook, Colonel, US Army, Special Forces (retired)*

Iraq in 2003 was a boiling cauldron—this was not the peace that many had hoped for and declared, but rather a nation heading toward an insurgency and an opportunity for multiple actors to pursue their own agendas. This book is mandatory reading to understand the nature of the United Nations, its capabilities, constraints, and political nature. Bob writes from a perch that few can understand or comprehend. It's a story of great potential and significant limitations—of what could have been and what was. He vividly illustrates the nature of power and influence and how the two can bring about good—or trample innocents in order to achieve objectives that conflict with perceived lofty ideals. It is also a reminder that our U.S. justice system, as imperfect as it may seem, often exceeds that of other nations, organizations, and non-state actors.

—*Barbara G. Fast, Major General, US Army (retired)*

I first met Lieutenant Colonel Robert Adolph, known to all as Bob, when I reached Sierra Leone in December 1999, as the first Force Commander of the UN Mission called UNAMSIL. I was immediately struck by his enthusiasm, infectious personality, professional competence, and desire to enter the dangerous interior of strife torn Sierra Leone, where the rule of law had not yet been established, and where the brutal rebels of the Revolutionary United Front (RUF) ruled the roost. To say that such an endeavour was fraught with danger would be an understatement, for the mercurial rebels, mostly under the influence of drugs, could commit the most heinous crimes without compunction. However, this did not deter Bob because his own personal safety was the least of his concerns. He was more interested at getting an accurate intelligence picture of what was happening in the field to enable the Mission to be forewarned. And, being a highly trained Special Forces officer with a penchant for intelligence operations, he succeeded admirably in this task. He was tactful yet firm with the rebels and succeeded in gaining their confidence while simultaneously gathering valuable intelligence. As the Force Commander of this hazardous mission, I could not have asked for better support from anyone. Bob has an eye for detail, which is visible from his vivid and extremely accurate description of his experiences in Sierra Leone. His racy writing style makes the book a highly compelling read. I strongly recommend this book be read by all those who have anything to do with UN Peacekeeping.

—*V. K. Jetley, Lieutenant General, PVSM, UYSM, Indian Army (Retired), First Force Commander of UNAMSIL in Sierra Leone, West Africa*

UN Chief Security Advisor Bob Adolph is a warrior, and one of our most gifted and essential citizens. He endeavored all throughout his UN career to improve safety and security measures for staff in the field. He sometimes clashed with colleagues, and most importantly, he often fought with self-interested superiors. Bob's book is in many ways a chronicle of those skirmishes. Some he won. Some he lost. When he lost in Baghdad, people died. His struggles within the UN are a testament to his personal code of conduct. There are UN civil staff alive today because of his successful battles against an often opaque and amorphous bureaucracy. His book helps clear away denials and common delusions - providing essential historical facts to inform and inspire. In a world made up of nations, there is no more powerful way to fight the forces of prejudice, intolerance, and injustice than by dedication to equality, citizenship, and equal rights. Bob is an exemplary UN staff member and leader. "Bob's Laws" available in the book's Appendix, are a true gem and an unusual self-improvement guide. This is a book inspired by Bob's own life: courageous and beautifully written. Every UN staff member should read this book. Every person should read this book.

—*Samar Issa, PhD, Assistant Professor, Saint Peter's University*

Surviving the United Nations

Surviving the United Nations

The Unexpected Challenge

by Robert Bruce Adolph

Lieutenant Colonel, US Army, Special Forces (retired)
& Chief Security Advisor, United Nations (retired)

With a Foreword by *NYT* Best-selling Author
Ralph Peters

NEW ACADEMIA PUBLISHING

VELLUM

Washington, DC

Library of Congress Control Number: 2019953723
ISBN 978-17333980-0-8 paperback (alk. paper)
ISBN 978-17333980-4-6 hardcover (alk. paper)

 An imprint of New Academia Publishing

 New Academia Publishing, 4401-A Connecticut Ave. NW, #236,
Washington, DC 20008
info@newacademia.com - www.newacademia.com

For Naima

IN MEMORIAM

The Dead

The twenty-two innocent people murdered by a jihadist suicide bomber at the UN Headquarters in Baghdad—the Canal Hotel—on 19 August 2003:

Sergio Viera de Mello, Nadia Younes, Fiona Watson,
Jean-Salim Kanaan, Richard Hooper, Manuel Martin-Oar,
Christopher Klein-Beekman, Reham Al-Farra, Martha Teas,
Leen Assad Al-Qadi, Ranillo Buenaventura, Reza Hosseini,
Ihsan Taha Husein, Basim Mahmoud Utaiwi,
Raid Shaker Mustafa Al-Mahdawi, Gillian Clark, Arthur
Helton, Alya Ahmad Souza, Khidir Saleem Sahir, Saad Her-
mis Abona, Omar Kahtan Mohamed Al-Orfali, and
Emaad Ahmed Salman Al-Jobody

and

Richard Manlove
Our Friend – Mentor – and Colleague

Table of Contents

List of Illustrations

Foreword

A Necessary Book

Our forebears from the Middle Ages may not have imagined our "magic" technologies, but neither could they have foreseen our miraculous and wasteful abundance of books. The book has declined from an item to be cherished to a toss-away even libraries scorn and discard. Despite the advent of the Internet, more books are published each year than ever before. A few are good, most are not, and many of them are dreadful. We are lured to buy (but not necessarily to read) the latest screeds by outraged "patriots" or memoirs of the semi-famous ghost-written for them by the semi-literate. There are books on every subject, but few that change our minds, let alone our lives. Nonetheless, the two most familiar words in the realm of book reviews are "must read."

No, we mustn't. Few books are truly worth our time. Even fewer are necessary. Bob Adolph's book regarding his early years as a senior United Nations security chief is an exception. It is, in truth, a necessary book.

We need this book because the UN is much discussed, but little understood. It may be the world's most contradictory major organization. The UN is sometimes shamelessly corrupt and yet noble in its purpose. The corrupted serve beside others who are great-hearted and self-sacrificing, committed to improving the human condition. Well-placed bureaucrats hire luxurious villas and dine splendidly, while UN aid workers live in tents amid epidemics, famines, and lawless wars. The UN wastes fortunes and saves countless lives. It provides a platform for dictators and serves the cause of freedom. It blusters, betrays, and protects.

The UN is sometimes appalling, but always essential.

Following a twenty-five-year enlisted and officer career in the US Army's Special Forces and Military Intelligence communities (where I first brushed up against him), Bob was hand-picked by the UN to serve as security chief at a succession of missions in war zones and failed states. He knows the UN at its best and worst.

Those who have been fortunate to encounter Bob think first of his raw energy and exuberance. Then they recall his courage and curiosity, his quick mind and relentless generosity, his skill and judgment, and not least, his decency. He's a very good man who served in some very bad places, in uniform and in a plain khaki shirt. And he had to write this book. The ghosts rise from its pages.

Books often tell us more about their authors than the authors meant to reveal. In this case, you learn that Bob is in thrall to fairness. In these pages, he portrays the UN in all its complexity, a mash-up of pluses and minuses that ultimately benefits humankind.

Beyond that, there is the remarkable drama of a life well-lived — and well-described.

Ralph Peters, *New York Times* best-selling author of *Beyond Terror* and *Endless War*

Author's Note

UN Security Advisors identify man-made and natural threats, assess both vulnerability and risks, and offer recommendations to UN leadership on how to best mitigate the dangers to staff members in often life-threatening mission areas. Their ultimate objective is the preservation of those staff members' lives so that they, in turn, can do their jobs—feed the hungry, house the homeless, protect women and children, facilitate peace where there has been none, eradicate disease, and so much more. These are worthwhile and noble endeavors.

US Army Special Forces soldiers (Green Berets) are traditionally trained to operate far behind enemy lines in austere environments with limited support and while working closely with indigenous peoples. With the advent of both the Iraq and Afghan Wars, their missions began to lean hard toward the more kinetic variety. Special Forces' physically and mentally demanding schooling includes survival skills, hand-to-hand combat and close-quarters battle, languages, cross-cultural communications, methods of instruction, light and heavy weapons, communications, medicine, engineering (explosives), operations & intelligence, and much more. Green Berets are considered some of the best-trained and finest-educated soldiers on the planet. They are known globally as the "quiet professionals."

Preface

The United States of America in large measure created the UN. But in fact, the UN is not one but several different agencies, funds, and programs—many of which are independently funded, so little surprise, they often act independently. The humanitarian agencies are perhaps best represented by the World Food Program, UN Children's Fund, and UN High Commissioner for Refugees.

The UN also includes several specialized agencies like The United Nations Educational, Scientific and Cultural Organization, Universal Postal Union, International Civil Aviation Organization, World Bank, International Monetary Fund, World Meteorological Organization, World Intellectual Property Organization, International Atomic Energy Agency, World Trade Organization, International Labor Organization, and many more.

The most public face of the UN is the Secretary General, who presides over the UN Secretariat, which is predominantly located on the island of Manhattan in New York City. Within the Secretariat, the Secretary General enjoys great power, in my experience, perhaps too much. Major divisions within the Secretariat are the Departments of Peacekeeping and Politics, Offices for Disarmament and Drugs and Crime, as well as my old organization, Safety and Security. There are of course many more.

However, perhaps the real power within the UN is found in the ever-bickering Security Council, which is dominated by the "Big Five." These are the United States of America, France,

Great Britain, Russia, and China. There are ten other countries represented on a rotational basis that are elected by the General Assembly. The UN General Assembly is composed of all the nations of the world.

The UN is in many ways the culmination of an aspiration—that the nations of the world can attempt to live with one another in relative peace and harmony. Of course, such is a pipe dream. There is no peace and there is certainly no harmony. However, the aspiration lives on, and at least in my estimation, demands committed pursuit.

Former UN Secretary General, Dag Hammerskjold, was quoted as saying, "The UN was not created to take mankind to heaven, but to save humanity from hell." Based on the horrors of the 20th and early 21st Centuries, we still have a long hard road ahead. My point is that if our forebears had not created the UN, we would be compelled today to do so out of necessity. Despite its known faults, the UN is essential to humanity's pursuit of a better and hopefully more peaceful future, while at the same time caring for those who need it the most—the destitute and vulnerable.

If you read this story all the way through to the Epilogue and Afterword, you may find possible answers to several questions raised in the narrative concerning the UN, its staff, and leadership.

Key Acronyms and Abbreviations

CAO	Chief Administrative Officer
CASEVAC	Casualty Evacuation
CSO	Chief Security Officer
DMZ	Demilitarized Zone
DDR	Disarmament, Demobilization, and Reintegration
DO	Designated Official for Security
FAO	UN Food and Agriculture Organization
HC	Humanitarian Coordinator
HOM	Head of Mission
INGO	International Non-Government Organizations (humanitarians)
RR	Resident Representative
R&R	Rest and Recuperation Break
RUF	Revolutionary United Front
SA	Security Advisor
SG	Secretary General (UN)
SIOC	Security Information and Operations Center
SMT	Security Management Team
SLA	Sierra Leone Army
SRSG	Special Representative of the Secretary General
UK	United Kingdom (Great Britain)
UNAMSIL	UN Assistance Mission in Sierra Leone
UNDSS	UN Department of Safety and Security (replacing UNSECOORD)
UNDP	UN Development Program
UNICEF	UN Children's Fund
UNMO	UN Military Observer
UNOHCI	UN Office of the Humanitarian Coordinator in Iraq

UNSECOORD	UN Security Coordinator (or the officers working for him)
WHO	World Health Organization

In Appreciation

I wish first to express sincere gratitude to my long-deceased parents. We were a large poor family. It was a full-time job and more just to keep food on the table and a roof over our heads. Still, Mom and Dad somehow managed. Their untold sacrifices gave us kids a fighting chance for something better.

From my youth, I wish to thank childhood friend Steve Kastner in San Francisco, California, and later Jim Miller and George Minasian in Newburyport, Massachusetts. I also wish to thank Kenny Archie, my first real boss and the first person who ever expressed a belief in my ability to accomplish more than sweep floors, wash windows, and clean toilets. Although, I was reportedly very good at all three.

Regarding my enlisted and officer service in the US Army, I wish to express my personal thanks to Sergeant Major Miguel Ramirez, Sergeant Major Mike Vining, Master Sergeant "Fast" Eddie Fisler, Master Sergeant Phil Hanley, Major General Harley Davis, Colonel Ila Mettee-McCutchon, Colonel James "Nick" Rowe, Colonel Edward Doyle, Colonel Matt Parelli, Brigadier General Richard "Dick" Potter, Major General William "Bill" Garrison, Lieutenant General Sydney Weinstein, and former Chief of Staff of the US Army General Peter Schoomaker. These men—and one woman—at one time or another either assisted me personally or by their example, inspired me to attempt to be better than I am.

From my nearly fifteen-year civil career with the United Nations, I wish to express special gratitude to UN Under-Secretary General and former US Assistant Secretary of State Greg Starr, a great boss and good friend. I also wish to thank my superb multinational staff while I was serving as the Chief of the Middle East and North Africa at UN Headquarters in New York during the "Arab Awakening." None of us got much sleep through five country evacuations, the war in Iraq, NATO bombing of Libya, slowly building disaster in Syria, a kidnapping in Yemen and much more. These outstanding individuals include Leopoldo Avellenal, Valentine Aldea, Bud Collins, Diarmuid O'Donovan, Richard Arnold, Richard Manlove, and Doctor (PhD) Samar Issa, as well as the sixteen UN Security Advisors and Chief Security Advisors and their staffs, serving on tough duty in some of the world's most necessary and often-thankless jobs.

I also desire to say thanks to my local assistants—Aya in Sierra Leone; Jamal and Safa in Yemen; Mazzin and Fatin in Iraq; Elias in Ethiopia; Mahmoud, Ahmed, and Aya in Egypt; Ayman in Jordan; as well as my entire national staff, especially Heike, in Indonesia. The job would have been impossible without their loyal, kind, and generous support.

I must express special and deep appreciation to Colonel (retired) Terry Cook. He and I went through much together early in our military careers both personally and professionally. We made a point to stay in touch with one another over the decades, even when on opposite sides of the globe. Nobody could ask for a better or more loyal friend. His story concerning the early days of the American-Afghan War has never been told, and it should be. His fundamental on-the-ground contributions were the *sine qua non* of our initial stunning successes in that seemingly never-ending conflict.

Regarding my greater stable of old military comrades, thanks to Colonel and Doctor (PhD) Charles "Denny" Lane, Colonel John "Dago" Dagostino, Professor and Lieutenant Colonel Benjamin Lawton, Major Rick Desmond, Deacon and Captain Pat Snyder, FBI Supervisory Special Agent Jeff John, US Coast Guard Captain Bob Innes, Attorney Greg Lamarca, and Lieutenant Colonel Tim Grimmett. At various times in my life, the above-mentioned men have served as bosom buddy, personal advisor, confidant, and teammate, as well as friend. Several of the above also reviewed and commented on my early drafts.

I owe an extra special thanks to Prof. Ben Lawton of Purdue University, a long time friend, advisor, and confidant. He not only encouraged my writing of this book, but also did considerable hand-holding during the long and difficult writing process. His personal and professional contributions to this work are incalculable.

Although this book is dedicated to her, I also wish to thank my wife, Naima, for her encouragement and unflagging support; Haysam Fahmy for his incessant prodding; Hala Rharrit for her keen eye and sharp mind; and of course, Shems, for inspiration.

Also with regard to this opus (reviewers and fact-verifiers), I wish to express appreciation to Richard Manlove, James Rawley, Stuart Groves, Gerry Ganz, Stephen Mariano, Barbara Fast, Mick Lorentzen, Chris Shorter, Samar Issa, Leopoldo Avellanal, Andries Dreyer, Ben Lawton, Brad May, Terry Wolff, Steve Bucci, Denny Lane, Joe Kilgore, Terry Burke, Rudy Juanito, Tom Tutt, Vladimir Plecko, Erni Soplantila, Jim Abelee, Terry Cook, Alan Brimelow, Annette Leijenaar, George Minasian, Marco Smoliner, John Schot, Ron Sheckler, Connor O'Hara, Richard Cook, Scott Herbert, Bob Duffy, Tom Lee, John Warner, Marty Stanton, Frank Pedrozo, Richard Mitchelson, Jean-Luc Massart, Enrique Oribe, Chris Ankerson, KC Reddy, Rich Garcia, Mike Barnes, Jamal Outaifa, Akber Khan, Radies Rademeyer, Naudole Mataitini, Dave McIver, Dave Bongi, Tim Headington, Maria Traficanti, Vijay Jetley, Michael Moran, Tony Banbury, Elena Tartaglione Steiner, and last, but hardly least, well-known American movie producer David Giler.

Several of my reviewers were with me during some tough times in dangerous places. They not only helped perfect my poor prose, but also assisted me in correcting errors in fact. A few chose to remain anonymous because they are still on active duty with either the US Government or United Nations. They know who they are and thank you.

A special thanks is also due to Susan Clawson and Joan Kennedy. Susan edited my early drafts, and Joan served as copy editor of my near-final manuscript. Both performed well beyond the call of duty. Each is clear-eyed, as well as exceedingly knowledgeable.

I owe a huge debt of gratitude to Doctor (PhD) Anna Lawton, my publisher at New Academia Publishers in Washington, DC. She is intelligent, kind, thoughtful, and understanding. I could not have asked for better.

I feel bound to thank the former Middle East Director of Habitat for Humanity International, Richard Cook. Richard gave me a third chance at service when he hired me on as a security consultant in support of his offices in Beirut, Lebanon, in 2018 as I was nearing the completion of this book. It felt good getting back into harness in support of such a superb humanitarian organization.

Appreciation is also certainly due Sierra of sierrasketches@gmail.com. She created the maps for this memoir, and her artistry is undeniable. Moreover, she met every deadline without complaint.

I need to acknowledge the three literary agents who declined to represent me concerning the initial drafts of this book. They were Henry Thayer, EJ McCarthy, and Scott Miller. On reflection, my fledgling efforts were too full of anger and hurt. Moreover, my organizational structure and descriptions of events needed considerable work. Their rejections compelled me to look at my efforts with greater objectivity and strive all the harder at the craft of writing. Thank you.

I also owe a much-belated apology to Miss Down, my high school French teacher. If I had only known then what I know now, I never would have been such a pain-in-the-ass.

I could not then see how learning a foreign language could be relevant. Once again, as many times previous, I was wrong.

It is important to express my heart-felt appreciation to the institution of the US Army as well. I joined up as a private shortly after completing high school at the rock bottom of my 1971 graduating class with a low two-digit draft number at the tail end of the Vietnam War era—a poor, long-haired, much-confused, and largely uneducated kid. I retired nearly twenty-six years later as a lower-middle income, short-haired, still much-confused, but far better-educated Lieutenant Colonel of Special Forces in 1997. The Special Forces, Military Intelligence, Psychological Operations, Civil Affairs, and Foreign Area Officer communities served as my tutors.

An old comrade of mine once reminded me that along with one hundred thirty-two other enlisted men we began Phase One of the Special Forces Qualification Course in November of 1972 at Camp McCall, North Carolina. He subsequently pointed out that only eighteen of that original group successfully graduated Phase Three completion training the following year. Becoming a Special Forces soldier, and earning the right to wear the Green Beret, was one of the proudest moments of my life. More than that, I later had both the honor and privilege to serve beside some of the bravest and most dedicated soldiers on the planet within the US Special Operations Community. Their mettle would be proven time and time again on battlefields in Iraq and Afghanistan, and several other less-well-known locales. It is fair to say that I got the absolute best of the bargain. On much reflection, I was a marginal soldier who was enormously fortunate to rub elbows for a time with a phalanx of genuine and enduring heroes.

Finally, I would be much remiss if I did not thank brilliant authors Ralph Peters and Robert Kaplan. Both encouraged the writing of this book, assuring me that somebody somewhere would surely be interested enough to read it. We shall see…

Figure 1. Map of Sierra Leone

1

The Road to Sierra Leone

Peace is not the absence of war; it is instead the presence of justice.
—Bob's Laws

I was an American soldier for well over two decades. Following my retirement from active military service, I was at a loss for something worthwhile to do. In retirement, I missed the meaning and purpose the military had given my life. The same is no doubt true for many old soldiers. For nearly two years I tried writing, teaching, and military contracting. None of these gave me the same feeling I had experienced in uniform. Something was missing. Although not conscious of it at that time, I ultimately sought out a second profession that provided me what I needed most.

This unlikely record of events concerns my initial period of service with the UN. It is unlikely because, looking back on my fledgling years with the organization, I find it difficult to believe it all happened, and yet it certainly did. There are simply too many credible and usually sober eyewitnesses to confirm the facts. This sometimes-tragic history involves multiple rape victims, child soldiers, blood diamonds, kidnappings, invasions, emergency evacuations, refugee camp violence, gun fights, jihadist suicide bombings, the abuse of power, institutional corruption, political expediency, and betrayal.

I never imagined that my choice of the UN might nearly result in my own death or the death of someone I loved. I was wrong.

It was 21 August 1999. I had been serving in Sarajevo for nearly a year as a defense policy advisor to the fledgling government of Bosnia-Herzegovina. My year-long contract was generated by the US State Department and performed by Military Professional Resources Incorporated, a private military contractor. Essentially, we were attempting to assist the three formerly warring factions build a national and—we hoped—unifying army in the wake of a terrible war. I drafted the Defense Planning Guidance and Army Plan. These are both keystone national-military policy documents.

The previous work year had been long and tedious, producing unquestionably questionable results. The Roman Catholic Croats, Orthodox Christian Serbs of *Republika Serbska* (a Serbian enclave within Bosnia) and Bosnian Muslims had demonstrated little trust in one another or the future of the international community's cobbled-together nation of Bosnia-Herzegovina. Their mistrust of one another was real and justified. Much blood had been spilled. Essentially, the country seemed to be headed nowhere.

The war in the former Yugoslavia was punctuated with war crimes. An especially heinous act was perpetrated by the Serbs when they massacred over 7,000 Muslim men and boys in 1995 at a place now infamous, Srebrenica. More than 20,000 residents of the town and environs were also "ethnically cleansed," meaning they were either killed or forcibly driven from their homes.

Although the Serbs were clearly responsible for the tragedy, the UN also had to admit its own failings. The unfortunately named UN Protection Force proved to be unable to protect itself, much less the population of Muslims. CNN and other media outlets provided embarrassing video of UN "blue helmets" shackled to bridges by Serb forces, meant to dissuade American and allied military pilots from bombing them.

The residents of Sarajevo endured sniper fire from the ridgelines high above the city that failed to discriminate between combatants and noncombatants or women and children—killing anybody seen moving below. Not all the residents who attempted to negotiate what came to be called "Sniper Alley" survived.

Much later, after my arrival in the Balkans in the early fall of 1998, another conflict developed in an obscure province of Serbia called Kosovo—largely populated by ethnic Albanians, also Muslim—which now seemed poised to break away from Belgrade. In my spare time, I wrote a series of commentaries for the *Army Times* newspaper on the War in Kosovo.

My bosses at Military Professional Resources Inc. apparently found my work satisfactory. In the late summer of 1999, they offered me additional money and a twelve-month extension on my contract. The money was all right, and I enjoyed learning more about the former Yugoslavia and traveling in the region; the Balkans have a fascinating history. No matter the interest, the job could not keep me there, as one issue was unresolvable: The newly established government mandated by the international community enjoyed little popular support among the former warring parties. The tripartite presidency was utterly dysfunctional, and the assumed merger of the armed forces was anything but a reality. As of this writing, roughly eighteen years later, not much has changed. It was clear to me even back then that ending a war is one thing, but that attempting to ensure actual reconciliation was a very different objective requiring a different strategy. In other words, ending the war is not enough. The challenge of building a durable peace remains. I began looking for alternative employment.

The UN subsequently offered me a post as Chief Security Officer (CSO) for their unarmed military observer mission in

Sierra Leone, West Africa. I soon accepted. From my perspective, the UN offered me more than a job. It offered me the possibility of a second act in service.

Although having previously served on UN peacekeeping missions as a soldier, I had no experience working as a member of the civil staff. My prior UN service had all been as a volunteer while on active duty in the US Army. As I was to discover later, the differences between the military and civil sides of the UN are significant.

My previous peacekeeping tours had served to introduce me to that side of the UN. I say, "that side" because the UN is multifaceted. There are political, developmental, and humanitarian functions as well. But at the front end of my UN service, peacekeeping was the primary focus.

The unarmed variety of peacekeeping is a different sort of military mission. UN member states provide officers to serve as military observers. The most common term is UNMO, short for UN Military Observer. The general mission statement is to "observe and report." UNMOs observe the status of the peace and write reports for the gratification of the UN Security Council that establishes the mandate under which the mission operates. Essentially, unarmed UNMOs are placed on the ground between former belligerents. Their lives are then held hostage to the peace process. Although little-reported, it is not uncommon for military observers to die in the performance of their duties. I found this type of peacekeeping service, in the abstract, to be an honorable endeavor. The reality, though, was sometimes something else entirely. As a matter of historical import, approximately three thousand eight hundred peacekeepers have died in the performance of their duties around the globe.

Another type of peacekeeping involves the use of armed battalions. I had seen this permutation in 1990 while serving with UN Observer Group-Lebanon in the form of the UN Interim Forces in Lebanon, and two years later with the

UN Transitional Authority in Cambodia. My future mission would combine elements of both UNMOs and armed battalions.

The key assumption on the part of the UN Security Council when establishing a peacekeeping mission is that there is a genuine peace to keep. That assumption proved false in several countries. As many discovered over several decades of peacekeeping, genuine peace is often anathema to one or more parties to UN-brokered agreements, especially when such agreements are between warring factions within the same country.

The infamous 1994 genocide in Rwanda is merely one example. Majority tribal Hutus planned and executed the murders of up to one million minority tribal Tutsis, and directly under the noses of armed UN peacekeepers, who, following orders from New York, did little to stop the genocide. Although recent scholarship tends to mitigate Hutu guilt, the dead don't care.

Then there is the issue of the UN deploying armed troops of many nations to enforce a peace between formerly warring parties. This one is a very tough nut. The UN is not a capable war-fighting organization. One of the key reasons is that the troops sent by various nation-states are often not the best the country has to offer. Sub-Saharan African countries, for example, tend to keep their best troop units at home to protect the interests of the powerful.

I entered UN civil service on 22 September 1999, two years following my retirement from the military. I was excited and pleased. Because of my previous experience in both the US Army's Special Forces and UN peacekeeping, I felt reasonably confident that I could handle whatever challenges presented themselves. I was wrong.

My briefing officer in New York was Richard Manlove. Like me, he was a retired US Army lieutenant colonel. Our paths would cross many times in the future. In my briefing, I was informed that there was a very good chance the mission in Sierra Leone was about to get much larger, and far more complex.

I would receive no training prior to deployment. Essentially, my competence to serve as the mission's CSO was assumed based on the résumé I had presented to those doing the hiring in New York. However, there was nothing in that résumé that reflected anything other than an extraordinarily eclectic military career. On reflection, I wish there had been some security-based instruction. My training would all be on-the-job and much of it self-taught. So at least at the start of my UN service, I was, at least in my own estimation, largely technically incompetent and stepping into an arena that would test me in unexpected ways. It proved to be an inauspicious beginning.

I arrived in Sierra Leone less than a week later from Conakry, Guinea, onboard a Soviet-era Ukrainian-contract World Food Program helicopter, and without a visa stamp on my UN blue Laissez-Passer (UN Passport). The fledgling government had not yet quite gotten on its feet sufficiently to manage its borders properly. We landed at what passed for a helipad. I was accompanied by several UN staffers, as well as the new Regional Security Officer for the US Embassy in Freetown. I was tired. The trip from New York had been a long one.

Riding in Soviet-era helicopters is always an adventure. Two of them fell from the sky while I was serving in Cambodia. Although their pilots were first-rate (many had served in the Soviet Union's ill-fated Afghan War), their helicopter maintenance was questionable. Also, there was the issue of alcohol consumption. Soviet-era pilots and their crews seemed to love vodka, even when flying. In general, I prefer my pilots sober.

In addition, Soviet whirly-birds of this vintage tended to shake. They shake on takeoff. They shake at cruising altitude. They shake upon landing. It always seemed to me that when the blades were turning, they were just moments away from shaking apart, not like American-made helicopters at all. I always took safety procedures very seriously when flying in these aircraft. Luckily, and after what seemed a very long ride, I sighted Freetown Harbor from one of the port-side windows. Still, I did not relax completely until we returned to Mother Earth. Fortunately, the landing was uneventful.

The helicopter's back ramp lowered slowly to the attendant scream of hydraulics. Shirtless black men entered by the ramp and began wordlessly unloading cargo. The sky was overcast; it had rained earlier, and the late-afternoon air was cool. The passengers debarked by the port-side drop-stairs. UN agency vehicles were there to collect their staff. I was supposed to have been met by the incumbent CSO, but there was nobody there to greet me.

The new American Embassy Regional Security Officer must have noticed that I seemed lonely. He offered to drop me at the UN compound on the way to his embassy. I would discover later that the compound was nowhere near his embassy grounds. It was a genuine kindness. The only space available was in the back of a diplomatically tagged pick-up truck. I was glad of his generosity; we had only met briefly that morning on the helipad in Conakry. We were, at that time, strangers to one another. I tossed my gear in the back before climbing onboard myself.

The ride in the back of the pick-up took about twenty minutes through the streets of Freetown, the national capital. Those streets were rough and narrow. The truck shared that roadway with carts of all description, cattle, goats, bicycles, battered motor vehicles and lots and lots of people. Women of all ages were balancing heavy loads on their heads. Sidewalks were absent. There were great deep trenches on each side of the narrow streets, roughly waist deep. During the rainy season, if not blocked by refuse, those trenches were supposed to carry away the rainwater. Sometimes it worked. Other times it did not. I later heard credible stories of people falling into these cavernous culverts and drowning during rainy season downpours.

Sierra Leone is located eight degrees north of the equator. At these latitudes in West Africa, when it rains, it pours, and for months at a time (the rainy season extends from June to October). As I was to discover later, everything that can, will mildew. My clothes or anything else that remained stationary for more than a few days soon developed a green tinted sheen—Mother Nature working hard at entropy.

I noticed several electrical power generators, small and large, while proceeding to the UN compound. Their mufflers in several cases were nonfunctional, and therefore extraordinarily loud. They also, for the most part, belched unusually black, acrid smoke, which suggested that many of those diesel engines needed maintenance. I knew that Sierra Leone might be like many of the previous countries I had traversed. Locals would run an engine until it failed, and only then seek repair. Preventive maintenance was largely unheard of. My suspicion would later be verified by observation. The reason for all the generators was that Freetown at that time had no functioning power grid. If you wanted to power any electrical device, the purchase of a stand-alone generator was essential.

The smells were not altogether unfamiliar. I had not previously worked in sub-Saharan Africa, but I had served in the Third World, also known by the more politically correct moniker "Developing World." The stench of raw sewage was not uncommon in some of my former travels. That odor, along with the diesel fumes, filled my troubled nostrils.

I had accomplished an area study on the country before departing Sarajevo—an old habit instilled in me by military training. You see, if time permits prior to the deployment of a Special Forces team on mission, the unit would enter isolation for as much as a week prior in preparation. During that period an area study would be developed among the twelve members of the team. Essentially, an area study examines all aspects of a country or region that might impact mission accomplishment. Knowing the history of a country is often key to understanding its future.

Sierra Leone had been established on the west coast of the African continent in 1787 by Great Britain as a home for freed slaves. It is about half the size of the American state of Illinois and became a crown colony in 1808. From that time until 1961, when it became an independent nation-state, the country was ruled by the British. In retrospect, the native population was not well prepared for self-rule.

There was a succession of coups. Government changed hands several times. In 1991, Corporal Foday Sankoh, a former soldier of the Sierra Leone Army, began a military campaign (insurgency) against the national warlord of the moment, Major General Saidu Momoh. Sankoh led what came to be known as the Revolutionary United Front (RUF). The RUF generally focused its attentions on the inland—controlling diamond-producing areas, and the Sierra Leone/Liberia border area in the east and south. Momoh was overthrown in yet another coup the following year by Captain Valentine Strasser. Four years later, Strasser was ousted by his own defense minister. All the while, the RUF continued to expand its bloody insurgency against the central government, funded by what came to be known as "blood diamonds."

In 1996 a former UN official, Ahmad Tejan Kabbah, was elected President. The new President's first order of business was to sign a peace treaty with Sankoh that rapidly failed. Sankoh continued to maintain control of the most valuable diamond-producing areas. The following year, the fledgling President was overthrown by Major Johnny Paul Koroma and the Sierra Leone Army. Koroma immediately suspended the Constitution, outlawed demonstrations, and abolished all political parties. President Kabbah beat a hasty retreat to the country of Guinea, immediately to the north and east of Sierra Leone.

Two years later, the Nigerian-led Western African Intervention Force entered Freetown to cheering crowds. The cheers died quickly when the RUF later attempted to take Freetown by force. The UN Military Observer mission in Sierra Leone evacuated its staff northward to Conakry, Guinea. Its headquarters compound was subsequently burned-out by the RUF.

The West African Intervention Force subsequently retook Freetown. The RUF returned to the bush, while maintaining control of the diamond-producing areas in the south and east of the country. The UN then arranged a ceasefire. Later, in Lomé, Togo, an UN-brokered peace agreement was signed between Kabbah's government and the RUF. Not many in Sierra Leone believed that the peace agreement would hold. Fear was omnipresent. Nobody knew what the future might hold.

Confirmed reports spoke to many RUF atrocities. Because they had lost the previously held general election, their revenge was to cut off the hands of over 1,000 residents of Freetown. This equated in their minds to punishment for voting the wrong way. In addition, some persons thought to be friends of Kabbah's government were locked in their homes, which were then set afire, roasting them alive.

Rape was as common an occurrence as the sunrise, only far more frequent. No woman or girl was safe, no matter her youth, advanced years or infirmity. Drug abuse was common among the RUF, as was the drinking of locally produced palm wine. Many were child-soldiers, who had been stolen from their parents. Their utter brutality was the stuff of nightmares, only these terrors were all real.

Their unusual choice for hero was American rapper Tupac Shakur. Tupac T-shirts were worn by many of the RUF. The 25-year-old dead man—killed in a hail of gunfire by an unknown assailant in Las Vegas in 1996—was enormously popular. In a later surreal conversation with an RUF Commander,

I was told that Tupac's popularity was because he was black, prone to violence, and a drug user—just like many of the RUF. So they had a great affinity for the rapper. My shock at his answer was to be the first of many.

Adding to this level of complexity, the unarmed UN Military Observer mission was soon to transition to a much larger and far more complex peacekeeping mission with armed battalions. This is the Sierra Leone that I entered in the bed of a US Embassy pick-up truck.

They deposited me at the front of the UN compound—the same compound that had been razed during the RUF invasion of Freetown a year earlier. It was composed of a front gate manned by a local guard force with an intermittently walled area full of ugly, thin-walled, pre-fabricated buildings. Once past the guards, I entered the office of the CSO of the UN Military Observer mission. I learned little from him. Over the next few days I discovered that his office lacked even a rudimentary security plan. In addition, he seemed in a hurry to depart the country, which he did at the first opportunity.

During the previous invasion, my predecessor had reportedly been the first person out on the first helicopter—leaving the remaining civil staff to shift for themselves during the emergency evacuation. Although I was a fledgling security officer myself, even I knew that the security chief should be the last person out on the last helicopter of an evacuation, and only after everyone in the mission had been fully accounted-for on double-checked manifests.

I was just getting my feet on the ground in-country when I was directed to return to the US to attend the UN Hostage Incident Management Course in Glen Cove, New York. I had been in the mission area for barely fourteen days. The course was taught over a week's time by two senior Scotland Yard police officers who were also experienced hostage negotiators. We worked from early morning until late in the evening hours without pause, except for meals.

The Japanese government had provided a special financial grant to the UN Security Coordinator (UNSECOORD) to assist in better training those selected to serve as UN security officers. It was by any standard, some of the finest training I ever received. This course would prove to be very handy later in my UN career.

My classmates were all UN security officers serving from around the world. They all spoke English, but the number of nationalities was astounding, and from literally every inhabited continent. There were at that time three categories of officers: peacekeeping, which included me; those working for UNSECOORD; and the agencies. UNSECOORD officers served the whole of the UN system, and generally at the country level. Agency officers included those working directly for the UN Children's Fund, World Food Program, and UN High Commissioner for Refugees. Peacekeeping security officers served their individual missions.

While in attendance, a tragic incident occurred in the central African nation of Burundi—a convoy of UN humanitarian aid workers was taken prisoner and robbed by rogue militia. The criminals shot one and then another unarmed staffer, killing both. The lone UN security officer pulled an "unauthorized" side arm and shot two of the militiamen, permitting the remaining humanitarians to escape unharmed.

This incident led the Deputy UNSECOORD to authorize me to be issued a 9mm Smith & Wesson pistol prior to my redeployment back to Sierra Leone. However, before I could be issued a UN weapon, qualification was mandatory. Unfortunately, I developed a wicked cold on the last day of training. I felt like ten miles of bad road, but I made the effort. I went to the range and fired. Frankly, I was shocked to hit anything. My nose ran. I ached. My temperature was high, and my vision was blurry. I was utterly miserable. Somehow, though, I managed to qualify. It may have helped that as a young sergeant in the 10th Special Forces Group, I had specialized in light weapons that included familiarity with a dozen or more pistols of all sorts.

At the same time, I was handed a pistol and ammunition I was also issued a badge mounted on a stiff black leather belt clip. The badge was burnished gold with the blue UN symbol in the center, and printed above and below it, in both English and French, the words "Chief Security Officer." I placed the badge in my vest pocket and promptly forgot about it. This was the second time in my life that I had been issued a badge. The first time had been when I graduated from the US Army's Counterintelligence Special Agent Course in 1977, as a second lieutenant recently graduated from Officer Candidate School at Fort Benning, Georgia.

The return flight from New York via Brussels ultimately landed in Conakry, Guinea. The aircraft was going on to another destination somewhere in Francophone West Africa. After being deposited by a bus at the arrival terminal, I walked back out on the flight line to observe my bags being taken out of the cargo hold. My handgun and ammunition were in checked luggage. Losing a weapon is an anathema, even if it is the fault of sloppy baggage handlers.

Two uniformed airport policemen intercepted me. They spoke angrily in rapid-fire French. I understood them to say that I was not authorized to be on the flight line. I got that much, but it did not matter. I had to see my luggage—with handgun and ammunition inside—come off the aircraft, and before it left for its next destination. An argument ensued. My French is poor. Their English was non-existent. It was not going well.

They were probably on the cusp of slapping me in handcuffs and marching me off to the local lock-up when I remembered something. I reached into the pocket of my vest and pulled out the shiny gold badge that I had been issued in New York. I showed it to them—palm-up and about waist high.

There was a momentary pause as they looked downward and examined my badge closely. Their subsequent change in attitude was remarkable. You may recall that the badge said in French, Chef de Sécurité. That could be taken to mean I was the chief of security for the whole of the UN.

Apparently, this is precisely what they took it to mean. Both police officers came to rigid attention, while giving me their best parade ground salutes. I returned their salute accompanied with a grateful smile. They then escorted me planeside and allowed me to identify my luggage as it was removed from the aircraft. They then carried my bags to and through Customs, after clearing visa processing. They would not permit the customs agents to ransack my gear—I never heard of this happening before or since. They continued lugging my baggage to the hotel bus and placed me gently aboard. Both were standing at attention and saluting as the bus pulled away from the terminal.

I removed the badge from my pocket and looked down at it with genuine admiration. It possessed unexpected utility. I would not forget it. From that time forward, and while in the mission area, I always wore that badge prominently displayed on my belt, just like the New York City detectives in the well-known American *Law and Order* television series. It proved to be a very useful affectation.

October 22nd was notable. It was the date when the mandate for the new UN Assistance Mission in Sierra Leone (UNAMSIL) was published. The mandate was unique in historical terms. It was the first time that a peacekeeping mission was permitted to use violence to meet its stated objectives. The mandate authorized the use of force to protect the citizens of Sierra Leone from harm. I was stunned.

Having served on peacekeeping missions in Egypt, Israel, Cambodia, Iraq, and Kuwait, I knew something about the business. I had also published several articles about peacekeeping in professional military journals and magazines. I had never heard of the UN being given so broad a mandate in the use of violence. I was worried.

I planned to return to the US for the Christmas and New Year's holidays. Unfortunately, the RUF announced in the local newspaper that they intended to once again invade Freetown—this time over the holiday period. I felt that the potential threat might be real. I therefore canceled my home leave to remain at my post. The invasion never materialized.

While retaining the unarmed military observers of the old mission, the new mission experienced rapid growth in the new year that included the arrival of several armed infantry battalions, most of which were sub-Saharan African in origin, although India and Jordan were both significant contributors. In fact, the commanding general, known in UN parlance as the Force Commander, was an Indian major general. The new head of mission (HOM) was a former West African ambassador.

Unfortunately, the supervisory arrangement for security was ill-conceived. My direct boss was the Chief Administrative Officer (CAO). His boss was the HOM. But the UN Designated Official for Security (DO) was the senior head of the humanitarian and development agencies in Sierra Leone. Our peacekeeping priorities were not a match to the priorities of the UN humanitarian and development agencies, like the World Food Program, World Health Organization, and UN Development Programs. These agencies even had their own UNSECOORD Security Advisor. There is little doubt that the mission of which I was a part had very different objectives and appetite for risk.

One of the first contentious issues I encountered was the new HOM's choice of headquarters. The old accommodations lacked the necessary space for the expanding mission. I was informed that he had selected the former Sierra Leone Army main building and compound. The decision came to my office as a "done deal"—without consultation—that the army headquarters would best suit the UN.

I had been there previously and had doubts. I took it upon myself to examine the compound and building more closely. The local military guards reacted well to my UN-marked vehicle, a new white SUV bristling with radio antennas, when I drove up to the front gate. Between that and my badge, they let me in.

My first action was to conduct a perimeter walk, a military habit of long standing. The guards kept an eye on me, no doubt curious about my presence. The headquarters building had been bombed in one of the previous conflicts. Damage to the structure was extensive. Perhaps 50 yards distant from the building I noted a padlocked double door leading under what appeared to be a hillock. I noticed one of the guards nearby and called him over. I asked him if he could open the door for me. He nodded in the affirmative immediately, grabbing some keys from his pocket, and opened the padlock. He pulled the door open while standing nearby, perhaps to see if I required anything further. It was bright daylight outside. It was very dark inside, and there was no electrical power in the compound. I carried a small flashlight on a belt holder. I removed the device and turned on the lamp, so I could peer into the gloom, while stepping inside. My eyes took a moment to adjust. The hairs on the back of my neck suddenly reacted, and I felt a knot growing in my gut. The hillock was an ordnance storage facility.

I stared unbelievingly around me as my flashlight played across the interior. I could not see all the way to the back wall, but the storage area was large and in total disarray. There were outboard motor engines, cans of kerosene and gasoline, plastic explosives, antipersonnel mines, and all mixed with piles of corroded batteries, rockets, mortar rounds, machine gun belt ammunition and more.

One careless match would have launched this entire storage facility into low earth orbit. Since it was so close to the future UN mission headquarters, if it exploded, it would likely

kill or maim anyone there as well. I remember walking bold-
ly through that door, but gingerly tip-toeing back out. I was
nearly speechless.

I swallowed hard, while taking a deep steadying breath.
The man who had opened the door for me was still waiting
outside. I asked him in a quiet voice to place the padlock again
on the double doors. He complied. I then asked him, "You do
know how dangerous this place is?" He replied meekly, "Yes
sir, I tell them all the time." I never found out who "them"
was, nor did I care at that moment.

I returned to my office and wrote a formal memorandum
for both the HOM and CAO. In a nutshell, I stated the new
home for our headquarters should under no circumstances be
within the Sierra Leone Army compound and explained why,
making it clear how outrageously dangerous that ordnance
storage facility was. I also stated in clear and uncompromis-
ing terms that if the current decision remained in force, my
next communication would be to New York. That last comment, threatening communication with UN Headquarters,
was unnecessarily undiplomatic. The bottom line is that I was
wrong to add such a threat. Of necessity, and in my later UN
service, I learned to be a better diplomat.

My alternate recommendation for our new headquarters
was the Mammy Yoko Hotel on Lumely Beach. Unfortunately, the hotel had been looted in the invasion of Freetown and
would need significant and costly refurbishment. The HOM
and CAO eventually agreed.

One day while walking the perimeter of the old UN compound I noticed something odd sticking out of a knot in a
tree. I took the time to look more closely. It was the tail fin of a
rocket-propelled grenade of soviet manufacture. Apparently,
and perhaps during the first invasion of Freetown when the
UN compound had been attacked and razed, the grenade had
been fired and somehow lodged in the knot of the tree, but
did not explode. The warhead was still intact. Mission electri-

cians had thereafter used the tail fin to tie up electrical wiring leading from the generators. Dangerous.

I immediately instructed the electricians to carefully remove the wiring. Then I established a cordon around the tree and posted warning signs. Thereafter, I saw the CAO and told him the grenade was potentially dangerous and had to be destroyed-in-place. The problem was that we had no explosives to do the job. It was a straightforward task. A ¼ pound block of C-4 plastic explosive and blasting cap with a timed detonator would do the job. I had done similar work in my previous military career.

I then contacted an engineer unit from a West African country. They agreed to provide the explosives with two officers to emplace the charge the following Sunday morning. I accomplished the requisite notifications of UN staff; placed officers with hand-held radios on every possible approach; and sent flyers around the neighborhood to locals. Essentially, I meant to take every possible safety measure. I was confident in myself and my previous training. I shouldn't have been.

The engineers arrived Sunday morning as planned. I asked them if I could inspect the plastic explosive, blasting cap, and timer. What I saw did not inspire confidence. The explosive was dated stamped 1964. It was early 2000. I never worked with explosives that were over 30 years old before. The two officers told me that it was no problem. They would simply use more explosive than the ¼ pound block I had proposed. This was something they told me they had done previously to positive effect. What could possibly go wrong?

The resulting explosion was far larger and louder than I had anticipated. The engineer officers, proven wrong about the extra explosive used, left in a hurry, and with me holding the bag. Of course, I was responsible. The decision was mine. Although nobody was injured, the damage done was substantial. A portion of the perimeter wall had been destroyed; the tree had a nasty gash; the windows of the logistics section were blown out; and the server for our computers was off-line for the next 24 hours.

Yes, I know something of explosives, but I did not know everything about explosives. It was not my primary field of military expertise. However, I allowed my ego to get the better of me. I vowed never to make that kind of mistake again.

UN missions need money. Sierra Leone had no functioning banking system. The UN peacekeeping mission at Layounne, Western Sahara, over 1,500 miles to the north, had funds. I was asked to take the UN twin-engine turbo-prop aircraft, fly to Western Sahara, pick up two million dollars in cash, and deliver it back to my boss in Freetown. This was a very scary proposition.

First, two million dollars is a lot of money in this part of the world. There were many among the RUF who would have killed everyone in the mission for that amount of money; perhaps far less. Second, besides myself, I had only three other officers who were authorized to carry side arms. Almost everyone in Sierra Leone had automatic weapons. We were potentially badly out gunned. I anticipated little trouble picking up the money in Western Sahara. Getting the cash back to Lunghi International Airport, on the opposite side of Freetown Bay, would also likely be without incident.

The scariest part was moving the money in Freetown to our headquarters by vehicle. There were only two routes available to us. I ultimately directed my staff to pre-position two vehicles near the helipad. I would decide on the spot which vehicle I would take upon arrival, and subsequently which route I would take. If word got out that much money was coming into Freetown, there would have no doubt been an ambush and robbery.

Word did not get out. We were successful, but it was a very hairy exercise—one I had no wish to repeat. I suggested to the CAO that he contract a bonded courier company to move money into Freetown. I never wanted to transport money from outside Sierra Leone again, and I never did.

My next pressing task was to begin assessing Sierra Leone. From a threat perspective, the RUF's intentions were the determining factor. They had invaded once previously. They had threatened to invade over the holiday period. The threat appeared to be clear and present. At the first opportunity, I headed into the bush to see for myself what they might be up to. On this first trip, I spent a total of two weeks in RUF country. It was enlightening. I discovered that they were not all planning to turn over their weaponry to the UN mission, which had been the agreement made in Lomé, Togo. Clearly, not all their officers were enamored with the notion of peace. The reasoning of some was interesting, and perhaps at the human level, understandable.

One mid-level RUF Commander asked me straight out, "What's in it for me?" "Isn't peace usually preferable to war?" I answered his question with another. "No," he said, flatly. "Peace means that I lose my rank. I lose my position of respect. I command over a hundred soldiers. When I turn in my weapon, and my unit no longer exists, I no longer exist too. I have nothing else. I know only how to be a soldier."

The Commander was probably nineteen years old. From his perspective, his life was over before it had really begun. Many of his troops were child soldiers. In fact, the Commander was a former child soldier himself. He had, over time, simply aged out of child status. Peace for him involved the total loss of his identity, and begged the no-doubt nagging and unanswerable question, what next? For him, with no civilian technical skills, no formal education, and no hope of acquiring either, peace was a frightening, dark, swirling abyss of awful possibilities.

What would happen to the former combatants of the RUF? Where would they go? What would they do? Some felt they could never return home. Others were slowly becoming more aware that their many crimes, under orders or not, might be punishable under international law.

Then there was the pressing issue of money. The RUF had managed to support itself primarily through the exploitation of blood diamonds that had been removed from the alluvial diamond fields found by the Liberian border to the south and east. By way of explanation, alluvial diamonds are those that can literally be picked up off the ground or are located close enough to the surface to be reached by men using picks and shovels. The potential dissolution of the RUF meant no more diamonds. The RUF also engaged in armed robbery to raise cash.

I met several RUF soldiers—and I use the term "soldier" very loosely. They were not disciplined. They followed no rules of soldierly behavior. They complied with the orders of their superiors, or they themselves were beaten or killed. Still, many were exceedingly proud of their skills with what weapons were assigned to them. In other words, their weapons became joined at the hip to their egos—not altogether surprising for young men torn from their families at a tender age—and they were exceedingly dangerous.

Several had become stone-cold killers. Some kept track of their personal body count—enormously proud of the number of human lives they had taken, and while totally unaware of what monsters they had become. The RUF's infamy later became so well known that they were added to the US Department of State's list of terrorist organizations in 2001. But these were not true terrorists. They were instead children who had tragically lost their sense of right and wrong. Men without conscience had stolen their humanity from them.

I saw a different sort of human tragedy in Cambodia. I spent six months on temporary duty in that sad country serving as an unarmed UNMO. The mission was to conduct the country's first free and fair elections.

The UN pulled out all the stops, spending an estimated two billion dollars on the effort. When I arrived in early December of 1992, there was no government, no hospitals, no police, no jails, no courts, no national power grid, and few functioning markets. There were hundreds of thousands of refugees, and survivors of the Khmer Rouge "re-education camps." There were also thousands of landmine victims. The entire population had suffered severe physical and psychological trauma on a scale rarely seen in modern times. Only Mao, Stalin, and Hitler were more successful at industrial-grade state-sponsored murder.

The death and devastation created by the Khmer Rouge was unimaginable. As many as one point eight million people were slaughtered in the "Killing Fields" in the vain attempt to create a Communist-inspired agrarian utopia. Pol Pot, the leader, otherwise known as "Brother Number One," presided over the mass killings of physicians, schoolteachers, university professors, anyone who spoke a foreign language, even people who wore glasses and their offspring.

Anyone who might possibly have sufficient education to counter the twisted Khmer Rouge narrative was simply removed from this earth by the cheapest and most expeditious means possible. When bullets became too expensive, victims were bludgeoned, and in some cases, buried alive in enormous mass graves.

The tragedy of Cambodia was ever-present for me every day of the six-month deployment. I had never previously witnessed, up close and personal, human suffering on these enormous dimensions. The stupa outside of Phnom Penh piled high with the skulls of the dead... the killing fields that exposed more and more of the evidence of mass murder in the wake of every monsoon season—the rains washing away the dirt from the bones of the long-dead... the ubiquitous landmine victims... so many men and women missing arms and legs and begging for money in the streets of the national capital... Toul Slang Prison, where the Khmer Rouge tortured and killed thousands... the photographs of the dead fill the walls of that prison today, which has been turned into a national museum of the macabre. These images never leave me, although time tends to dull the sharper edges of clarity.

My decision to spend two weeks in the bush in Sierra Leone had been much influenced by my observations in Cambodia. Those experiences convinced me that the only way to truly understand what was happening in the country, and to better gauge the threat to the mission, I had to visit the major concentrations of RUF in the provinces. This trip, one of several, proved useful.

As my two-week intelligence-gathering tour wound down, I was contacted by my boss, the CAO. He wanted me to return to Freetown early. When I asked him for the reason, he stated that my immediate return was essential to sort out a problem concerning the vehicle parking lot at the new headquarters. Once again, as many times before and after, I was stunned to silence. In his mind the parking issues of the senior staff members were of critical importance. He thought that my time would be more appropriately spent on creating designated parking spots for the mission's department heads. It became pretty clear pretty quickly that he and I would seldom see eye-to-eye. Instead of flying back immediately to Freetown, I assigned the task to one of my staff, stayed in the provinces, and completed the tour.

Several other mission department heads traveled in the provinces as well. The majority would take a helicopter out for the day, and then visit one or two field sites before returning to the comforts of Freetown. In my estimation, they never actually learned much of importance because nobody could on such brief visits. My Special Forces training again paid huge dividends. If you really want to learn something in the field, you must remain for a while, and listen to what people have to say.

Traveling in the bush was uncomfortable, and sometimes dangerous. There were few hotels. When there were, they had no working fans or air conditioning. Mosquitoes were commonplace, as was the malaria they carried.

To add insult to injury, the local food was laced with bacteria to which I had never previously been introduced. That meant I spent a goodly amount of time in severe gastro-intestinal distress in a part of the world where functional toilets were in extraordinarily short supply. Over time, I discovered the safest thing to eat was over-cooked scrambled eggs. Thereafter, I had well-browned eggs for breakfast, lunch, and dinner, sometimes with white rice. I suspect that my cholesterol count went through the roof on this trip. Still, that was preferable to the messy alternative.

While transiting by vehicle between provinces, I observed the daily life of the people. Women generally trekked to water sources daily. They would accomplish the washing of both themselves and family clothing while there. When returning to their villages, they carried enormous jars full of water for drinking and cooking on their heads. The balancing act with those jars was nothing short of amazing. It also wasn't uncommon for women to go about bare-breasted; something I got used to over time. Clothing choices for both men and women leaned toward the very bright and colorful, often bearing intricate patterns.

Sometimes I traveled in the company of UNMOs. Sometimes I traveled alone. I saw few young men in the villages. I was told later that able-bodied young men often worked in the alluvial diamond fields in the hopes of striking it rich. Others had either joined, or been compelled to join, the RUF. Old men were a rarity. The male mortality rate was very high. In other words, men lived, but they did not live long.

The circumstances for the very young were heartbreaking. Malnutrition was rampant. There were few physicians. Childhood illnesses took many. Deaths from malaria and diarrhea were commonplace. Acute respiratory infections killed many more. I could not be around the children very long; their eyes conveyed such great need. They had so little. They had suffered long, and with no end in sight.

My general observation about the villagers was that they were universally dirt-poor. They barely eked out a living from the land. The long war had devastated the populace, and the RUF was feared by all. Village life was perhaps best characterized by the twin maladies of misery and uncertainty.

I saw some wildlife, too. These included forest buffalo, monkeys, baboons, and I may have even once caught a fleeting glance of a prowling leopard. The reason for animal scarcity was that the RUF shot and killed anything on four legs. For the RUF, quadrupeds equaled food.

The RUF was *the* power in the eastern and southern provinces. In addition to controlling the alluvial diamond fields, and in violation of the Lomé Peace Accords, they had established armed checkpoints on several of the major roadways. At these checkpoints, they extorted money from travelers, calling the payments tolls or taxes. In the early portion of 2000, the RUF checkpoints were generally reasonably hospitable to people like me. I was apparently unarmed; the 9mm handgun that I sometimes carried was always concealed by a vest. And I was, by appearance, a civilian. In other words, they fortunately did not consider me a threat. They felt that the real concern emanated from the growing armed military component of the mission.

But not all RUF checkpoints were welcoming. I remember approaching one in an UN-marked white SUV. I approached slowly in hours of daylight, lowered my driver-side window, and kept both of my hands in plain sight, while making no rapid arm movements—standard procedure. This checkpoint was different, though. Those RUF troops manning it seemed agitated and jumpy. I never discovered why. Their weapons, mostly a collection of older model AK-47s and Belgium-made FN FAL rifles, perhaps a dozen or so, were all pointed in my direction.

I stopped my vehicle perhaps five yards in front of the group arrayed from roughly 10 to 2 o'clock to my front. I placed the shift lever in the reverse gear, while keeping my left foot depressed on the clutch in the event a hasty exit was required. A teenager wearing a ratty T-shirt, well-worn camouflage trousers, and flip-flops broke from the group and began sauntering toward my vehicle. He carried a pistol in his right hand. He was not close enough initially for me to see what kind. He turned briefly and yelled something: I could not make it out. Two of the pack jumped and ran toward a small mud-cake building with a thatched roof, following whatever order had just be given. The air was tense with anticipation.

By his appearance and manner, the teenager was either drunk or stoned, or perhaps both. His eyes were glassy, and his lips were stretched into a wicked grin. He seemed to have difficulty focusing. He blinked a lot. I assumed that he was in charge. As he closed in on my vehicle, I noted that his fingernails and toenails had all been painted bright red. I guessed that this is what the guys on RUF checkpoints did with their down time. He kept his side arm pointed downward while tapping the trigger guard with his index finger. I knew that on his order, I would die.

There was no sense in killing me. But with child-soldiers, logic need not apply. Add alcohol and drugs, and a tough situation gets even worse. It would have been foolish of me to draw my own weapon. I was badly out gunned, and my vehicle was not armored. If they had seen my pistol, they might have reacted to the potential threat. The use of force was not a viable option. This was no movie, and I am not Chuck Norris.

I smiled and waved with my left hand out of the window, while keeping my right hand visible on the steering wheel. "Hi, there. My name is Bob. I work for the United Nations. I assume you all are with the RUF. I sure am glad that Foday Sankoh signed that peace treaty in Lomé. I wouldn't want to tangle with you guys." It is always good policy to be polite as well as complimentary at armed checkpoints manned by drug-addicted child-soldiers.

The teenager did not speak but kept up the tapping on the trigger guard on his pistol, like he was playing some absurd single-digit drum solo. I was committed to the role now. Luckily, this was not my first rodeo.

"You guys like to smoke?" The teenager tapping his trigger guard slowly nodded. The tapping never stopped for a second. I looked about. Some of the others had moved in a bit closer to my vehicle while I was focused on the kid with the handgun. I noted that they were nodding too.

I tried to speak in a conversational voice, but loud enough for all to hear, "I'll bet you all don't get into Freetown much, and good cigarettes are hard to come by. For that reason, I often travel with more cigarettes than I need. I am happy to share them with you." They closed in further. The rifle muzzles lowered to thigh-high. Things were improving.

The pistoleer had closed the distance. He was standing no more than a yard away. If possible, he looked even younger up close, not much more than fifteen or sixteen years old. Judging only from their appearance, he could have been the old man of the group. I could see now that he was carrying what appeared to be a WWII-vintage British Enfield top-break sidearm. I wondered where the hell he had picked up that relic.

I reached carefully with my left hand across my body in a wide arc that all could see and returned with a red and white carton of cigarettes that I had earlier placed on the seat beside me. The reaction was unexpected but welcome. I heard multiple squeals of delight. The teenager smiled at me while placing his pistol in the waistline of his trousers. His eyes remained unfocused and blinking hard. Still, he had the presence of mind to reach out. I very carefully handed him the carton of American cigarettes.

Rifles were suddenly on shoulders, and literally everyone was surrounding the young man with the pistol to garner their fair share of the spoils. At least for the moment, I was all but forgotten. I breathed an inward sigh of relief.

Credible reports from my staff tended to confirm that the RUF had engaged in human sacrifice and cannibalism based in local Ju-Ju beliefs (traditional magic). It gave new meaning to the well-known American commercial phrase, "It's what's for dinner." I had no wish to become the main course. Managing my own fear under these circumstances was personally demanding. Unexpected death was a real possibility at almost any time.

I ended up spending two hours at that checkpoint, talking with the RUF. They were totally without guile. They answered all my questions without any attempts at evasion that I could discern. I learned a great deal that day. I had discovered many years earlier that cigarettes, especially American cigarettes, can buy tons of good will.

I began developing a better feel for my job. My position was not about exhibiting power, which was true enough for armed police officers everywhere. My function was more about using soft power, like diplomacy. Essentially, working in UN security was all about being smarter than your potential antagonists and being better prepared. I concluded that if I had to go for my gun, I had already failed. It is of course impossible to foresee every contingency, which was why I was armed. However, in most cases, it was my job to avoid confrontation and find what the Buddhists might call the "middle path."

Some days following my intelligence-gathering trip, and once my reports were written and submitted to my chain of command, I took an all-too-brief R&R in Europe. While returning to Freetown, I remember standing in line to have my luggage ransacked by the customs agents in Conakry, Guinea. The customs officers were well known for their corruption. They happily accepted bribes. I was not so inclined, so my bags were about to be mauled. Having met her briefly onboard the flight, I knew the woman to my immediate front in line was an incoming member of the UN mission. She was British, and she was an unusually white, white woman.

The customs agent was rifling through her bag when he came across something that must have felt curious beneath a mound of clothing. He grasped the item of interest and pulled it free. He gazed at the thing in his hand with a look of growing horror. He held an anatomically correct, life-sized, 12-inch dildo complete with wrinkled scrotum. He dropped the very intimate device back into the woman's bag as if burned by it. He then glared directly at her in anger, as if to say, "Madame, in Africa we have men for this sort of thing." Head bowed, she glanced at him. She then glanced at me. The very white, white woman turned a shade of red I have never seen in nature. Once in the mission area, she expended considerable effort avoiding me.

2

Prelude

Maybe there is a beast... maybe it's only us.
—William Golding, *Lord of the Flies*

M y favorite nightspot in Freetown was Paddy's Chinese Bar and Grill. I usually arrived around 8:00 PM, after leaving the office. Workdays in Freetown were long; fourteen hours and more were common. Paddy's was a fantastical place. It was an open-air facility—an enormous tin roof decorated with dugout canoes and other West African paraphernalia over a huge slab of concrete. Paddy's served a fascinating mix of UN civil and military personnel, hustlers, peanut sellers, merchants, mercenaries, diamond and gold miners, humanitarian aid workers, prostitutes, foreign embassy people, and senior local police and military officers. All were seeking relief from the pressure of living in a town under constant threat from the RUF.

It was accepted as common knowledge that as many as 1,000 RUF had already infiltrated Freetown and had cached weapons and ammunition. The threat was real. Some of the RUF were probably in Paddy's every night, collecting intelligence from well-lubricated members of the UN military and civil staff. Unfortunately, there were few ways to tell just who was and wasn't RUF. They wore no uniforms and fit no ready description. The RUF of course had sympathizers among the city dwellers of Freetown. Also, the UN possessed no counter-intelligence capability. RUF spies basically operated with near-total impunity in and around the UN. Although I had no way of proving it, I was sure that the UN had inadvertently hired some RUF as local staff. In such circumstances, it was all but impossible to keep a secret.

The music in Paddy's was played on large loudspeakers and generally favored African American Hip-hop, R&B, and RAP artists. Prostitutes often danced with one another when they could not find a willing male.

The prostitutes of Sierra Leone were an interesting lot. Unlike hookers elsewhere, they all appeared to seek a single sugar daddy. Some were successful. I had noticed a few UN staff males, as well as others of the expatriate community, with the same women night after night. Ladies who had hooked up in this manner were considered the lucky ones. They did not have to hustle every night for new customers. Most of the "night fighters," as they were called by the mission's military component, were from Liberia, although there appeared to be plenty of locals as well.

In my first weeks of frequenting Paddy's I had been approached by nearly every hooker in the place. They were outrageously aggressive. Their come-ons were often the stuff of some of the worst porno movies I had seen in my youth. It wasn't uncommon for one of these girls to go through the motions of fellating a finger directly in front of me. Other techniques included grabbing my crotch under the table while promising the best massage and blowjob in town. All of them, of course, claimed the title of "best."

I was always polite but firm. Thank you, but no thank you! As part of my area study, I had read that AIDS in West Africa was climbing to epidemic proportions. Messing around with these women could easily result in a long, lingering, and lamentable death. It was an easy choice. I really enjoy breathing. After a while, they left me alone and began looking elsewhere. All succeeded.

Their professional attire was of special note. This is what everyone took to calling "Paddy's evening fashion show." Many wore clothing that seemed to come directly from the old Frederick's of Hollywood lingerie catalog. These included translucent blouses; long gowns with slits nearly up to the waist; push-up underwired wonder bras; spray-on blue jeans worn with spiked stiletto heels; way-off-the-shoulder dresses with outrageously plunging necklines; and the most mini of mini-skirts. One woman's nickname was "Pop-tarts," because her incredibly ample breasts always seemed barely short of popping out of their confinement—meaning her massively under-wired push-up bra. Every night was a sexual smorgasbord for those men foolish enough to sample the wares. Clearly, there were many fools in Freetown.

To my way of thinking, these women were every bit as much victims of the war in Sierra Leone as anyone else. I never met a woman who selected prostitution as a career choice. All of them had felt compelled to do it for one reason or another. Some were orphans, forced into the trade by ruthless men. Some had no other means of supporting themselves. Others had lost their entire families in the war. Still others were multiple rape victims. There were many reasons. But mainly, none felt like they were in control of their own lives.

Aside from common courtesy, I was polite to these women because of my need for information. Many of these prostitutes were "intimately familiar" with a multitude of local government officials, RUF members, embassy staff, and UN personnel, both civil and military. It did not cost much. Some were bored and tired of chasing johns. Occasionally, and for the price of a few drinks, I was well on my way to developing sources of information nobody else in the UN tapped (pun intended).

Why were they willing to help me? A prime motivation might have been their near-universal hatred of the RUF. The RUF took what it wanted, and without payment for services rendered. These women already suffered from a lack of options. The RUF in control meant that their options disappeared altogether.

There were many other potential sources of information to be had at Paddy's. The mercenary community was one. Mercenaries had been active in Sierra Leone for years and had once even saved the elected government when hired by the president. The outfit called Executive Outcomes had previously managed to fight the RUF to a standstill. Mostly former South African Army soldiers, these men had done a superb job against a merciless enemy.

Unfortunately, and because of no doubt well-intended international pressure, the president of Sierra Leone decided to dispense with their services following their initial successes. Immediately following Executive Outcome's dismissal, the RUF began its resurgence. Many citizens of Sierra Leone had reason to regret the government's bowing to international pressure. Perhaps in some cases mercenaries aren't so bad after all.

President Kabbah reportedly replaced the Executive Outcomes mercenaries with the Kamajors. The Kamajors were from the Mende ethnic group that was native to Sierra Leone. They were notable for their choice of combat garb, which included women's blonde wigs, dresses, lingerie, and other female-related paraphernalia, sometimes including full facial make-up and painted nails. The explanation for this unusual manner of costuming had to do with a belief that the wearer would thereby create an alternative personality that would be immune to bullets and shrapnel. Several of the Mende claimed that the female garb could even render them invisible. The Kamajors were not particularly successful against the RUF.

There was yet another offshoot of this sort of thinking. I cannot say for sure if they were Mende or not. They were called the "Butt Naked Boys." The Butt Naked Boys reportedly went into battle, as you already surmised, without a stitch of clothing. The ostensible rationale was for either invulnerability or invisibility—perhaps both. I was able to verify the existence of this unusual group in Liberia but heard only rumors concerning their activities in Sierra Leone.

Another rumor I could not verify was the existence of a young girl called the Angel of Death. Several unconfirmed reports claimed she was a mere 13 years of age and had been trained to use an ice pick to the base of the brain to dispatch captured enemies of the RUF. According to those rumors, she had killed hundreds in this manner. True or not, stories like these were widespread and served to terrify the already-frightened residents of Freetown.

Some of the former mercenaries under the Executive Outcomes banner remained in Sierra Leone to train the Kamajors, while others chose to take work providing security for the more extensive mining operations. Some others even netted jobs with the Sierra Leone Army as trainers. No matter where they were or what they were doing, they had information that I needed.

The information superhighway literally ran straight through Paddy's. Other sources abounded here as well. The international non-governmental humanitarian organizations, or INGOs, performed charitable activities throughout Sierra Leone. They included doctors, nurses, foodstuff delivery specialists, child-care experts, and much more. They came from various countries, and although holding different humanitarian approaches, all shared a common interest in their own survival. I felt that I could tap into their security concerns and exploit them as sources of information. Of course, they would exploit me as well, so at least the relationship would be mutually beneficial. I later arranged for the INGO community to receive security briefings every week from members of my staff, which were always well attended.

The bottom line was this: a few of these INGOs were in places where the UN was not currently deployed. If you wanted knowledge of these areas, they were the only sources available. You either cultivated these people or you lived in ignorance. I preferred the former option.

Unfortunately, this was a job that I had to accomplish largely on my own. None of my staff had been trained in intelligence collection. Moreover, collection of this type is something that had to be handled very delicately. The various ambassadors were also useful sources of information, but they because they often kept secrets and their home governments established their agendas, I did not always trust them.

There is yet another reason why my information collection efforts eventually bore fruit: I was a UN Chief Security Officer. The UN is generally perceived as neutral and unbiased by a host of nations and organizations, so my position placed me on the side of the angels for many. In other words, I was often trusted. I invested considerable time and effort to ensure that their trust was based on a solid foundation.

I would always enter Paddy's by way of the side parking lot, choosing a spot near the front where I could not be blocked in. I would sit at my usual table in the corner and with my back to a concrete wall, where I could observe nearly the entire establishment.

On a typical visit, I would choose to sit alone, even though I had become familiar with many of the regulars. My usual waitress would deliver an ice-cold beer, pouring it into a not-too-clean glass. I would remove the handheld radio from its belt clip and placed it on the table in front of me. I could monitor the radio better in this way. Sometimes the loud music would make it difficult to hear.

I did not need to decide what to eat. As a regular, and by pre-arrangement, my waitress would choose for me. Most of the time, her choices were good, and I always tipped her well. She, in turn, would ensure that my evening meal was reasonably well made, large, and fresh. I was usually hungry, especially if I had missed a meal, as often happened.

It would be an hour or more before the food arrived, and I would be on my second beer of a three-beer self-enforced limit. I did not drink much in those days, but I dislike soda, and the beer at Paddy's was very cold. After a day in the West African heat, a cold beer was just the thing. I set myself a three-beer limit because I was always on duty. I had to remain sober and clear-headed; radio calls demanding my attention and presence were common, and they could come at any time.

Some matters were well beyond my limited authority. For example, a Chinese UNMO drove his UN vehicle off the road in Freetown and through a local business in the hours of darkness, nearly killing an entire local family of four. The Chinese presented unique difficulties regarding driving vehicles. I had seen this problem before in Cambodia. Many Chinese officers had little experience driving motor vehicles. Back then, the primary means of transport in China was the bicycle. For this reason—their lack of driving experience—they commonly became a road hazard to themselves, the vehicle occupants, and the public. One of these officers had three major vehicle accidents to his credit in almost as many weeks.

China was supposed to send officers who could read, write, and speak English, which is generally the peacekeeping mission's primary language of choice—to produce reports and talk over radios. Driving skills are necessary to patrol their assigned sectors. Chinese officers often fell well short of the mark in all these areas. Unfortunately, these officers were often unable to contribute much to the mission. Nothing could be done about it, though. China was one of the "Big Five" on the UN Security Council along with the US, UK, France, and Russia.

At one of my more memorable daily briefing sessions, the news was especially tragic. The briefing officer spoke clearly and concisely—never letting on how the story affected him personally. He reported that the day prior, a busload of locals had been ambushed not far from Freetown. The men had been beaten and robbed. Two had been shot dead. The women, young and old alike, had been taken into the bush and gang raped. Three female abductees had been taken as sex slaves or bush wives. One of the girls taken was barely twelve years old. Such accounts were tragically commonplace.

Only a week earlier, and while in the provinces in early February, I had met and spoken with a woman who had a six-month-old baby taken from her while she was gang-raped by eight or more RUF toughs. When they were done with her, she recovered her child and limped back to her small village that I just happened to be visiting.

Accompanied by an Indian military physician, I went to see her. After the doctor gave her an examination and treated her for cuts and abrasions, she began speaking in a surprisingly calm voice while she breastfed her child. I listened intently while she told us what had happened to her. When she finished her horrific tale, she gazed into the doctor's eyes and asked the question that had been plaguing her thoughts, "Will my breast milk be safe, if any of those boys have AIDS? Is my baby in danger because of what had happened?" Neither of us knew the answer. Not knowing what else to do, I gave the woman all the money that was in my wallet before we left. Tragically, she was only one of thousands of victims of RUF sexual assault.

Blistering angry, I felt helpless as I walked away. There was no functioning police force or judges in the provinces, nor were there any jails. Nobody was engaged in attempts to bring these killers and rapists to justice. What few police there were in the provinces were mostly unarmed and grossly underpaid. Going up against the RUF would have been foolhardy. Just staying alive was a full-time job for a Sierra Leone provincial policeman.

Moreover, the UN-brokered peace agreement had unwise-ly given Foday Sankoh the country's vice-presidency, as well as control over the alluvial diamond fields. The RUF could act with impunity, as it was essentially then part of the govern-ment. As much as I wanted to help the woman, I knew that she was merely one of many who had suffered a similar fate. My job was elsewhere.

Mundane problems abounded as well. Most of my staff had not been paid their salaries in months, an experience I had also suffered when I first arrived. I was fortunate to have significant savings. Although the mission could seem to orga-nize payment of Mission Subsistence Allowance (one hundred thirty-five dollars a day), salaries—paid out of the sluggish bureaucracy in New York—were a long time coming. It was tough on my staff with families. I lent money out-of-pocket to those who were worst-off, knowing that eventually I would be repaid.

One night in Paddy's, I was joined by the mission's con-tracting officer. Over beers, he told me about his day. While accomplishing due diligence regarding bids on the fuel con-tract, he discovered what he felt to be an unusual bid. He took his concerns directly to the HOM. He told me that one of the key names associated with this outfit was someone with his same last name.

What the contracting officer wanted to know was whether this person was any relation. After all, the surname in ques-tion could be as common in his country as "Smith" or "Jones" is in Great Britain. After what the contracting officer described as some weak attempts at evasion, the HOM finally admitted that the person associated with the fuel company was, in fact, his son. The company did not get the fuel contract, but only because the contracting officer insisted on doing his job.

Shortly after we moved into the Mammy Yoko Hotel, and as the mission continued to expand, I noted one morning a fantastic creature walking down the hallway outside my office. She was an attractive and clearly voluptuous woman dressed in an incredible skin-tight multi-colored full-body dress with matching enormous headscarf. Her garment was so tight I marveled that she was able to walk. She was all swaying breasts, hips, and bottom with greatly overdone make-up. This was, I was informed later, the new head of one of the minor administrative units of the mission. She had recently arrived from the HOM's former duty station in the diamond rich Central African Republic (formerly the Central African Empire). The performance of her small unit declined precipitously from the day she arrived.

A brief time later I mentioned in a security staff meeting that I was going to submit a complaint to the CAO concerning that unit's recent dismal record of efficiency and effectiveness. The close protection officer of the HOM, a member of my staff, asked to see me alone following the meeting. This is when he advised me behind closed doors to hold my peace because the woman was servicing the HOM at least two evenings a week. Someone had apparently made special arrangements so that this woman from his previous UN duty station would be able to continue her nocturnal activities in Freetown. Of course, now it all made sense. It's good to be the Head of Mission!

Before long, I noted an oddity concerning the mission's political department. It was one hundred percent populated by sub-Saharan Africans. The reason why I considered this strange is because I had served on three peacekeeping missions previously. On those missions, diversity in the political section, and everywhere else, was always the case. Moreover, diversity is demanded within the UN Charter. I asked the obvious question at a meeting with the head of that department. I was told that, "... only Africans can hope to understand African problems." This statement struck me as complete horseshit. Such was certainly not held as true anywhere else in the world. Why only in sub-Saharan Africa?

In the early days of the mission I became friendly with

one of the members of the political department. She was European. She did not long remain once the new HOM was enthroned. She told me behind closed doors that she must return to New York. I asked why? Speaking in a lowered voice level, she told me that the HOM used her for moving around furniture before and after meetings in his office, and little else, except for a growing rash of embarrassingly menial chores. She also shared with me that, in her opinion, that the HOM was an outrageous chauvinist, and likely a closet misogynist as well. She was a very smart, well educated, and capable woman, who was, until the HOM's arrival, a mainstay of the political department. I agreed with her choice to return to UN Headquarters in New York. I had noted similar behavior on the part of the HOM as well.

By early March, my staff had grown to twenty internationals, and well over one hundred local staff, including the guard force. I was holding one of the daily 9:00 AM meetings in my office. There was standing room only. It was at this meeting that one of my senior officers suggested to the group that it would be prudent to "hot iron" their underwear before putting it on. I confess, this news required more explanation. I asked the obvious question, "why?"

He told the assemblage that there was a local insect called a Tumba fly, which laid its eggs in damp hanging laundry. The unsuspecting would sometimes put on their undies once dry. So far, this story seemed unremarkable. Except—as he went on—these flies had burrowing larvae. The larvae would burrow into the very soft and sensitive skin of one's posterior. The officer speaking pulled his pants down partially on the spot, while turning his hindquarters to his security brethren. There was a collective gasp from the all-male crowd. His ample buttocks were pockmarked with the remnants of what appeared to be some very ugly pustules. This no doubt was an important safety tip that everyone took to heart. I know I did. I never thought to ask what happened to those who would go "commando."

A brief time later, I woke up to find that my right eye was swollen shut, and as red as Rudolph's nose. This was alarming because the state of medical care in Sierra Leone was at that time rudimentary at best. The mission doctors came as part of the military contingent. Once I successfully made myself minimally presentable, I made a beeline for the Indian Medical Clinic. My condition, an eye swollen almost to the size of a baseball, moved me immediately to the front of the line. My condition stumped all three of the doctors who examined me. None of them had seen a condition like mine before or had a clue as to how to treat it. I was getting worried.

Since the medical professionals were unable to diagnose my ailment, I took charge of my own health and wellbeing. I instructed the military doctors to give me a broad-spectrum antibiotic along with the most powerful anti-inflammatory agent they had in stock. I theorized that the infection was possibly bacterial in origin and that therefore the antibiotic should help. Also, the anti-inflammatory was a no-brainer, in my estimation. My eye was unquestionably inflamed! I thereafter went to work in my office and horrified everyone who beheld me.

That same evening, when just occupying my usual table at Paddy's, my waitress took one look at me and stated matter-of-factly, "Bob, you were bitten by a champion bug." She went on to explain that the champion bug likely crawled up underneath my mosquito netting. She assured me that I was in no danger of losing my eye, and that the swelling and redness would recede over the next few days. She was right.

Insects provided other, and more serious, health hazards. Malaria is common in Sierra Leone. I remember two variants: One was the garden variety—fever, chills, headache, sweats, fatigue, nausea and vomiting. The other was cerebral malaria. That one was especially nasty, and while including some of the more unpleasant previously mentioned symptoms, also brought coma and seizures, which unless correctly diagnosed and treated, could result in death. This disease is historically credited with killing more people than any other pathogen on the planet. Malaria is today, as it has always been, a scourge on humankind. With global warming, the malarial zone grows every year.

Hoping to avoid this malady, I put considerable thought into what my own defense against malaria would require. I mostly wore light-colored long-sleeve shirts with long, light-colored pants and boots, thereby exposing the least amount of skin to the blood-sucking female mosquito that carries the malarial parasite. Experience had suggested to me that mosquitoes were attracted to darker-colored fabrics. Years later I heard that mosquitos hunt in infrared. So dark colors absorb additional heat, therefore attracting more of the dangerous insects.

Over my bed, I arranged not one, but two insect-repellent-impregnated mosquito nets. One net might be torn or develop a hole. It is unlikely that a tear or hole might occur in precisely the same spot, hence the use of two nets. When traveling in the provinces, I used an insect repellent high in DEET content. DEET had proved itself effective to me on multiple previous occasions. If the proof is in the pudding, I never contracted malaria, when many I knew did. I suspect that it was my overabundance of caution that made the difference.

Several of the military contingent used a medication called Larium or Mefloquine. It was supposed to be an anti-malarial drug. Unfortunately, it had some nasty side effects. My military liaison officer took the stuff. He told me later that his side effects were considerable, and consisted of confusion, vomiting, hallucinations, diarrhea, chills, fever, anxiety and more. He quit its use after several weeks of experimentation.

Near my small ground-floor apartment off the main road into town, there was a Christian church, and across the street, a Muslim mosque. Also nearby were the small offices of a woman who practiced Ju-Ju, or traditional magic. Over many weeks' time, I noted that several of the same people were attending both Christian services and Muslim prayers. I also noticed later that a few of those same individuals frequented the offices of the Ju-Ju magic practitioner.

For a while I was stumped, and then one of the local staff members explained it to me. The people of Sierra Leone are immensely practical. Jesus strikes many as a very good man, and perhaps even the son of God. They have also come to respect Mohammed, the Prophet of Allah. But before Jesus and Mohammed, there was Ju-Ju. It just seemed to make sense to some citizens that it would be wise not to place all their eggs in one basket. As a result, on Sunday they were Christians. On Friday they were Muslims. And the rest of the week, something else: all in all, a highly pragmatic approach.

By late March, I was meeting once a week at Paddy's with a very senior Freetown-based police officer with whom I had become friendly over time. I gladly paid for his food and beer, as his salary was an embarrassment by way of comparison with the UN, and he had a wife and children. He was also a superb source of security-related information, and I liked him very much.

Into his third or fourth drink, he said something out loud I had never thought to hear. His head wobbled a little to the side before saying, "Bob, I wish the British were back." I was stunned. The British had given Sierra Leone its freedom from colonial oppression years earlier. He went on to explain, "The British had their ways, sure. But at least when they ruled here, my children could go to school. There was no RUF. My wife could go to market without fear of being robbed or raped. The police and courts were respected. The roads were safe. Now there is only the war that never seems to end, and the foreigners that come here only for the diamonds and gold."

Many of my classmates in the graduate program at American University's School of International Service in Washington, DC, were from Africa, the Middle East, and Asia. Several came from countries that had suffered colonial oppression and exploitation. The achievement of freedom from former European colonial oppressors was often celebrated with fireworks and national holidays in their home countries. Much of the curriculum that I studied was focused on the terrible practices of racist colonial powers that economically exploited native peoples.

Now here I was, sitting across the table from my friend, in a bar, in Freetown, who had just said that which could not be repeated in polite Western academic society. From his perspective, peace and order were immensely preferable to local self-rule, when the price was war, war, and more war. I nodded my understanding. I said nothing. I could think of nothing to say. His words still give me pause for reflection today.

On the odd Sunday, I skipped work to drive to a beautiful beach south of Freetown. Copying the activities of the RUF, local children would sometimes set up a checkpoint on the beach road composed of sticks and string to extort money from passersby. Many mission personnel threw the kids pocket change.

The beach was popular with UN staff. Locals ran the beach as proprietors—providing thatched-roof huts, boat rides, cold beer, and fresh-caught seafood lunches. Those few Sundays were memorable for me. I swam, lay in the sun, and thoroughly enjoyed the idyllic surroundings. For a brief moment, I could almost forget the mounting danger.

The mission continued to grow. Every day seemed an endless round of briefings, consultations, and meetings. The UN can't do anything without a meeting. Also, several UN senior staff seem to feel the need to speak in meetings, even when they have little relevant to add to the conversation. In other words, much of my day was wasted, and there was only so much I could fairly off-load on my staff.

I was regularly sending copies of my security reports to New York. These reports told a troubling tale. In my estimation, the RUF would at some point once again invade Freetown. There seemed to be a clear breach between the RUF field Commander, Sam Bokary, and Foday Sankoh. Bokary was also known by his self-chosen *nom de guerre*, "Maskita" (Mosquito). He enjoyed being associated with the deadly insect because, throughout human history, the mosquito-borne parasites had killed uncounted millions. He took sick pride in bragging that he had personally taken the lives of hundreds by his own hand.

My sources indicated that he had cut a deal with Charles Taylor, the dictator of Liberia to the south of the country, to supply him stolen Sierra Leone blood diamonds. Therefore, Bokary simply had no incentive to surrender his position in the east. Essentially, he was now more into the illegal diamond trade than acting as the leader of the RUF military component. He simply had no interest in peace. There was no profit in it for him. At some point, he ceased working for Foday Sankoh and began to work for President-for-Life Charles Taylor in Liberia. At that point, the pursuit of money, rather than ideology, ruled the actions of a significant portion of the RUF.

I could prove none of the above. This was merely my analysis, which I shared with my boss, the HOM, and New York. Years later my assessment concerning Charles Taylor's involvement, and his relationship with Bokary, was validated by investigators from the International Criminal Court in The Hague.

Due to the threat posed by the RUF, and because there simply wasn't enough time to get everything done, I pushed the standard UN work week of five days (Monday thru Friday) into Saturday over the objections of those few officers working for me who had permanent UN contracts. I listened to their complaints, but never seriously considered relenting. Within a week, my boss, the CAO, extended the work week into Saturday for the entire civil staff of the mission as well.

One evening, while heading from my office to the parking lot at the end of a long day, one of the newer members of the mission stopped me and asked if we could speak. I reluctantly agreed. I was looking forward to a cold beer at Paddy's and was annoyed at the delay. We returned to my office and shut the door at her request. After taking a seat, she told me that she knew the HOM was deeply involved in the illegal diamond trade both in his former duty station of the Central African Republic, and now, here in Sierra Leone as well. She was reluctant to tell me how she came by this information. I did not know what to say.

My terms of reference (formal job description) primarily focused on the preservation of the lives of mission civil staff. I was not a cop, although several of my staff were former police officers. I had no criminal investigative mandate, and certainly not concerning the HOM.

I thanked the woman and told her I would look into it. That seemed to satisfy her. She sauntered off, no doubt feeling better for having unburdened herself to me. But I was left holding the bag. What was I to do now?

I took the woman seriously, with little choice but to kick it upstairs. I sent a message to New York from my personal e-mail account using a non-UN computer, and asked what to do with the startling information that I had just been given. The response came a day later. The e-mail note from Richard Manlove said simply, "Tell nobody." That was it. There was no advice beyond keeping the allegation against the HOM secret. To my knowledge, no investigation was ever conducted. The UN was nothing if not surprising. Richard no doubt gave my report to the Deputy UNSECOORD. What she did with it, I cannot say. Of course, if one wishes to remain ignorant of criminal behavior, then choosing not to investigate it will surely result in the desired blissful ignorance.

On a more personal note, my feelings of isolation and loneliness increased daily. My military training resulted in my keeping a professional distance from my staff. My long work hours and overriding mission focus meant that I had little time to develop genuine friendships. These circumstances meant that there was nobody in whom I could confide. At least in the early part of the mission, trust, the essential pre-condition to friendship, was rare. I never fully appreciated the comforting cocoon I had lived in while serving within the US Special Operations Community, where I knew that I could trust nearly everyone.

There were perhaps reasons. Sierra Leone was a strange and violent war-torn land, populated by peoples of whose culture I possessed only limited understanding. My UN colleagues were all from different countries themselves. Some shared my values; some did not. At the outset of the mission we were all strangers to one another, and my job tended to keep it that way. I had little time, and I kept secrets too. I would like to say that we were all united in a common cause—the attempt to bring peace to Sierra Leone. The facts of the matter, which would soon become evident, tended to suggest otherwise. I had only rarely felt so alone.

I did not dwell on these feelings. But they were always there, like a splinter deep under the skin, seemingly ever-present, and in this case, all but impossible to remove.

I should probably mention at some point that I had always hated my last name, "Adolph." Growing up a military brat in the post WWII America with that name had been a genuine curse. At every new school, and there were many, some bully a head taller and 20 pounds heavier inevitably called me "Hitler." My reaction was always the same: I punched him. Tragically, I did not know how to fight in my youth. To add insult to injury, I was a small kid. I almost never won a fight growing up. But I kept punching anyway. And every time someone called me Hitler, I hit them as hard as I could, followed by an immediate and humiliating ass-kicking. I came home from school with a bloody nose more times than I can count. After a while, the bullies lost interest in me and began picking on others. I think they tired of bruising their knuckles on my fortunately hard head.

In perhaps a vain attempt to transform chicken shit into chicken salad, a seemingly life-long pursuit, every time I picked up a ringing phone on duty, I answered with my surname, "Adolph." I would never get rid of the name, but I could choose to embrace it, and try and make it into something to be proud of.

By the time April arrived, there was another issue at hand. While attending the US Army's Command and General Staff College nearly a decade earlier, I had formally studied strategy development. Since my arrival in Sierra Leone, I had been looking for a political-military road map document—something to spell out just how the peace process was to be implemented. I was shocked to discover that there was no such document and if there was a strategy, I never met anyone who could explain it to me. Frankly, I was beginning to wonder if I was a good fit for the UN.

As a department head, I was considered a member of the mission's senior staff. One day, and in capacity, I attended a teleconference with New York. I was told that it was an important event. Every department head would be present along with their note-takers. I came solo with my pocket notepad. When I arrived outside the conference room, there was hardly a spot to stand. Everyone was in the hallway. When I asked the problem, I was informed that the HOM's secretary had gone to lunch and had taken the key to the conference room with her. Reportedly, she was not scheduled to return for another half hour. Nobody knew how to contact her. The problem was that the very important teleconference with New York was scheduled to begin in less than five minutes. What to do?

The solution, to me, was obvious. I asked a small portion of the assembled mass to please stand clear of the entranceway. When they had, I executed a simple side kick that I'd learned many years earlier while studying the martial arts. Essentially, my military-booted foot struck a blow about an inch below the doorknob. The result, though, was a good deal more than I expected. The door literally flew off its bottom hinge. The knob went clattering to the floor. The wood splintered loudly apart, not because my kick was so powerful—it wasn't—but because the door was so very poorly made; mission procurement hard at work.

I then pivoted to the front and grabbed what remained of the door that was still attached to the upper hinge and pushed it aside. Stepping back, I turned around to invite the group to enter. The looks on many of their faces showed nothing short of silent amazed surprise. They began filing in, once recovered. My boss was one of the last to enter. As he passed, he snarled, "I will deduct the cost of that door from your paycheck." To which I responded with a genuine smile, "I would expect nothing less."

A few days later, a humanitarian aid worker from one of the INGOs came to me with a request to provide training on the conduct of emergency operations. I was happy to do so, even with my uber-busy schedule, but I was curious how this organization defined the word "emergency." As I soon discovered, this group of aid workers was badly frightened, and for very good reason.

This group had taken-in dozens of child-soldiers in the hopes of rehabilitating them back into Sierra Leone society. These young men, generally ages 12 to 18, were all former members of the RUF. Many of them had been stolen from their parents at gunpoint. Several had admitted to killing. They were some of the scariest people alive. Many were drug- and alcohol-addicted. Most had limited—if any—impulse control. All were prone to violence in a split second, and for little cause. Essentially, violence was all they knew.

The RUF's recruitment techniques were ghastly. A RUF

patrol would enter a village and round up everyone at gun-point. Then they would cull out those young boys, generally teenagers, whom they wanted for their ranks. The RUF patrol would also take one of the village's old women with them. The boys and the old woman would then be taken to a remote location outside the village, where each of the boys would be compelled under the threat of death to engage in a gang rape of the elderly village woman. The RUF knew that the best way to keep what they stole would be to ensure that the boys themselves felt that they could never go home because of the shame of what they had done.

Child-soldiers were horribly psychologically damaged by their RUF experiences. They were often beaten or killed if they failed to comply immediately with the orders of their superi-ors. It was not uncommon that their orders involved killing or maiming others. The RUF also used drugs to terrible effect. Drug and alcohol usage were encouraged as a control mech-anism. These teenagers—over time—were utterly inured to violence. In other words, violence—for most intents and pur-poses—became part of their very being. They had been made extremely dangerous. The humanitarian aid workers caring for these youngsters felt themselves at significant risk. Their perceptions were accurate.

I agreed to provide a class to the aid workers who were caring for these damaged young men. I did so at their com-pound. The timing was fortunate. Only a week later, Foday Sankoh visited the site. For reasons that confound, he told the assembled group of child-soldiers that he had personally pro-vided considerable funding to the INGO (an out-and-out lie) and then suggested that the money might have been stolen by the aid workers themselves.

Unsurprisingly, after Sankoh left, the former child-soldiers rioted and attempted to attack the aid workers. They failed to harm anyone. Luckily, I had focused a sizable portion of my class on the establishment of well-planned and well-practiced escape routes with safe areas. I knew that they would never wish to harm a child, even a former child-soldier. I was aware through personal experience that attempting to reason with child-soldiers was often a lost cause. They are almost pure raw emotion. That left only the escape-and-safe-area option. I taught the aid workers to develop secret escape routes out of their compound so that they could return another day in the attempt to help those who clearly needed it the most. Fortunately, it worked.

On yet another day, the representative of a well-known medically oriented humanitarian aid organization from Europe entered my office. We were previously acquainted. Following the usual pleasantries, he told me that he was considering sending two of his medical personnel (doctors) to the easternmost province. He asked me what I thought of the idea. In halting French, I said, "Mon ami, je pense que c'est une très mauvaise idée." In English that means, "My friend, I think that this is a very bad idea." I explained that the eastern provinces were crawling with RUF under the command of Sam Bokary, who had taken people hostage before and might again. In my estimation, sending physicians out that way was an unwarranted gamble.

Two weeks later, the same man was back in my office to inform me that his two physicians had been taken hostage by Sam Bokary. He asked me somewhat sheepishly if I could "confidentially" assist him in gaining their release. Why did my assistance have to be confidential? His organization was passionate about its independence. They simply could not afford to be publicly beholden to the UN; hence, my involvement must be secret.

Of course, I immediately agreed in principle. Lives were at risk. But not being a free agent, I first had to gain permission from New York. That permission was rapidly granted by the Deputy UNSECOORD in a subsequent telephone conversation. Both physicians were subsequently released unharmed and thereafter repatriated to Europe on one of the first available flights out of Sierra Leone. UN involvement in securing their release was never mentioned in the Press. Success!

However, from that time forward, every time I entered Paddy's and sat at my usual table, a free beer appeared. My waitress informed me that on the instructions of the representative of that well-known and highly independent European humanitarian aid organization, she was to henceforth ensure that the cost of my first beer was always placed on his tab. *Merci bien.*

On those rare occasions when there was time for lunch, I most often went to the Crown Bakery in downtown Freetown. It was one of the very few restaurants open at mid-day that served safe, decent food at reasonable prices. Safe food in this context means lacking bacteria that would force an individual to spend inordinate time making obeisance to the white porcelain gods.

There were often young men outside of the Crown Bakery selling photographs of the many atrocities committed by the RUF during their invasion of Freetown over a year earlier. I bought a set, not out of morbid curiosity, but out of professional interest. It is important to know your potential adversaries. The photos were not for the squeamish or faint of heart. I will only say here that anyone whose stomach is not turned by these images should consider professional counseling.

Several beggars also congregated outside the Crown Bakery. These panhandlers were of a different sort, though. They all lacked hands. Their appendages had been hacked off by the RUF. Most wore ratty shirts or blouses with large double pockets—men, women, and children—to receive donations. I always carried extra money on me for this purpose. I could not then or now imagine how one gets through life without hands. I felt enormous sympathy for them accompanied by enormous helplessness. The men responsible for these heinous crimes still walked the earth free.

It was time for the morning roundup in my office. The briefing officer was speaking: "Chief, we have an unconfirmed report that one of our military patrols surrendered their weapons and were taken at an RUF checkpoint yesterday near Magburaka." I reacted sharply, "How is that possible? Why would an armed UN patrol surrender their weapons to the RUF? No professional soldier would do such a thing." Still, I knew it was true. The soldiers had given up their weapons, and probably without a fight. This was not the last time that members of the military contingent would be taken by the RUF. In fact, detentions by units of the RUF of the UN military contingent soon became an embarrassing rash. Mission soldiers were soon grabbed in Makeni and Kailahun as well. Why was it so easy for the RUF?

The peacekeeping soldiers who were in Sierra Leone mostly represented sub-Saharan African nations. Unfortunately, there are few genuinely professional armies south of the Sahara. Moreover, many were not psychologically prepared for a fight. Their various governments told them that they were in Sierra Leone as peacekeepers. But what if there was no peace to keep? What if the Lomé Peace Accords were a sham? How would these soldiers react if faced with real battle?

In addition, military officers in some sub-Saharan African armies acquired their commissions based on loyalty to a given national leader, usually tied to a single ethnic group or tribe, and not because of professional competence. Several of the sub-Saharan African senior officers of the mission did not inspire confidence.

I have been asked many times over the years how I define good leaders. Surprisingly, it is not complicated. Simply put, they all do two things very well: 1. Good leaders know their job. Because they know their job, they are respected. 2. Good leaders also take care of their subordinates. Because they take care of their subordinates, they often win their loyalty.

Leaders who have earned both the respect and loyalty of

their people are almost always successful. It could not be otherwise. Although I always took these two lessons to heart, I had yet to learn to master my ego. As any good boss can attest, mastery of one's ego is also an essential element in good leadership. I still had some work to accomplish on that score.

Matters became further complicated when the UN Security Council gave the mission a mandate that included protection of the civilian populace. How could the military component of the peacekeeping mission hope to protect civilians when they were unwilling and/or unable to defend themselves?

The story of these soldiers being taken hostage would spread like wildfire among the local population. The people of Sierra Leone had been hoping against hope that the UN mission could be their salvation. What would they think when they found out the truth—that the UN military was a paper tiger?

The Force Commander concentrated considerable effort into the attempt to put backbone into his subordinate peacekeeping commanders. But there was probably no chance of success. Confidence came with training and familiarity. Many of these battalions didn't even speak the same language. Even if they did, they had no secure communications means and no intelligence collection system worthy of the description. If it came to a fight with the RUF, the Force Commander was going to find himself standing in some very deep shit.

It was mission impossible and therefore doomed to failure unless the Lomé Peace Accords were real. Unfortunately, there was no evidence to support such an absurd notion. Lomé was very likely a sham—an illusionary peace established without justice, providing a general amnesty to those who had engaged in the mutilations, rapes, and murders of the country's citizens. I suspected that peace without justice was probably not possible, that "Peace is not the absence of war; it is instead the presence of justice." This thought was added to my collection of what I believe passes for wisdom that can be found in the appendix of this book under the tongue-in-cheek title, *Bob's Laws*.

The other major military problem was that the peacekeeping forces were arrayed to support the UN Security Council's mandate: Those units were not deployed to play a combatant role. They were deployed instead to support the Disarmament, Demobilization and Reintegration (DDR) process of RUF soldiers. That process, where these soldiers were supposed to turn over their weapons to representatives of the mission, sparked violence in several regions. It became abundantly clear that the leadership of the RUF had no intention of keeping the promises made by Foday Sankoh at Lomé.

All reports from the provinces—formal and informal—were negative. The RUF was on the move, but to where? More importantly, what were their intentions? Because the mission had no genuine intelligence collection mechanism, we had to be creative. Earlier in the year, I had requested that the military contingent provide my office a military liaison officer. The Force Commander agreed. I was fortunate to get a very good man in the form of a captain of the British Royal Marine Commandos (the one who had the trouble with the anti-malarial medication).

I called him into my office, instructed him to change into civilian clothes, and then head straight-away to the helipad to catch the World Food Program helicopter that was going east that day. We needed airborne reconnaissance. Coordination had already been accomplished with the pilots. They were former military, too, and understood the requirement. The captain did the job and then some. He returned with information that substantiated my worst fears.

This was the corroboration I needed. My informal sources at Paddy's had told me the exact same thing some days earlier, only they could not confirm the timing. Between the information provided by them, the security staff and our military liaison officer, it was—in my estimation—a lock. The murderous RUF was coming, and soon.

3

Another Invasion

How ridiculous and how strange to be surprised at anything which happens in life.
—Marcus Aurelius, *Meditations*

It was 3 May 2000. The previous day several UN military units had been seized in different provincial towns. Getting accurate numbers always seemed to be impossible. The RUF invasion of Freetown, which I had long anticipated and reported to my masters in both Freetown and New York, was beginning. I received a radio report from my staff that as many as seven peacekeepers had been killed. That number was later reduced to four. It hardly mattered. Things were about to get ugly.

In addition, we had to move a group of UN staff out of Kenema by helicopter. Our security officer there, Erni Soplantila, reported fighting in the province between RUF and UN forces. I had selected Erni to head our office in Kenema because he was a consummate professional and an able leader.

Erni also reported the possibility of an attack on the city. After reviewing his reports and others, I concurred with his assessment. Once I got permission from the CAO, I directed Erni to evacuate all UN staff out of the town and back to Freetown as soon as possible. What made this situation dicey was that the communications between Kenema and Freetown were spotty at best. Military communications, upon which we relied, were in many cases dysfunctional. We relied on military units for communications because we did not have enough of our own. Everything was on back order.

I was investigating the deployment of troops on the main road leading to the capital in my vehicle. My last stop was the Jordanian Special Forces Brigade, which I had made a point of visiting often. Their Commander was a very good man, and they were a cohesive fighting force. After enjoying some sweet tea with the senior officers, the Commander pulled me aside to tell me something privately. He explained that he felt it was impossible for him to fight. I asked the obvious question, "Why?" He said that there were West-African battalions deployed on his flanks and that he simply did not trust them. He also stated that he believed they had inflated their troop strength. In other words, he believed there were far fewer soldiers present than their leadership had reported. I shared that concern.

On one of my previous visits to the provinces, I had been briefed by a senior military officer from the same country, who claimed to have nearly 1,000 soldiers under his command and in that immediate vicinity. Very undiplomatically, and unable to contain myself, I laughed out loud. I had no doubt that the UN was paying for 1,000 soldiers. But if there were even half that number present, I would have been shocked. The UN was paying for many "ghost soldiers."

So when the Jordanian Commander shared his concerns with me, I understood immediately. He told me his primary responsibility, given this reality, had to be the lives of his soldiers. I nodded my head in sad agreement. He was, of course, correct. Finally, he mentioned that he had already spoken with King Hussein. The King, he told me, supported his decision not to fight under these circumstances. It was a done deal. But that meant we were wide open to another invasion.

I returned to my offices in Freetown, alerted my staff, and subsequently made verbal reports to both the Force Commander and CAO. The fantasy that the military component of the mission could or would fight had finally been laid bare.

Richard Manlove had just arrived in Freetown. He was dispatched from UN Headquarters to assist me in handling the multiple detainments involving the military component. He too was a graduate of the course on hostage negotiation held in Glen Cove, New York. In later years, he went on to author the global UN Policy on Hostage Incident Management. Richard was taken hostage roughly six years earlier when serving as the chief security officer for the peacekeeping mission in Liberia. Experience always tells.

We met in my office and rapidly came to an agreement on how we would proceed. He focused wholly on the expanding detainment aspects, and I concentrated on the possible evacuation of the civil staff. I had formally recommended the evacuation out-of-country of non-essential personnel, but no decision had yet been taken by my superiors.

The RUF would soon begin its second invasion of Freetown. Richard, who shared my concern, said he would contact New York. I later found out that he informed the Deputy UNSECOORD that my previous reports had been accurate, and that the HOM was nowhere to be seen. Subsequently, the deputy contacted a senior official at the Department of Peacekeeping Operations. They, too, had apparently been unable to reach the HOM.

Before leaving my office, Richard did something unexpected: he apologized. My face must have betrayed my confusion and surprise. Richard explained, "Bob, some of our colleagues in New York were skeptical of you. You are on your first assignment with us. You were an unknown. You reported that an invasion by the RUF would very likely occur. The HOM sent periodic messages to HQ saying that there were few security-related issues, and that the Lomé Peace Accords were proceeding as anticipated. If anything, the situation here might even be worse than your reports suggested." I was thankful for Richard's honesty. It explained much I had not previously understood. I was new to the job, an unknown quantity, but apparently no longer.

Richard occupied one of the few rooms in the Mammy Yoko Hotel that the mission maintained for visitors. Since my duties required my presence at the headquarters 24/7, and he knew that I had no place to sleep except my office, he offered to share his room with me. That offer later came to include several other security officers as well, sleeping on cots. Thankfully, his was one of the few rooms in the Mammy Yoko with a functioning toilet and shower. Both would come in extraordinarily handy in the days ahead.

I was in my office. If memory serves, it was 5 May. On my recommendation, we brought all international civil staff members into the Mammy Yoko Hotel. They numbered over 200. I arrayed the Indian Military Police Company around the outer perimeter of the hotel, while using the local guard force to secure the inner perimeter. The Force Commander had entrusted me with temporary operational control of his Military Police unit, for which I was very grateful.

It is difficult for me to convey the genuine terror that was rapidly becoming evident in Freetown. The city's residents were in a panic. They knew that the RUF was on its way. They knew that the RUF was a merciless enemy. They knew now that the UN military was ineffectual. They already knew that the fledgling Sierra Leone Army was all but useless. They knew too that there was nowhere to go—Freetown borders the Atlantic Ocean. They also knew that neighboring countries were not friendly to refugees. They were trapped, and death was knocking at their door.

One of my staff came to me with a code cable. I had never received a code cable. The use of this UN communications means was the province of the most senior members of the mission—above my pay grade—and supposedly secure. I read it with care. The cable directed me to conduct an evacuation of non-essential civil staff personnel. It was my understanding that such cables would usually be addressed to either the head or acting head of the mission, not me.

This was not how I understood things were done. Permission to conduct an evacuation had to be requested by the HOM. That request had never been sent, at least not to my knowledge. What the hell was going on?

The HOM was not even in the mission area. In fact, I had no idea where he was. He was in the habit of disappearing for days at a time, only later to reappear unexpectedly. The Force Commander was the acting HOM in his absence. His soldiers would not be affected by an evacuation order. I was to evacuate the international civil staff, and only those designated by my superiors as "non-essential personnel." Of course, nobody wants to be tagged "non-essential." Some might fear job loss if they were so identified. For many of the citizens of the developing world, UN jobs paid better than anything else they could hope for at home.

Weeks earlier, I had asked the CAO to stockpile food, water, and fuel against the possibility of our having to use the Mammy Yoko Hotel as a concentration point prior to evacuation. He did none of these things. Therefore, we did not have enough food, water, or fuel to last long. In addition, there were not enough functioning toilets for so many people. The fledgling headquarters was still under renovation. People were sleeping wherever they could find a dry, cool spot on the floor.

To add further insult to injury, I asked my boss to close the hotel bar. He declined. Apparently, he did not understand that fear and alcohol consumption make poor bedfellows. Fights were therefore expected, and in fact occurred.

In an especially memorable incident, the CAO called me to his office and instructed me to speak to the local staff. They were genuinely terrified. They requested evacuation with the international staff. His subsequent refusal led to a near-lynching. Now he wanted me to speak with them. I pointed out that, outside of my office, I had no direct or indirect supervisory relationship with the local staff. Why me?

The answer, although never stated out loud, was that he was afraid to do it. I had seen the look of fear before in my previous career. The CAO's eyes betrayed him. I spoke with the local staff in a group later that day, not because I was directed to do it, but because they deserved answers. Their concerns were real. The RUF was murderous, and on their way. I was aware that under UN rules we were not permitted to remove local staff members from their own country.

What the CAO had perhaps not considered was that the mission was permitted to move local staff internally. I made inquiries to see if I could borrow some trucks with drivers from the Indian military contingent. If the situation went from bad to worse, I had a plan in my back pocket for the relocation of local staff out of Freetown using those trucks.

Of course, it would never be that easy. Local staff had families. Their total numbers could easily climb into the many hundreds. We could have been easily swamped by the resulting human tsunami. There were also problems with water, food, and fuel availability. But again, if it got bad enough, I could at least take what I hoped was some positive action to move the local staff and their family members out of harm's way.

A mission logistician came to me in my office with his arm wrapped around a local woman whom everyone who frequented Paddy's Chinese Bar and Grill knew to be a prostitute. He handed me a document that he claimed to be a marriage license, and then introduced me to his new wife, the hooker. It was his understanding, he explained to me, that I was required to evacuate family members of UN staff. He was wrong, of course; this was a Non-Family Duty Station. There were not supposed to be any family members present in the mission area, period. After I explained how he was mistaken, he left much disappointed. The young lady on his arm also appeared more than a little miffed. I couldn't help but wonder what she had promised him had he successfully removed her from danger.

Shortly after that, the CAO sought me out near the helipad. He had the head of the political section (a former West African foreign minister) in tow, who was accompanied by a young man I did not recognize. He introduced me to the son of the former foreign minister, whom he wanted me to evacuate with the international staff. Nobody followed the rules. I agreed, on purely humanitarian grounds, and because he was not a citizen of Sierra Leone.

Another staff member showed up with, literally, a monkey on his back. Apparently, he had purchased the animal locally at great cost, developed genuine feelings for it, and now wanted me to clear his pet onto one of our evacuation helicopters. This one was easy: "No!" I had a momentary vision of a frightened monkey careening around inside a loaded helicopter full of terrified people. It wasn't a pretty sight.

My staff informed me that the HOM had just flown in and was now awaiting my presence in his hotel suite. I did not know what to expect, but for some reason I tucked the code cable with the evacuation order in my shirt pocket. The door was slightly ajar when I arrived. I knocked, announced myself, and entered.

The HOM was literally spitting mad. Without preamble, he shouted at me, "Who authorized you to conduct an evacuation?" I said nothing, but pulled the code cable from my pocket, unfolded it and handed it over. He looked at me, then the cable, put on his reading glasses, and began scanning. I waited. I think he had to read it twice. His face first showed disbelief, then anger, then something else I cannot describe. The man was small, and he seemed slowly to grow even smaller. His shoulders slumped. His head bowed. His knees gave an inch or more. I thought he might faint. Then it struck me: He had no idea. He was clueless. Nobody in authority in New York had spoken to him. He had not requested evacuation. His boss, the UN Secretary General, had apparently decided to evacuate the mission without consultation with his own HOM.

I suspected that his previous code cables to New York, claiming that the peace process was on-track, had come home to roost. The man was visibly crestfallen. I excused myself, saying that I must return to my work. He said nothing. I backed away, grateful to be out of his presence. Now, this was my interpretation of events. I cannot be sure that this is what in fact happened. The HOM might offer up a very different story.

In any case, the RUF was on its way; of that there could be little doubt. The peacekeeping troops of the UN, although armed, had not stemmed the tide of fighters. In fact, many UN troops were taken captive, and a few had been killed.

The reaction of the international community in Freetown — INGOs, contractors, and embassy personnel from some of the European countries present — was predictable. Many showed up at the Mammy Yoko Hotel, sought me out, and begged a ride out of town on one of our helicopters. I had no mandate to move them out of harm's way. I was only responsible for the safety of the civilian staff of the peacekeeping mission. Still, I never said no to an international.

Now, to UN staff members reading this book, it would seem abundantly clear that I was often exceeding my authority. This is no doubt true. However, and in my defense, any former Special Forces officer would have done the same. We are trained to take the initiative, and to place mission accomplishment ahead of all other priorities. There simply was no time for me to check with my boss every time a key decision was required. Lives were at risk. Over two decades of training kicked in. I did what I thought best on every occasion. However, on much reflection, I perhaps should have made a greater effort to involve the CAO in evacuation operations.

Then again, upon even further reflection, I noted that difficult decisions on the part of UN managers is often left with a subordinate or brought to the desk of a superior. Making decisions in a UN context is perceived as dangerous. Decision avoidance is a seemingly near full time preoccupation of many UN supervisors. I saw this preoccupation playout numerous times in later years. It is remarkable. If one never hopes to be held accountable, then, never decide anything. And if you do, don't ever leave your fingerprints on it. So the CAO may have been more than happy to have me bear the brunt of decision-making in the context of the evacuation. The fact is, we will never know for sure.

My superiors in New York had only recently informed me that I could evacuate non-UN internationals in UN aircraft, but only on a cost-reimbursable basis. Unfortunately, events were moving far too quickly to accommodate the financial administration required that would have resulted in reimbursement for seats in our aircraft. On purely humanitarian grounds, I was personally committed to evacuating as many internationals as could fit into available seats, and I so informed my staff. Luckily, our new heliport was immediately adjacent to the Mammy Yoko.

One of our problems was that we were no longer going to Conakry, Guinea, which was reflected in our Security Plan. We were now going to Banjul, The Gambia. I had received a report earlier in the day that every available hotel room in Conakry was already occupied by UN agency personnel or INGOs who had already evacuated. I subsequently called the UN boss in The Gambia, a small, West African country a little over seven hundred miles to the north of Sierra Leone. She agreed to take care of the over two hundred peacekeeping civil staffers I was shortly sending her way. The soldiers of the mission would remain, as would I and many of my staff. We had a job to do.

I requested IL-76s from the airfield at Brindisi, Italy, to be dispatched in a hurry to Lunghi International Airport, located on the opposite shore of Freetown Bay from our current location. My request was approved. The Soviet-era jumbo cargo aircraft now bearing UN markings were on their way. There were rumors of a possible British intervention force to stop the RUF. I hoped that the rumors were true. It was clear to me that the RUF was not going to be stopped by UN troops.

I had earlier approved a request of the British High Commissioner's office in Sierra Leone to use our helipad to evacuate some of his staff. This humanitarian-motivated action later got me into more trouble with the HOM. He felt that he should have been asked. I would have been glad to, had he been available.

I received another report that the entire Zambian Infantry Battalion surrendered to the RUF without firing a shot. I was initially stunned. As a former US Army officer, I could not imagine why an infantry battalion composed of roughly five hundred armed soldiers would surrender without a shot being fired. The eventual answer came as another surprise.

An even more worrying report arrived in my office. The former Soviet pilots (Ukrainians) now operating our helicopters under UN contract refused to fly the evacuation from the Mammy Yoko helipad unless I first agreed to extract some of their crew mates from a local brothel across town, and in the dark, with the locations of RUF units currently unknown. When I say that it had to be done in the dark, I am not engaging in hyperbole. There was no functioning power grid in Freetown. It was literally very dark and therefore extraordinarily dangerous. The common usage of child soldiers by the RUF compounded everything as well. Children with automatic weapons had proven to be notoriously unpredictable and ruthless killers. There was nothing in the UN playbook to help me sort out what to do next.

I called on two of my staff and tasked them to take my vehicle, drive across town, and recover the contract pilots forthwith. I pulled out my UN-issued 9mm pistol from the pancake holster in the small of my back and handed it to Richard "Mitch" Mitchelson. I knew that he knew how to use it. I said, "Don't come back without them." Mitch was accompanied by Graham "Fish" Mahuika. My handing over an UN-issued pistol to a member of my staff was a violation of policy. The thing is, I absolutely trusted these two. Mitch and Fish were, without question, highly competent, dedicated, intelligent, and perhaps most important to me then, willing to assume significant personal risk to accomplish a vital mission.

Following a more than two-hour white-knuckle wait, the pair returned with the errant air crew. Mitch returned my pistol while stating unequivocally, "I will never do anything like that ever again!" I believed him. But now the evacuation could proceed apace.

Next, I received a report that the RUF had cut the road leading to Lunghi International Airport. Fortunately, our MI-26 helicopters were sufficient to move our evacuees. A road movement was not necessary. The IL-76 jumbo cargo aircraft landed at the now cut-off airport. They were met by an advance security team I had dispatched from the Mammy Yoko earlier by air. That team took charge of the transfer process from the rotary-wing to fixed-wing aircraft on-site. Given the circumstances, I thought it went remarkably well. Our evacuees were soon airborne and out of harm's way. I breathed a huge sigh of relief.

However, the day after all non-essential personnel were supposed to have been evacuated, I discovered that some persons reflected on our manifests were not in Banjul, The Gambia, as I had thought. It was later reported that two former ambassadors from West African countries now working for the mission had locked themselves in their offices instead of reporting for manifest call. I discovered later that they were concerned about the possibility of losing their UN jobs and decided on their own to ignore their instructions to depart. Neither was disciplined.

In addition, I discovered that the mission's head of human resources, on the instructions of the CAO, had pulled some staff members off the helicopters just prior to takeoff. In so doing, the critically important manifests were made useless. My office was required by New York to send a final count by name and nationality of all those who were air-lifted to safety. Both family members and nation-states were intensely interested. My final report was delayed more than twenty-four hours because of the uncoordinated and rash actions of my boss. The manifests thereafter had to be re-created from scratch in Banjul.

The British intervention, called Operation Palliser, began on 7 May. Their intelligence officer, a British Army lieutenant colonel, had sought me out prior. He was a member of the Operational Reconnaissance and Liaison Team. We spoke at length, sharing intelligence-related information concerning the RUF. We met daily thereafter over a breakfast of black coffee, stale toast, and soon-to-be rancid jam in the Mammy Yoko Hotel. The Brits knew things we did not. We knew things they did not. The sharing was mutually beneficial.

A British parachute battalion (1st Paras) and elements of the elite Special Air & Boat Services soon took Lunghi International Airport to facilitate their primary mission, which was the evacuation of all "entitled persons." These were primarily UK citizens. However, the RUF did not know what the British military mission was. For all they knew, the UK forces were deployed for combat. The RUF invasion of Freetown halted. They subsequently retreated when they came face-to-face with a genuinely disciplined and well-trained military force that was configured for combat, even though no shots were initially fired in anger. Their mere presence, in my estimation, was enough to give the RUF pause. It is fair to state that if the

British had not intervened militarily, the result would have been a massacre. I was personally very thankful.

A day later, a mob of Sierra Leone citizens, angered by the now-aborted invasion, proceeded to Foday Sankoh's home in Freetown and sacked it. I received a report subsequently that the UN's Nigerian contingent had whisked him away—and out of harm's way—barely ahead of the mob. I went there the following morning out of curiosity. What I found was instructive: The first floor of Sankoh's home was a wreck, but the refuse told a tale. There were broken drug bottles, syringes, and drug paraphernalia everywhere. This could explain much. Sankoh was well known for his mercurial personality; his mood swings were the stuff of legend. If he was himself drug addicted, that might account for his wildly erratic behavior. Years later, hearing he had died while awaiting trial for his many heinous crimes, I shed no tears.

Although we were much relieved by the British military success, there were still many hundreds of UN military prisoners taken. We called them prisoner-detainees. There were not prisoners of war (there was no declared war), and they were not kidnap victims. To qualify as kidnap victims there had to be a ransom demand, and there had been none to date; therefore, prisoner-detainees. Solid reports stated that the prisoner-detainees of the Zambian Infantry Battalion were to be taken to Foya, which was a small, lawless town just inside Liberia, near the borders of both Sierra Leone and Guinea. Foya was infamous as a trans-shipment point for guns, drugs, and blood diamonds—a very dangerous place.

Somehow, we had to recover the Zambians. Now that the invasion threat was over, I worked up a hasty plan with some of my staff to take two helicopters carrying vehicles and a few of my most trusted officers to Monrovia, the capital of Liberia, then ruled by the former rebel leader and by-then tyrant, Charles Taylor. Taylor was a brutal and merciless dictator who would years later be convicted of crimes against humanity by the International Criminal Court. Going to Liberia was risky, but it was a risk that had to be taken. The Zambians were being taken to Liberia by the RUF; therefore, if we were to bring them home, we had to go there too.

It was 15 May when the HOM left for Monrovia to conduct direct negotiations with Taylor. He had approved our plan. Richard went with him. They traveled in the UN twin-engine turbo-prop. I came later with two mission helicopters, MI-26 and MI-8. Unfortunately, we had to leave our weapons in Freetown. We were authorized to carry our pistols only in Sierra Leone. We did not like going into Charles Taylor's Liberia unarmed, but there was nothing that could be done about it. To do so would have been a clear violation of international law. Without a pressing reason to bring weapons, I felt the need to comply.

Why were we so concerned? Samuel Doe, the previous president of Liberia, had been brutally tortured and executed by Taylor in what can be only described as a near-carnival atmosphere. It is fair to say that Taylor and his henchmen viewed killing as casually as morning coffee. The surreal and gruesome video is still available on YouTube. Casual killing also tends to be indiscriminate. Clearly, there was cause for worry.

The trip south was uneventful. We landed at Roberts International Airport outside of Monrovia on a cool rainy afternoon. I instructed my staff to remain in the helicopter. It was my intent to accomplish a quick personal reconnaissance. When the tailgate lowered, I stepped onto the tarmac carrying a large black-and-white golf umbrella over my head. From the tailgate, I walked to the front of the airframe heading toward the tower walkway, when suddenly five soldiers in full combat garb burst forth from the building with raised weapons.

I stopped in my tracks, still on the tarmac, short of the walkway now filled with charging soldiers. They looked like they meant business. But what was their intent? The five literally surrounded me and stopped, all the while pointing their weapons at my midsection. Nobody spoke. I held my umbrella high to avoid the rain, and while trying to figure out what to do next. Erni Soplantila saw the ruckus from the cockpit and through an open window, shouted out to me, "Chief, you must look REAL dangerous." I heard peals of laughter from within the helicopter. I wasn't smiling, though. One twitchy trigger finger and I would have been history.

We had landed at the wrong airport. Our pilots assumed that we should land at Roberts. It was, after all, the international airport, and we came from a place outside of Liberia. The problem was that we were supposed to land at Spriggs Payne Airport, which was a good deal closer to Monrovia. Once we were informed of the error by the tower, and the five soldiers pointing weapons at me decided I was little threat, we took off again for the short ride to Spriggs Payne.

The mission to recover the Zambians was ultimately successful. Most of the soldiers made it back home to tell the tale, but sadly, not all. Per the mission spokesman on 29 May, and after all those held by the RUF had been released, the final casualty tally was 11 dead and 25 wounded.

While we were still in Liberia, British forces came under RUF attack near Lunghi International Airport. The RUF had regrouped. In a subsequent series of firefights, the RUF was forced to withdraw while sustaining heavy losses. They would not make that mistake again.

Following my return to Freetown, I took the opportunity to confront the Zambian Infantry Battalion Commander regarding his decision to surrender to the RUF. I asked him straight out, "How the hell could you surrender your soldiers and arms without a fight?" He immediately began to explain in a confidential tone that the battalion he commanded was not the "infantry battalion" promised by his government in their Memorandum of Agreement with the UN Department of Peacekeeping in New York. Instead it was a composite unit composed of a ragged mix of cooks, clerks, mechanics, and many other noncombat specialties. In other words, his government had sent several hundred men in uniform to Sierra Leone, but they were not a trained and cohesive fighting force by any stretch of the imagination. I had to wonder, how many of the other peacekeeping military contingents were similarly manned?

It was widely reported in the Media that the tyrant Charles Taylor had brokered the deal for the return of the Zambians for the UN. I found this assertion particularly troubling. In my analysis of the situation, Sam Bokary, the RUF's field Commander, was in fact working for Taylor in the illicit blood diamond trade. It was also my suspicion that the captured Zambian Infantry Battalion was brought to Liberia on the orders of the tyrant. The notion that Taylor did anything that was not in his own self-interest struck me as patently absurd.

Major General Vijay Jetley, the Force Commander, was directly responsible for all military matters pertaining to the implementation of the mandate. He was a good man, who was focused on mission accomplishment and the attempt to bring peace to people who sorely needed it. A few months after the invasion, he was in the process of writing a draft document entitled Report on the Crisis in Sierra Leone. A quote from that document follows: "…they have not only tried to scuttle the peace process but also try to denigrate me and the country I represent, to promote their own personal ambitions and personal interests." "They" in this report references a West African contingent of the mission. This report was stolen and leaked to the Media. His goose was quickly cooked.

Unfortunately, Major General Jetley's deputy was from the same West African country as the HOM. Therefore, the Indian two-star was sandwiched hard between him and his boss. In my estimation, he never stood a chance. Jetley's deputy on several occasions simply refused to obey orders, when those directives ran against self-interest. Military matters cannot be conducted successfully in this manner.

Major General Jetley was subsequently removed from his post by the UN. He was replaced by a general officer from a sub-Saharan African country. The Indian government thereafter withdrew their support from the mission. The Jordanians later withdrew their troops as well. Was the Force Commander forced out of his post because he told the truth? I think I know.

These events hardened my developing opinion that corruption in much of sub-Saharan Africa is not *a* way of life; it is, for many, *the* way of life.

Maps by sierrasketches@gmail.com

Figure 2. Map of Yemen

4

The Road to Yemen

When you come to the fork in the road, you need to take it.
—Yogi Berra

I wrote a three-page letter to the Deputy UNSECOORD explaining the circumstances. Following our return from Liberia, I was told by the HOM that my services on the senior staff of the peacekeeping mission were no longer required. I was not dismissed outright, just thrust aside. My actual boss, the CAO, said not a word in my defense, not that I had expected him to stick out his neck for me. I could have stayed with the mission as CSO and managed parking issues for the CAO, but that is something I was unwilling to contemplate. Under these circumstances, I explained to New York that I no longer felt I could be effective in Sierra Leone. Nothing like this had ever happened to me before. There was no reference point for me to steer by. This was my first and only time—for all intents and purposes—being fired. I felt horrible.

We conducted a messy, but ultimately successful, evacuation of over two hundred non-essential civil staff of the mission ahead of the RUF invasion. The proof of success is that no UN civil staff became casualties. Moreover, I accurately foretold the RUF invasion of Freetown. I was alone in this opinion. The HOM was in total disagreement, as was the entire senior civil staff of the mission, following his lead. Apparently, the key people who did agree with my assessment, once it was confirmed by Richard Manlove, were in New York. They ordered the evacuation against all then-existing UN security policy. The HOM could not vent his anger on New York. I, on the other hand, must have been perceived as an all-too-easy target.

A colleague suggested that I was removed from senior mission staff status because I committed the unpardonable sin of publicly embarrassing the HOM, by being right about the invasion. I can't say for certain, although I noted that thin skins were common enough among the higher-ranking UN staff. However, and on much reflection, I must admit to having been very much a fish out of water in my first security assignment with the UN.

I have been told by knowledgeable others that this was the only time in UN history that a mission was evacuated without a request from the field. It wasn't long before New York sent me a new contract. Apparently, they agreed with me, that I could no longer be effective in Sierra Leone. I had lasted roughly nine months in my first UN civil staff posting, an inauspicious beginning to my inchoate security career.

When the news spread that I was soon to be reassigned, the Indian contingent decided to throw me a going-away party. Their offer was gratefully accepted. However, I told my benefactors that they would have to pick-me-up and then later drop-me-off, after the party. I avoid drinking and driving. They agreed. An Indian batman (military officer's personal servant) was placed at my left for the entire evening. When my glass was less than half full, the batman immediately refilled the glass with scotch and ice.

I have no memory of how I got home that evening, nor do I remember being placed in my bed. I do remember being presented with a matched set of ceremonial kukri knives, a gift from the battalion of Nepalese Gurkas that was part of the Indian contingent. The Gurkas were fine soldiers, feared by the RUF.

I was in my office packing for the trip to my next assignment. I had already turned in my pistol, as I would not be permitted to go there armed. Mitch dropped by to see me privately. He knew that I was feeling dejected. Perhaps to make me feel better, he told me that if I were still in the US Army and had successfully conducted an evacuation without civilian casualties under such outrageously difficult circumstances, I might have been presented with a medal and placed on the short list for promotion. But in the UN, I was all but fired. I appreciated his attempt to improve my mood. It worked. We both chuckled at the irony.

There was something else, too. As my departure from Freetown neared, I still felt alone. Within my former institution, the US Special Operations Community, my subordinates, contemporaries, and superiors all shared a sense of brotherhood. Our values united us in ways that would be difficult for civilians to comprehend. For this reason, I rarely felt pangs of loneliness. There was always someone I could speak to, to confide in, but no longer. My sense of isolation in my first UN assignment, with only a few exceptions, was profound.

I spent my last evening in Freetown with the US Ambassador to Sierra Leone. His residence was built on the side of a hill overlooking Freetown and the sea. He invited me up for dinner and drinks. His objective was to ask my opinion concerning the failure of the peace process. Although our conversation was far-ranging, my opinions are easily enumerated. The peace process failed for five main reasons: The UN Security Council had given UNAMSIL a thoroughly unrealistic mandate based on assumptions that proved to be false. The RUF could not be trusted—they were murderers, torturers, rapists, diamond thieves, and drug addicts. The RUF was never brought to justice for their many heinous crimes. The UN military component was weak and fragmented, and undercut from within by self-interest. Finally, Charles Taylor, Sam Bokary, and others wanted to continue profiting from Sierra Leone's alluvial diamond fields.

The next day, my new posting would take me to one of the most isolated and little-known places on the planet: the country of Yemen. Fortunately, I already enjoyed some limited on-the-ground familiarity with the greater region. I'd had the privilege of commanding a Special Forces Underwater Operations Detachment many years previous with the 5th Special Forces Group, which was oriented on the Middle East. Although my linguistic abilities are very severely limited, I also studied rudimentary Arabic language in that assignment. Moreover, and in the wake of Operation Desert Storm, I served briefly as the Host Nation Liaison Officer to the Saudi Arabian Ministry of Defense and Aviation in Riyadh. Finally, my first graduate degree was in International Affairs (Middle East Studies) courtesy of the US Army's Foreign Area Officer Program. Still, I knew that the minimal knowledge I possessed was insufficient, and so had begun an area study several days earlier.

Yemen is over twice the size of Wyoming and occupies the extreme southwest corner of the Saudi Arabian Peninsula, with the Red Sea to the west, Saudi Arabia to the north, the Gulf of Aden to the south, and the country of Oman eastward. The country is a study in extremes, from vast wasteland deserts in the interior to high mountains in the north and west with over 1,000 miles of coastline. The city of Sana'a is one of the highest national capitals in the world at 7,500 feet. Altitude sickness is not uncommon for new arrivals. Some of the beaches on the Red Sea coast are gorgeous, if little-visited, and therefore unappreciated.

Unfortunately, annual rainfall is barely enough to support the native population. This problem could be ameliorated by better water management and improved arable land usage. Tragically, most of the arable land is not used for raising edible crops. Instead, the preponderance of the land and limited water resources are used in the cultivation of khat. Khat is a leafy plant possessing mild narcotic properties. The entire country comes to a halt every afternoon between 2:00 PM and 3:00 PM to chew the leaves of this plant in communal groups, large and small, divided only by gender. Women and men both chew khat, but they never chew khat together!

Yemen has a history that harkens back to the Old Testament. The Queen of Sheba, who may have seduced King Solomon (or perhaps the other way around), was by legend Yemeni. Ethiopians also claim her, though. The Ethiopians claim that the offspring of King Solomon and the Queen of Sheba was a son, Menelik I. The Ethiopians believe that Menelik was the first in a 3,000 millennium-long line of their emperors, ending with Haile Selassie in the last century.

Yemenis and Ethiopians might both have some right on their sides. It has been suggested that Sheba's domain might have included the general land mass of both countries. The Bab Al Mandab Strait separating ancient Sheba from ancient Ethiopia is a mere twenty-two miles across, and the queen is said to have ruled over a well-established trading empire.

Yemenis and Ethiopians also both take credit for being the birthplace of coffee. In this argument, I think the Ethiopians have the stronger case.

Modern Yemen, and I use that term "modern" loosely, is decidedly tribal in character. There is a president. There is a Parliament. But Yemen is not democratic in the Western sense of that word. The choice of president and parliamentary members is decided in large measure based on tribal realities. As in sub-Saharan Africa, the idea of the nation-state, to which citizens owe their first loyalty, never took strong root in Yemeni soil. First loyalties in Yemen are to self and family, followed by village and tribe. The nation-state runs a distant fifth, if it is even in the running.

Yemen was and is split—perhaps fractured is a more accurate description—in several ways. There is the fracture between the Shia and Sunni branches of Islam that more recently devolved into a civil war with the Sunni side supported by Saudi Arabia and the United Arab Emirates. There is yet another fracture between north and south. In fact, during the Cold War, Yemen existed essentially as two separate countries: a semi-Marxist south and a very loosely democratic north. They later reunited under the leadership of President Ali Abdullah Saleh, as cagey a political operator as any you might find, following the war between the two sides.

The largest fracture, of course, is a consequence of the many tribes of Yemen. Every tribal group, or confederation, has its own goals and aspirations, which often are at odds with the goals and aspirations of the central government in Sana'a. There are three major confederations, the Hashid, Bakil, and Madhaj. The strength of each rises and wanes with intermarriage and shifting alliances. The problem with tribes is that they are exclusive, and not inclusive. This means that Yemen is, and will remain, fragile.

That fragility became all too evident in 2015, sparking the war currently raging within Yemen at this writing. This conflict is generally between the shifting tribal alliances; the Shia Houthi and those who were loyal to the former Yemeni President Saleh; Al Qaeda in the Arabian Peninsula; and a reasonably new but ultimately dysfunctional central government. Saudi Arabia joined the battle because the Houthis are from the Shia branch of Islam that is supported by Iran. Iran is a historical enemy of Saudi Arabia. For this reason, Saudi Arabia and the United Arab Emirates conducted repeated bombing raids in Yemen that resulted in significant international condemnation. But all this would be years in the future.

I arrived in Yemen in early July of 2000, directly from Sierra Leone via Frankfurt, Germany, where I had served as an intelligence officer during the Cold War. I was told that my presence was required immediately because there had been a murder of a UN staff member during the four-month lapse since my predecessor had departed. Unlike my former position with peacekeeping, where I had a large staff and complex responsibilities, I was now responsible for providing security advice to eight UN humanitarian and development agencies, while creating a comprehensive security plan and then keeping it up to date. It seemed simple at the outset, but it certainly did not remain so.

The airport was, except for the tower, made up of medium-height beige buildings. As I was to find out later, most of Yemen falls within the category of variations of the color beige. The bus dropped us just outside the terminal. There followed a rush to the half-dozen stalls manned by all-male officials in ill-fitting uniforms, who would examine our visas for entry into the country.

I was unwilling to muscle my way through the rush. Nor was I willing to push aside women dressed head to foot in black garb, the abiya. No queues formed. There was only the crush of humanity, pushing and shoving their way to the front while waving their passports in a vain attempt to gain the attention of the officials.

The officials for their part seemed enormously bored. Many were unshaven. Most smoked cigarettes. They spoke among themselves in loud voices. They sometimes yelled for the crowd to back away from their stalls. The mob might pull back for a moment following such outbursts, only a few moments later to begin to edge their way back to the front while attempting to push their passports forward across the top of the official's desk.

Personal space that Americans are so accustomed to was non-existent in the melee. I was surrounded by the press of humanity, with all its attendant odors. The combination of body sweat, bad breath, and cigarette smoke would have gagged a maggot. Passengers denied the opportunity to smoke aboard the flight all lit up as soon as they cleared the bus.

There was a glass separating the luggage collection area from those attempting to gain access to Yemen. I observed several possible relatives of passengers waving. I then noticed a smallish man in a blue suit waving to me and pointing at a tiny placard he held in his left hand. The placard bore my misspelled name—"ADOLF." I waved back, and he in turn pointed toward the first stall, apparently directing me to head in that direction. I was fortunate. I was already near what passed for a queue near the second stall. I started to make my way, repetitively saying excuse me "min fadlak" in Arabic.

The airport was malodorous depending upon which way the wind blew. Unfortunately, the local government had located the capital city's sewage processing facility nearby. The airport sometimes stank of the worst of humanity's leavings.

The ride from the airport into Sana'a was interesting. There were children as young as ten years old driving dilapidated pick-up trucks while sitting atop some sort of booster seats. Vehicles shared the road with donkey carts and pedestrians. There were lots and lots of older vehicles, and from predominantly European manufacturers. Newer vehicles were almost always from either Korea or Japan. The SUV was the general vehicle of choice.

Yemeni male dress was unusual, even for the Middle East. Men wore the usual regional headgear, a khafiya or pashmina shawl, but often, in addition to a thobe, also wore over it a Western-style sports coat. Moreover, many men left the manufacturer's label on the sleeve. I have no idea why. Sandals were the most common footwear. Also, most men wore a jumbiya (a curved broad-blade knife) centered over their belly and held in place by a wide and often colorful belt.

Yeminis are generally of short to medium height. A six-foot-tall Yemeni is a rarity. Also, dentistry seemed in its infancy in Yemen. Bad teeth—discolored, missing, and crooked—were commonplace.

The driver sent by the local office of UN Development Programs located both my bags and loaded them into his vehicle. I had only field clothes with me—boots, cargo pants, multi-pocket vest, and long-sleeve shirts with billow pockets.

This was all that was needed for West Africa. As I soon discovered, working for the UN humanitarian and development agencies was nothing like working for peacekeeping.

I was initially authorized two staff members: a local security assistant and an administrative assistant. Only the administrative post was filled. Later, I later gleaned financial support from the Security Management Team (the heads of UN agencies) to hire a communications specialist too.

Most Yemeni women, including our UN local staff, were covered head to foot in black cloth and wore a black veil as well. Normally only their eyes and hands showed. This assignment would stretch me in unanticipated ways.

5

Setting up Shop

People who think with their epidermis or their genitalia or their clan are the problem...
—Christopher Hitchens

I had been in-country only a few days. I stayed at a local hotel while searching for a reasonably priced apartment. A driver had been detailed to take me around to be introduced to the eight heads of agency in Sana'a at their places of business. Most had their own offices, which were well separated from one another. Each was jealous of its independence, even while existing under the flag of the UN.

The introductions went well. I was slowly getting acquainted with all the members of the Security Management Team of the country. On a day in the second week of July, I had just completed a meeting with one of these heads of agency when, while heading back to my vehicle, I was accosted by a woman in a hallway. I saw her coming at me, her cheeks flushed and clearly angry. There was a wall behind me, so there was no escape. Whatever she was going to do seemed to be aimed at me. Eyes flashing, she stopped inches in front of my face before speaking in an over-loud voice. I remember little of what she said. There was something about a robbery, that she was the victim. There was something more about a phone call for help, and something else concerning someone's non-availability. She was screaming at me. I had no idea why. I went into "bunker mode." She was not the first woman to be upset with me. I crossed my arms in front of my chest and lowered my head, while trying to listen intently for a break in the tirade. The whole episode might have taken a minute or two. Somehow, it seemed much longer. Every attempt of mine to speak was immediately shouted down, so I never did get to say anything. She finally completed her rant, turned on her heel, and strode off, leaving me shell-shocked in her wake.

I found out subsequently that the woman who had just verbally assaulted me was a senior UN international staff member. Her walled villa had been broken into and robbed a week earlier. She had reportedly made repeated phone calls to the UN Security Advisor, who had already left the country on reassignment. I, of course, was still in Sierra Leone at the time of the robbery. So when she called for help, nobody answered. No one within her agency had informed her of my predecessor's departure. She had no idea when I arrived. Her anger was completely understandable. I looked forward to seeing her again, assuming she would permit me the opportunity to explain.

I later found a decent three-bedroom apartment in a building less than a five-minute drive from work. I also soon discovered that my sub-Saharan African field garb was inappropriate for Yemen. The heads of agency I served generally wore suits and ties. I asked one of the UN drivers to take me to the place where they got their suits made. He took me there gladly. The tailor, his cousin, sized-me-up and over the next few weeks made me a half-dozen suits for a little over fifty dollars apiece. I still have one of these in my closet more than eighteen years later. The tailor used material that wears like iron.

There is no central water delivery system in Sana'a, so everyone got their water by truck. Water tanks were installed on rooftops. For a fee, the trucks periodically filled the rooftop tanks, and everyone in my building, for example, got their shower and tap water by way of a gravity feed. The water was not suitable for drinking. For drinking, everyone used bottled water—the only safe alternative.

Electricity was installed throughout the city of Sana'a. Unfortunately, the local power plant could not hope to produce enough electricity for all. Therefore, nightly outages were very common. I kept two flashlights handy at home and placed candles in several used wine bottles around my apartment, just like you see in some old French movies. The many differing colors of candle wax eventually melted unevenly while making a pattern over the bottles that was oddly attractive.

One of my first missions was to the Kharaz Somali Refugee Camp run by the UN High Commissioner for Refugees agency. I had seen refugee camps previously in Cambodia, the Gaza Strip, Lebanon, and elsewhere. This camp, in my estimation, was far worse than all the others. For reasons I do not understand, the central government placed the camp in the absolute middle of nowhere in the southern Yemeni desert, a roughly three-hour drive over rough dirt roads outside of the port city of Aden. Daylight temperatures were often above 110 degrees Fahrenheit. At night, the temperature dropped precipitously. Refugee toilet facilities were open trenches. Living conditions were at their most basic. Shelters were constructed from plastic canvas material provided by the UN that hung loosely on what little wood was available. There was only sparse vegetation. One water well served the whole camp.

In one hut, I saw a baby who could not have been more than a few weeks old, literally covered from head to foot with flies. The mother was lying on a filthy foam pad beside the child, holding a piece of ragged cardboard while attempting to use it as a kind of make-shift fan in a forlorn attempt to keep the squadrons of insects at bay. The baby's eyes were swollen shut from what appeared to be a serious eye infection, and the child would not stop crying. The mother was clearly exhausted. I felt great sympathy for her and her child, but they were merely one small family among many in similar circumstances. Life in a Somali refugee camp in the southern Yemeni desert is unimaginably hard.

How bad must Somalia be that these people felt better off in Yemen than at home? Somalia—even back then—was one of the world's best-known failed states. Clan warfare was everywhere evident and accelerating. In the camp, poverty attended by misery seemed the refugees' only birthright.

The World Food Program provided food to the camp, which consisted of the basics of rice, sugar, flour, cooking oil, and little else. Meat of any kind was a luxury that most simply could not afford, although some of the refugees took to raising goats. I returned to that camp many times.

As I soon discovered, kidnapping was a common event in Yemen. Hostage-takings almost always targeted foreign nationals. The method used was unusual. Since the kidnappers targeted only Western foreigners, small groups that were most often village and/or tribal affiliated would come to the national capital and literally go on the hunt. They patrolled the streets in vehicles looking for somebody that appeared foreign. This technique often worked.

Why Western foreigners? Kidnapped Westerners made the best hostages because they could be used as leverage against President Saleh's administration. The kidnappers were not actually interested in extorting money from the national governments of those taken, as would be common in many other countries. In Yemen, the ransom was usually something only Saleh could provide. Although demands for money sometimes occurred the kidnappers often demanded a water well, school, or road—something of benefit to a whole village or tribe. Kidnappings would later occupy quite a bit of my time and attention.

One of my first formal acts as the new UN Security Advisor was to establish the Yemen International Security Forum. I sent invitations to every embassy in Sana'a, asking them to attend periodic meetings at the UN compound to share information relating to the security concerns of the group.

This initiative began slowly but was eventually successful for several reasons. Other than the Americans, no other embassy had a security professional on staff. The security portfolio was handled by either an untrained staff member or a military attaché. I worked for the UN, and every embassy represented in Sana'a was a member state. For this reason, I was perceived as having no agenda other than security, so I was considered reasonably safe. To my knowledge, I was the only person formally trained in the basics of being a hostage negotiator in all of Yemen. Finally, and more importantly, security-related incidents would later rise sharply.

I made a point of maintaining a positive relationship with the American Embassy's Regional Security Officer. We met often to compare notes. He envied my ability to travel anywhere I wished in the country to further the interests of my job. He, on the other hand, was faced with several restrictions that greatly limited his movement. US embassies used to be excellent conduits for information-gathering around the globe. Unfortunately, they have now become more like bastions due to sometimes over-arching security concerns. However, those concerns were valid in Yemen.

Not long after sunrise on the morning of Friday, 13 October 2000, I woke up suddenly to sound of an explosion, loud and not very far away, that literally shook my bed. The blast was clearly close, but either distance or layers of concrete shielded me from the worst of it; my windows were still intact.

I dressed hurriedly, while placing my small personal camera in a cargo pocket on my trousers. An immediate investigation was called for. I took the elevator to the ground floor and made my way to the older model UN-marked security vehicle parked nearby. I did not have far to go. In my first circuit of the block where my apartment building was located, I saw smoke rising from the vicinity of the British Embassy, just off the main street. Driving closer, I saw that a portion of the compound wall had been destroyed by a detonation.

Surprisingly, Yemeni troops were already present. I wondered at the superb response time. The Yemenis were not usually so prompt, and on a Friday morning, (Muslim holy day) too. I parked my vehicle across the street and walked to the incident site. Although a loose cordon of Yemeni troops was established, I walked straight into the compound. No uniformed Yemeni tried to stop me. An officer sporting the collar insignia of a colonel strode up. He might have thought me someone important, and I did not dissuade him of that opinion. After a brief greeting in Arabic, I asked the colonel in English what had happened. He responded immediately. He said that the embassy's electrical power generator had blown up.

I was immediately taken aback. How could he have made such a determination so quickly? The colonel followed me as I walked closer to the incident site. My examination only took a few seconds, but the correct answer was obvious: Although the power generator was indeed badly damaged, and a portion of the perimeter wall was down, the blast pattern made it clear that the source of the explosion was external to the generator. I looked back toward the colonel and told him in no uncertain terms that the cause of the explosion was a bomb. His face betrayed little in response.

In my estimation, the colonel was either uneducated in basic blast analysis, or he had already been given marching orders from higher-ups in his chain of command. The British Ambassador pulled up out front a few moments later. I was walking carefully about the incident site taking photographs. There were several Yemeni soldiers inside the embassy compound perimeter, where they had no business being, stomping on forensic evidence while violating sovereign British soil. The colonel had left me and was now conversing with the just-arrived ambassador. I continued taking photographs internal and external to the compound wall, and then in and around the power generator. I later took photographs of both the interior and exterior damage to the embassy building as well.

The ambassador apparently noticed me after his conversation with the Yemeni colonel. He waved me over. We were well acquainted with one another. His embassy was a member of the Yemen International Security Forum (the Forum). By this time, I served as the coordinator for that body, an elected office. Most of the Western embassies had become members. Security matters in Yemen were considered very serious, but aside from the regional security officer at the US Embassy, I was the only full-time international security professional assigned in the entire country.

We greeted one another with a handshake and then together surveyed the damage. He was seemingly in a chipper mood, smiling and greeting the Yemeni soldiers within his embassy compound. The ambassador looked at me, while saying that he was very glad that it was the generator that was the source of the explosion. Apparently, he accepted the colonel's assessment—which was that the embassy generator had exploded.

I took the man gently by the arm, held it tight, and said, "Sir, there is no question. This was a bombing." The ambassador shook my hand loose while standing more erect and then faced me directly. He reiterated the colonel's line. I was unmoved, insisting what I knew to be true, as true. The look on his face changed dramatically. It was sinking in. His embassy had been attacked.

I thought the choice of timing odd, though. The only persons inside the embassy on that day and at that time were a few Yemeni compound guards. Nobody was injured. The timing suggested that the bomber wanted to make a point but had little desire to hurt anyone—not standard extremist behavior at all.

There was another element of the attack that was puzzling, also relating to timing: The previous day, a Yemeni watercraft loaded with explosives had detonated near a US naval destroyer, the USS Cole, in Aden Harbor. The blast killed seventeen American sailors. The two bombings, so close together, suggested either coordination or opportunity exploitation. There could be little doubt that the USS Cole bombing was intended to create casualties. On the other hand, the British Embassy bombing, less than twenty-four hours later, seemed clearly designed to avoid casualties. Curious.

I made three suggestions to the ambassador. First, that he contact London and inform them that his embassy had indeed been bombed. There was simply no question of it. Second, that he request elements of the Anti-Terrorist Unit associated with Scotland Yard to lead the investigation into the bombing. I did not trust the Yemenis to do a thorough job of it, nor did I trust their conclusions. Finally, I suggested that he cordon off the area around the incident site with engineer tape or whatever his embassy might have on hand. Yemeni soldiers were already in the process of inadvertently contaminating the site. Those soldiers needed to be removed to locations outside of the embassy grounds.

Why was I making such recommendations? There was no security officer assigned to the British Embassy. I had previously, and on several occasions, made recommendations, at their request, to the security focal point (a diplomat) regarding various security-related matters. Those recommendations had been made in the context of their membership in the Forum. Essentially, I was the "UN" security guy, and because all nations represented in the Yemeni diplomatic community were members of the UN, it provided my office a patina of neutrality and legitimacy, just like in Sierra Leone. My security recommendations were perceived as unbiased. I had no profit motive and no nationally driven agenda. I was neutral, and therefore accepted by the membership as credible and trustworthy.

Following the two bombings, we held an emergency meeting of the Forum. There was standing room only. When I entered the conference room, I noted three ambassadors from donor nations in attendance. No one of that high rank had ever previously attended. Following the attack on a Western embassy, national capitals were demanding detailed and timely updates. Might one of the other Western embassies come under attack as well? The Forum in short order had become one of the most trusted sources of security-related information in the country.

I quickly popped downstairs from the conference room and broke into a meeting being held by my boss: UN Resident Representative and Designated Official for Security James W. Rawley. He did not look pleased at the interruption. I explained why—that there were attendees at the Forum meeting of ambassadorial rank who were also from nations that donated significant funds to UN humanitarian and development programs. James immediately excused himself from his guests and launched toward the conference room to greet his ambassadorial-rank colleagues. The Forum worked.

I provided a copy of my incident site photos to the Scotland Yard Anti-Terrorist Squad upon their arrival a few days later. They promised to return them; they never did, as I knew that they wouldn't. When requested, I also provided a second set of photos to senior Yemeni police officials. I had a third and fourth set made for me and my boss, James.

Bombings were hardly the only security matter to occupy my time, though. The UN headquarters in Sana'a was eventually the epicenter for twenty-eight separate demonstrations protesting either the mistreatment of Palestinians in the West Bank and Gaza Strip by the State of Israel, or the sanctions

leveled against Iraq by the international community. I usually knew the protesters were coming because I made several
liaison visits to the local deputy chief of police. Protests required police approval. Once the deputy chief became aware
of a demonstration coming our way, he called my security
assistant, who called me. I notified James and the other UN
agencies in Sana'a.

Protests in Yemen tended to be very different from demonstrations conducted in places like the US or Europe. In Yemen,
nearly every man is armed with an assault rifle (usually AK-
47 variants), pistols, and of course the ubiquitous jumbiya. I
had never previously managed an organizational response to
demonstrations, which made my learning curve steep.

I first requested that the Yemeni Police remain outside
the UN walled compound. I then arrayed the local contract
guards near the main entrance. The object was to keep direct
contact between the police and demonstrators, and not the
UN guard force. It was a good plan that failed.

The protestors arrived outside the UN compound. They
often carried placards. They also came in vehicles. I noted
that some of those vehicles sported machine gun mounts.
Sometimes women covered in black head-to-foot abayas also
participated. But as it turned out, there was almost always
a group of senior protestors—all older men, usually accompanied by mean-looking armed bodyguards, who wanted to
meet with James to make their complaints known to the UN
Secretary General (SG) in New York.

I have always disliked crowds. They are unpredictable. I
doubly dislike large armed crowds of protestors. For my part,
I could not permit armed men inside of a UN facility. Weapons are forbidden there. Also, it was not unusual that twenty
or more protestor representatives wanted to enter. This number was a good deal more than I could reasonably hope to
handle if the situation turned ugly. What to do?

I left the relative safety of the walled compound to speak directly with the protest organizers. My security assistant acted as interpreter. I heard their request to enter the compound, and agreed to permit it, but established some ground rules: No weapons of any kind inside the UN compound, including jumbiyas. No more than ten representatives could enter the compound to meet with my boss. Like it or not, everyone would be searched for weapons prior to entry. If agreed, I told the protest representatives that the head of the UN in Yemen would gladly see them and hear their words. Finally, if their issues had been committed to paper, we would that day send those documents to the SG's office in New York for his consideration.

More than two dozen times during my tenure in Yemen, we dealt with armed protests in this manner. Nobody was injured on my watch—this is a considerable point of personal pride for me. There were plenty of tense moments, but we always managed to avoid confrontation that would have certainly led to violence. The key, in my estimation, is that we treated protest leaders with respect, while permitting them to fulfill their mission—to lay their issues before the UN. Had we in any way frustrated their desires, the outcome might have been disastrous. In no small part this was a reflection on the positive working relationship I had with James. We reasoned together to find solutions. Not like the CAO or HOM in Sierra Leone at all. Essentially, we made a good team.

6

Heartbreak

Unable are the loved to die, for love is immortality.
—Emily Dickinson

It was 3 June 2001. It was my parent's Fiftieth Wedding Anniversary celebration. The entire family attended: six boys and three girls, all grown-up. Also present was a large assortment of uncles, aunts, second, and third cousins, as well as an unruly herd of close family friends.

I took leave and flew into Boston from Yemen via Germany for the event. By pre-agreement, we siblings had thrown in together to fund a large boat, band, and huge buffet meal for the day-sail. My mom and dad were both very happy. It was a gorgeous day in Newburyport, Massachusetts.

The whole family was only very rarely together. My brothers and sisters were spread out all over the US, and of course, I was usually deployed overseas, first as a soldier, and then later with the UN. Bottom line—I was only rarely anywhere near home.

The boat had left the pier only a few minutes earlier when it happened. The music was playing. The caterers were preparing food. A line formed at the bar. Several well-wishers were on deck enjoying the sea breeze as the vessel made its way toward the mouth of the Merrimac River that led to the Atlantic Ocean.

Mom was dancing with one of my nephews when she collapsed to the floor without warning. I heard someone call out. I was the first to get to her and immediately accomplished a visual check. My military medical training took hold. She exhibited no external wounds but was clearly in distress. She appeared paralyzed. I could think of nothing to do. I checked her pulse. Her heart was beating. She continued to breathe. CPR was not called for.

Not knowing what else to do, I sat on the deck and placed her head gently on my lap while stroking her head with a free hand. I was only vaguely aware of the things going on around me. I was conscious of the fact that the boat turned around and headed back to the pier. I also overheard someone calling for an ambulance to meet us when we docked. The hospital was a mere five minutes away.

I gazed into my mother's eyes. I perceived that she was in little pain, but I saw fear and confusion in her eyes. This was not a heart attack... perhaps a stroke? I told her to keep breathing, as if she could will it so. But the light of life gradually left her eyes over the next few minutes. I watched her slip away... helpless. She died in my arms, just as the boat docked and the ambulance arrived.

The paramedics took my Mother from me bare moments after her departure from this earth. I rose and disembarked to shore. I watched the ambulance depart for the hospital, while heading for the parking lot to use my own car to follow. I noted that one of my sisters was looking after Dad. That was good. He needed care. He was frail.

I knew that my mother was gone but stubbornly refused to admit it to myself. The emergency room physician pronounced shortly after her arrival at the hospital emergency room. I got there just in time to receive the news. I felt numb. The tears would come later, when I was alone.

The next few days were very difficult. My father had suffered a stroke himself previously. He could not speak clearly or easily. In halting language, he asked me—as the eldest—to take charge of all matters pertaining to the funeral arrangements and to write and present my Mother's eulogy. I felt the great weight of all that responsibility, but immediately told my father that I would do my absolute best.

The whole family was crushed. My mother was a tiny woman, but she possessed an out-sized personality and was much loved. I did as I was asked: I managed the funeral arrangements with the aid of my many siblings and wrote and presented my mother's eulogy at her funeral service in Newburyport's largest Catholic Church. The ceremony was very well attended.

Although unexpected, my eulogy provoked considerable laughter. Essentially, I attempted to tell the story of a woman who in large measure raised nine children all but single-handedly. We moved often between naval installations in Virginia, Connecticut, Maine, and California. Our father was a US Navy enlisted veteran with over two decades service. Predictably, he was often absent from home. That left our mother with the near-impossible task of caring for a large and unruly brood of children and teenagers, the eldest separated from the youngest by fifteen years. It is something of a miracle that she managed to ensure our collective survival until we all reached the age of eighteen.

It is fair to say that our home was often something of a mad house. For a time, six brothers shared the same small bedroom sleeping on three sets of bunk beds. As the eldest, I took a top bunk to ensure that I would awake dry the following morning. My youngest brothers had not yet been broken of the habit of bedwetting. Our three sisters, when they came of age, eventually synchronized their menstrual cycles together. The ensuing verbal battles between the girls and my mom were colossal.

Mealtimes were riotous. Laundry day was every day. Lines outside bathrooms were commonplace. Nobody had privacy.

Fights between siblings, physical and verbal, were a frequent occurrence. The noise level seemed often ten decibels above a Metallica concert. None of us got the attention we wanted, but all of us got the care that we needed.

My father moonlighted as a TV repairman. Mom also took part-time jobs, as did I. There was always just enough money to keep food on the table and to purchase clothing. My brothers, of course, received all my hand-me-downs.

As the eldest, I had the dubious honor of changing more diapers and bottle-feeding more babies than most mothers will in three lifetimes, and before I turned fifteen. I was, in the early days, my Mom's only helper. Essentially, I became the live-in babysitter too.

In the eulogy, however, the stories that evoked laughter might have accurately encapsulated my mother's life. She was so many things. She was loving. She was tough. She was funny. She was headstrong. She was caring. She was fierce. She was usually pregnant. She was, in a greater sense, a force of nature... because she had to be!

As I prepared to return to Yemen following the ceremony, I remember thinking that my mother was, in an odd way, fortunate. It was her fiftieth wedding anniversary. She was surrounded by those who knew and loved her. Her children were all present. She was dancing happily when struck down. She felt little pain that I could discern. My mother departed this life with her eldest son holding her gently in his arms. If I am any judge, it was a good death.

My return to Sana'a was gratefully uneventful. My mother's loss had hit me like a sledgehammer. I needed time to grieve and heal.

7

The Refugee Camp and
Yemeni Bureaucracy

But the wolf... the wolf only needs enough luck to find you once.
—Emily Carroll

On one of my first missions to the Somali refugee camp, early in my tenure, I noted a strange incongruity. The World Food Program was providing well over 10,000 rations a day in support of the camp run by the UN High Commissioner for Refugees. The problem was that, in my estimation, there were at no time more than 6,000 refugees present. One of the benefits of having served in the US Army was that I had often seen large formations of soldiers. Essentially, and in gross terms, I was practiced at counting noses. My many missions to the refugee camp were—up until that time—always in support of the refugee agency. That meant my reports were written for the refugee agency heads in Aden and Sana'a, and not the World Food Program.

After completing one of these early missions, I paid a courtesy visit to the head of World Food Program in Sana'a. Over a cup of coffee in his office, I told him of the incongruity—the numbers in the camp, at least in my estimation, in no way reflected reality—and that many more rations were being provided to the camp than were needed. There was an uncomfortable 10 second delay before the man spoke. His face displayed concern and perhaps even fear. Finally, he asked the only question that was on his mind; whether I had written up the fact in my official report to the refugee agency. I had not. It was merely a personal observation that I thought should be shared with him. His question spoke volumes to me. He clearly had already known that there were far too many rations going to the Kharaz Camp, and he hadn't to date taken the necessary corrective action. My observation—spoken out loud—would force his hand.

A few months later, I was asked to provide security advice for the conduct of a refugee camp re-count—to attempt to determine the exact numbers of Somali refugees, so that they could make subsequent adjustments in the numbers of rations needed to sustain that population. I was vaguely aware that I might have stirred things up. The potential for violence here was significant.

Perhaps an explanation is in order. The disparity between the actual numbers of refugees and the numbers of rations being provided represented a potential difference of several thousand. Those thousands of rations possessed a monetary value. Somebody in the camp was likely selling those excess rations on the black market and pocketing the profit. That somebody, or those somebodies, would lose a great deal of money if an accurate re-count was taken. This was going to be a hazardous undertaking. Moreover, I had no idea how to go about it. I had never supported the conduct of a refugee camp recount. I also had no idea who might be benefiting from the theft of the excess rations. The Somalis? The Yemenis? Both? Not only that, but it was quite possible that something untoward might happen to anyone foolish enough to ask too many questions.

I later contacted the UN High Commissioner for Refugees organization in Geneva, Switzerland, and spoke with their security focal point. He apologized, but he stated that they had no advice, no lessons learned, and no best practice files to share with me in planning for the security of staff members conducting a refugee camp recount. I also contacted my department in New York. They too could provide no advice or assistance. I was surprised. I was on my own. However, I would soon become accustomed to feeling this way—and acting alone.

I devised a security plan with the able assistance of UN-HCR staff and executed it. On the chosen day, the first order of business was to inspect the Yemeni camp guards. They turned out in uniform and platoon formation carrying medieval-looking wooden batons studded with nails. I confiscated those batons on the spot. I had no authority to do so. I did it anyway. I was learning a lesson about authority in places like these. If others perceive you as in charge, you are in charge.

Authority is a double-edged sword, though. With it comes responsibility. Responsibility in the UN context is often avoided because it equates to potential liability. Nobody wants to be liable for negative outcomes. So if you're willing to accept the liability, few will challenge your authority. I was willing. I would not permit the Yemeni guards to use nail-studded batons on the Somali refugee population that included many women and children. The Yemeni soldiers later showed up with standard wooden batons. These, I approved.

I took several other precautions to better protect those coming in close contact with the refugees. These precautions proved necessary and effective. There were some tense moments, of course. But most were manageable. Bottom line— no staff member or UN implementing partner was injured. The recount was conducted successfully.

We determined the accurate number of refugees occupying the camp, and subsequently the daily ration count was appropriately adjusted downward by the World Food Program. Regrettably, the process put four refugees in the hospital, but none suffered permanent injury. I arranged for an ambulance to be parked nearby, just in case. As previously mentioned, not all refugees shared an interest in the success of our endeavor.

Not all my duties were so exciting. One of my most frustrating chores involved repetitive attempts to secure permission from the Yemeni Government's Communications Ministry to import additional radio equipment, and to secure more dedicated frequencies for the use of those devices. It is basic security policy that redundant means of communications are essential. I did not initially think this would be a problem. Yemen had signed a well-known international convention that essentially said that the government should approve, at no cost, the UN's being assigned the needed frequencies, while also being granted permission for the importation of related equipment.

However, the Yemeni Communications Ministry disapproved every request I sent their way. In response to my many missives the answer was always the same: The UN must pay for both frequencies and import licenses on radios and associated equipment (antennas). No mention was ever made by the Communications Ministry concerning the legally binding convention that had been signed by the Yemeni Foreign Ministry, even though I had included a copy in both English and Arabic in my most recent request. I subsequently made an appointment to see the communications minister himself, and asked my boss, James, to come with me to provide the necessary senior emphasis. Nothing we said made any impact. The communications minister refused to consider allowing us frequencies or radio importation permission unless we paid for the privilege.

Over time I came to understand why. Each Yemeni ministry existed as a stovepipe bureaucracy, with the result that the ministries seldom spoke to one another. The point where they did intersect was in the national president's office. So it would take President Saleh to order the communications minister to comply with the convention.

The president never interceded on our behalf. Ministry appointments were divided up based on tribal affiliation. This means that President Saleh handed out ministerial posts as a form of patronage, and in return for political support. Each minister thereafter could use their position to make money. Essentially, each ministry became a cow to be milked. Lower-level appointments had little to do with competence, and everything to do with family and/or tribal connections. In other cultures, this would be called corruption and nepotism. In Yemen, I came to see it merely as the "tribal reality." President Saleh was assassinated on 4 December 2017.

I taught many classes while in Yemen, and to very diverse groups. Since I had very little by way of UN training for my post, and in the early days of this assignment, I purchased several professional books on security matters for self-study. They helped. Most of what I taught, though, I developed myself. My classes included kidnapping prevention, personal security, radio-telephone procedures, physical security, evacuation protocols, security management team functions, rape prevention to classes to women, and much more.

During one of my presentations, an attendee asked a question. The group laughed at him. They considered his question stupid. I intervened in support of the man with the query, stating categorically that "there is no such thing as a dumb question." This, of course, was a lie.

I knew this was a lie because of an incident I recalled from attending Phase One of the Special Forces Qualification Course. I was sitting in a classroom lecture on field-expedient methods of land navigation. I was tired. I had slept poorly the previous night and had to stand fire guard too. Our tents were warmed by oil-burning heaters. They sometime caught fire, hence someone had to remain awake to warn sleeping soldiers if a blaze occurred. This is my poor excuse for what transpired in the classroom the following day.

The senior sergeant teaching the class on land navigation started his presentation with the seemingly incontrovertible statement that "there is no such thing as a dumb question." Well into his speech, he discussed a method that could help someone who was lost determine which way is north and south. My hand shot immediately into the air. The sergeant recognized me. I stood, and in a loud and self-confident voice asked, "Once you know which way is north and south, how do you determine which way is east and west?" The words no sooner cleared my lips than I knew my question was one only an idiot would utter. Tragically, it was out there. There was no calling it back. The silence was deafening for what seemed an eternity. Then, all at once, the laughter burst forth. My classmates were rolling in the aisles. I must have been red-faced. I felt the flush on my cheeks. I stared straight ahead at the sergeant on stage. He was livid. He was not laughing. His loudspeaker-amplified southern-accented voice, laced with both sarcasm and distain, drowned out the laughter. "You shithead," he spit out. "You made a liar of me after all my years on the teaching platform. There is such a thing as a dumb question, and you just asked it. You will give me fifty push-ups on every break from now until all hell freezes over. Do you understand me... you stupid sum-a-bitch?" I nodded my agreement that I was indeed a stupid sum-a-bitch and sat back down quickly—suddenly wishing for a hole deep enough for me to crawl into and disappear.

There is such a thing as a dumb question. I am living proof.

8

Road Trips

Go wide, explore and learn new things…
—Mustafa Saifuddin

My smartest move in Yemen was to hire Jamal Outaifa as my security assistant. Jamal was typical Yemeni in appearance. He had a swarthy complexion with jet-black hair. He was also short, perhaps only five feet, five inches tall, and maybe weighing one hundred twenty pounds. What was not typical about him was that he had been educated in the US. He held a bachelor's degree in computer science from a university in Michigan. His English-language capabilities were therefore good. Moreover, and since being hired shortly after my arrival, he had proved to be dedicated, intelligent, resourceful, and loyal. I could not have asked for a better assistant during my time in Yemen than Jamal Outaifa.

Our boss, James, came to depend on Jamal as much as I did. After a while, he would not permit both of us to go on a mission simultaneously. One of us always had to be available to him in Sana'a. Much of my success in Yemen was a direct consequence of his advice and support. We remain friends to this day.

The security vehicle that I inherited was a decrepit, older, two-door model. I purchased a new full-sized SUV with my meager security budget as soon as I was able. Driving about

Sana'a often proved dangerous, particularly at night. Women of course were dressed head-to-foot in black. Functioning streetlights were uncommon. There were few designated crosswalks. Women crossed the street wherever it was convenient, and seemingly always directly in front of my SUV. Only by exercising enormous care did I avoid hitting and injuring a local woman during my tenure. But there were many close calls.

Jamal took me into the tribal lands of his birth, a village and tribe named Ra'ada, a couple of hours' drive outside of Sana'a. There we engaged in the Yemeni manly art of target-shooting with assault rifles, all-male communal meals, and a wedding where the groom had never met the bride. The groom was in his early 20s and very happy that he was at last to have sex for the very first time. The grin on his face looked like it was pasted on. His soon-to-be-wife, I was told, was a girl of 15. Obviously, this was a family-arranged marriage. Child brides far younger than 15 were not uncommon.

Weddings were sometimes dangerous events in Yemen because they were almost always accompanied by automatic weapons "celebratory fire." At one wedding, an attendee killed both the bride and the groom when his weapon got away from him after initially jamming. Deaths by weapons fire at weddings were reported in the local newspaper, on average, monthly. Still, no matter how unsafe the practice, nobody in government ever suggested doing away with the tradition.

On one of our several road trips outside the confines of the capital city, we ran into a police/military checkpoint. The officers at the checkpoint told us that they had orders to protect foreigners, and that they were mandated to accompany us to our destination. Unfortunately, they needed money for fuel. In fact, it was my belief that they needed money for khat. Jamal later confirmed that belief. I, of course, was expected to pay up. A mildly heated discussion ensued, with Jamal acting as interpreter. I told them we did not require their escort services. They told me that they had to follow their orders.

The winning argument was ultimately mine. I asked them to inspect the words in Arabic and English that I painted on the side of my SUV in addition to the classic UN markings. The words said, "United Nations Security." I told them that I did not require security escort because we ourselves were Security. That position seemed to stump them. They let us pass without escort.

It was on one of these early trips outside the national capital that I noticed the blue plastic bags. They were everywhere. Apparently, someone in authority had the monopoly on their sale. Most businesses, like grocery stores and fruit markets, universally provided their goods in medium-sized blue plastic bags. It also seemed that these bags were subsequently discarded as trash. It appeared that there were millions of them caught up in nearly every bush and stunted tree. I took to calling them the blue birds of Yemen. They were ugly—modernity's unintended gift to a several-millennia-old tribal society.

On another of our trips out of Sana'a we noticed what appeared to be a crowd standing around the base of something that looked like a flagpole, only without a flag. There was something large hanging from the top. I asked Jamal to pull over to find out what was going on. As we got closer, I made-out what was hanging from the pole. It was a man's body. He was hung by the neck. I guessed that he had been there for a day or two. His skin was mottled, nearly black, and bloated. Crows were busy consuming the softer parts around the eyes and lips. The crowd was composed of many men, some few women and several children, observing the grisly sight.

I asked Jamal to speak with them to find out what crime the man had committed that his corpse should warrant such treatment. Jamal returned in about five minutes with the story. The hanging man had been caught having sex with children. He was killed for it, and then denied a proper Islamic burial.

We left. I have no idea how long that body hung in that fashion. Jamal later went on to explain that this manner of death (hanging) was meant as a punishment for the pedophile, but also a warning for others that might feel thus inclined.

On yet another excursion, Jamal took me to a weapons market in northern Yemen. I found it much like the one I had previously visited in Pakistan's northwest frontier back in early 1997. Everything was on offer for a price. A hand grenade could be acquired for as little as five dollars. Chinese-made AK-47s went for under a hundred. Russian-made handguns were available for less than fifty. Weapons were inexpensive in the country because they were everywhere. No man in Yemen feels complete unless he owns a gun.

In all my travels about Yemen, I was in every case well-received and asked to return by my tribal hosts. Why? In my many years of Special Forces service, I had learned that it is critically important to demonstrate respect for the cultures of others. In many cases, that respect is best initially demonstrated through a show of good manners. Of course, good manners are culturally specific. I always made a point of good manners, because everywhere I went the local people were always watching me. Why? Foreigners, especially Americans, are only rarely seen in the tribal areas. The Yemenis were understandably curious.

The Toyota Land Cruiser was the king of the Yemeni road. Tribal sheiks who had access to the funds universally chose it for their personal use. This vehicle had all the status and prestige of a Cadillac or Lincoln in the US. The locals called the Land Cruisers by the nickname "Monica" in honor of Monica Lewinsky, President Bill Clinton's former White House intern and paramour. The goings-on in the country of my birth were of great interest to even the most isolated tribes in the country.

I eventually took to carrying lots of local coins in the console of my vehicle. There was a good reason. Sana'a had beggars. Most were women wearing ragged abayas. Some held babies in their arms. They generally waited at stoplights. As I brought my vehicle to a halt for a red light, they would walk up and knock on my driver's side window. Veils covered the entirety of their faces except their pleading eyes. I found them impossible to ignore, so would reach into my console to fish-out some change to place into their outstretched hand. It was little enough.

Then there was the Tuesday morning that started like any other day for me. I was scheduled to depart on mission to both Eritrea and Ethiopia in twenty-four hours. My administrative assistant had acquired flight tickets. I had also recently acquired the necessary visas, and they were now reflected in my UN blue Laissez-Passer. I had never previously visited either country and was looking forward to the trip. I often enjoy experiencing novel places.

My mission was to secure an agreement between UN-Yemen and the peacekeeping mission in Eritrea. Evacuation planning was one of my primary tasks. To conduct a possible evacuation of UN staff from Yemen, the peacekeeping mission had to send their mission aircraft to Yemen, upon request, and on short notice. Eritrea was not an ideal choice for evacuation, but given regional realities, it was the best we could probably hope for. The peacekeeping mission had two Soviet-era Antonov twin-engine cargo aircraft. In the event of an emergency evacuation, both aircraft could be dispatched to Sana'a to gather our international staff and family members, and then return them to Asmara, where the peacekeeping mission would provide safe haven. At least that was my plan. Now I had to nail down the agreement of the mission on paper in the form of a formal memorandum of agreement.

Eritrea had recently won its independence from Ethiopia through a long and brutal civil conflict. A peacekeeping mission was subsequently established in Asmara, Eritrea's capital city. Peace had not yet completely taken hold, though. Violent incidents were common along the still-simmering border areas between the two former antagonists. But the national capitals were generally stable.

I would eventually make this trip, only later. The horrendous event, which would impact the lives of so many, occurred that September day. Although I could not know it at that time, that calamity would continue to impact my life and the lives of many millions for years to come.

I was watching the news while packing. I saw New York's Twin Towers aflame. But how could fires break out in both towers simultaneously, I thought. It didn't make any sense. The video feed cut, and then I saw a commercial-size aircraft fly directly into the structure. I found the images I was seeing initially difficult to believe. I sat down. I suddenly did not trust my legs. The news presenter said that this was another aircraft flown into the second tower. Now it began to make better sense to me. The resulting explosion was startling, even on TV. It was an extremist attack on the US... maybe Al Qaeda? The later report of a similar attack on the Pentagon took the wind out of me. It took me a while to recover myself.

I later became very angry—so many innocents were killed. As an American, I wanted to see my nation strike back at the attackers. Yes, I wanted revenge. Revenge may not be rational, but it is completely human. I never could have imagined, though, how poorly my government's leadership would go about the subsequent target-selection process.

I called James and postponed the East Africa trip. I had to take some time to assess how the tragic events of 9/11 might impact UN security in Yemen. Fortunately, the rapid growth of Al Qaeda in the country would not occur until after my departure.

9

A Memorable Gunfight

The psychological components of war have not gone away—
dominance, vengeance, callousness, tribalism...
—Steven Pinker

I was driving home from the gym. It was late afternoon on 29 September 2002. The sun, hanging low in the sky, was casting long shadows across the roadway. I generally worked out in the afternoon after leaving my office around 3:00 PM (my workdays began at 7:00 AM). I heard gunfire in the distance but was unconcerned. Not unlike south Chicago, gunfire in Sana'a is relatively common. But as I came closer to my apartment building, the noise level and rapidity of fire both increased. By now I thought I could discern the unique sound signature of fully automatic AK-47 assault rifles.

As I turned one of the final corners near my apartment, I saw what appeared to be muzzle flashes coming from my multi-story apartment building. I had no idea what was happening, but it was clear to me that someone was shooting down into the street. In the distance, I could see what appeared to be a police checkpoint roughly seventy-five yards from my compound. The police saw me coming and tried to stop me. Their waving of arms was almost comical. I refused to stop, gritted my teeth, and went barreling through their checkpoint at high speed. The Yemeni cops scattered, as I knew they would. I had to get inside my apartment building.

I brought the vehicle to a halt to the sound of screeching tires and tortured brakes. The staccato gunfire never waned. I only hoped that I would draw little attention. I was still in my work-out garb, long black cotton pants and short-sleeve gray sweatshirt with white running shoes. I grabbed my light-weight rucksack, hurriedly opened the car door, then sprint-ed for the near wall. It provided both cover and concealment from whoever was firing from the building.

I looked around to try to take stock of my surroundings. I saw men in Yemeni police uniforms firing up into the build-ing from behind official-looking vehicles. I also observed men dressed in Yemeni tribal garb nearby firing up into the build-ing. I was on a side street, away from most of the action. The driveway entrance to my building's parking lot was only a few yards distant. I got low and moved as rapidly as I could under cover of the compound wall. When I made the drive-way entrance, I stopped to look toward the building. There was nobody there. I took a deep breath, swallowed hard, and forced myself to sprint the roughly 20 yards to the building entrance. By this time, I had placed the rucksack where it be-longed, on my back, although I do not remember doing it. I felt the hand-held radio's hard edge on my shoulder blade as it bounced about.

Someone must have seen me. The sound of fire came from above as rounds hit the pavement to my right and bits of con-crete and tar were thrown into the air. Nothing hit me. I made the safety of the entrance in record time, which was surpris-ing, as I am a poor runner. At that point, though, I was so scared I might have given Usain Bolt a race, even considering my advancing years.

Once inside, I took a couple of deep drafts of air. I was sweating profusely. I looked toward the elevator, then at the stairs, and was momentarily stumped. Which means should I take to my floor? The elevator offered an easier ride. But the elevator door would open at my floor on the unknown. The stairs were safer. I was really missing the pistol that I had carried in Sierra Leone. Being unarmed in the middle of a gunfight has distinct disadvantages. I felt utterly vulnerable, but I had to keep going.

I started the climb two steps at a time, but then chose to slow my pace. I wanted to arrive on the fifth floor capable of meeting the unknown. That was my intention, but by the time I got there, I was out of breath again. The fact that Sana'a was over a mile high ensured that the air was thin. The combination of age, adrenaline, and altitude worked against me. I took a moment to steady my breathing before launching into the abyss. My mouth was unimaginably dry. My hands were shaking, and my breathing was ragged. I wiped away the sweat from my eyes with a dirty hand.

I was just above the fourth-floor landing. All was silent; there was a lull in the fighting. I climbed the stairs carefully, while attempting to see over the fifth-floor landing. Straight ahead I noticed the door to the French military attaché's apartment was ajar. From the appearance, it had been kicked in. Was there anyone still inside?

To the left was my place. The door was closed. The door to the right was also closed. That was my destination. I moved as quietly as I could to the open door first. I had to know if there was anyone there. I gently pushed the door open further to peer inside. It remained quiet. There was nobody immediately visible. The windows had been shot out. The ceiling was pockmarked with bullet strikes, and a chandelier that had occupied the ceiling now rested on the dining room table in shattered remains. I cannot explain why, but I knew, or more correctly felt, that the remainder of the attaché's apartment was unoccupied. Whoever had kicked down the door had moved on, perhaps looking for a better firing position on a higher floor.

Sensing now that, for the moment, there was no danger here, I pivoted rapidly and made my way to the apartment that was my destination. I knocked on the door and called out her name. The response was muffled but nearly immediate. I heard the interior latches at work, and the door swung inward. Olga stood in front of me holding her baby girl close to her breast. Both mother and daughter were in tears, and badly frightened.

At my appearance, Olga's smile shone through. She was clearly very glad to see me. I have no memory of what I said next, probably something intended to be comforting. Unfortunately, the lull in the fighting ended. The bursts of fire were not controlled, but long and ragged. We heard the dull thud of rounds impacting concrete on the front side of the building. We also heard what might have been return fire from a pistol, perhaps from the vicinity of the rooftop. It was impossible to tell for sure.

I took Olga gently by the arm, while directing her to the nearest bathroom, and away from exterior windows. Interior bathrooms can often provide additional insulation against bullets. I placed her and the baby in the bathtub—more insulation—after acquiring a blanket for them from her son's bedroom. He was fortunately not yet home from school.

First, using my hand-held radio, I sent out a general call to all UN staff members in Sana'a, advising them to avoid the general location of my building until I provided an "all clear." Second, I called Frank, Olga's husband, on my cell phone. He worked at the UN High Commissioner for Refugees agency in Sana'a. I told Frank what had occurred and instructed him to stay at work until my next call, which would permit him to come home. I assured him that his wife and child were in good hands and safe. I lied. But it was a lie with a purpose. It kept Frank safe from harm. The fact was that I was not armed and could not have done much if armed men wanted to enter Frank and Olga's apartment. Third, I called James and provided a quick situation report.

I was about to call Jamal, when I heard him calling my name in the hallway. His voice is distinctive. I recognized it immediately. I opened the door, so he could join me in Olga's apartment. I was very glad to see him. We re-locked the door and piled some furniture in front of it as well. It wasn't much, but it might be just enough to stop or delay entry. Anyway, it was the best we could do under the circumstances.

Jamal then told me that he had been in his car nearby when he heard the firing. Once he discovered that the source of the automatic weapons fire was my building, he headed straight there, but while on the way, he noticed a fully loaded children's school bus headed in that direction too. Recognizing the potential danger, he raced ahead of the bus in his vehicle and brought his car to a stop directly in front of the school bus. The bus driver had no choice. He halted. Jamal instructed the bus driver not to enter what had become a free-fire zone. His quick thinking may have saved some young lives that day. I later ensured that he was presented a letter of commendation for his bravery and quick thinking.

Some minutes later, when the firing let up, I asked Jamal to check the area surrounding the apartment building to ensure that the firefight was indeed over. I remained with Olga and her baby. Jamal returned perhaps fifteen minutes later and confirmed that the fight was done. He also told me that he had seen the bodies of four dead. In conversation with local police authorities he discovered that several more were wounded and had been taken to the hospital.

What happened? As I discovered later that same day, two sons of a powerful sheik parked their vehicles near the British Embassy. The embassy guards asked them to move. An argument ensued. A physical assault occurred. Guns were drawn. Firing began. The battle became mobile—moving down the street and around the corner to my apartment building. This absurd altercation over parking spaces was the genesis of the gunfight.

The reason I saw both persons in tribal garb and persons in police uniforms firing into the building was because a man from one tribe will not fire on members of his own tribe, even if they are in police uniform. Instead he will automatically take up arms against anyone firing on another tribal member.

The following day, sometime in the early evening, I heard a gentle knock at my apartment door. It was Olga standing there holding a bag. I invited her in. She declined the invitation while handing me the bag. In her lilting Tajik accent, she said, "Bob this is for you from me, a gift, not from Frank." I looked inside the bag. It contained three bottles of extremely hard to come by 12-year-old scotch. I tried to refuse... to say that I was just doing my job... to make the point that I should not accept such generosity. She would have none of it. She insisted! I reluctantly caved in. She went home to her family across the hall. I cracked open a bottle and poured myself a welcome drink.

A few days later, and after filing my reports with the UN and the Forum, I attended a diplomatic dinner. The American Ambassador was present. The story of the gunfight at my apartment building was still fresh in everyone's minds, which made me a minor celebrity. I was asked over dinner to provide a verbal synopsis for those who had not read my reports. I did so and ended my brief narrative with the casualty count of four dead, and an unknown number of wounded. The American Ambassador immediately questioned my veracity. Apparently, his sources, which were likely governmental, claimed that there were no deaths.

My jaw tightened. I am not accustomed to being doubted within a professional context. I forced my facial muscles to relax before speaking. Without putting too fine a point on it, I made the case that we were there, and he was not. I also shared with him the fact that I trusted Jamal with my life, and therefore believed his report that there were four dead. There was simply no question of it. Finally, I made the additional point that government representatives had often been caught telling self-serving lies. I suspect that the ambassador did not like my tone. He was clearly accustomed to more subservient behavior.

The fact that the ambassador preferred to believe his Yemeni interlocutors over credible eyewitness accounts was interesting. I had noted this predilection previously among senior officials. The phenomenon is remarkable. When ranking bureaucrats are faced with reports that contradict policy, or their opinions and beliefs, they often tend to double-down and deny the truthfulness of even eyewitnesses on the ground. Essentially, people believe what they wish to believe. This observation with different wording later became enshrined as Bob's First Law.

10

Kidnappings

Conflict and resolution are two sides of the same coin.
—Harish Sippy

I finally made the trip to Eritrea and Ethiopia that had been canceled because of the appalling 9/11 attacks. Richard "Mitch" Mitchelson, my trusted staff member in Sierra Leone, had transferred to the UN peacekeeping mission headquartered in Asmara. It was very good to see him again. The mission was ultimately a success, and in no small part due to his assistance. I received the promise of the aircraft that I wanted in the event we were compelled to move the UN international staff and their families out of harm's way in a hurry in Yemen.

I made other notable trips out of Yemen. One was a week-long mission to Muscat, to write a baseline security plan for the UN in Oman. They had no assigned security officer, and therefore needed the assistance.

Another was to Dubai to attend a regionally based, week-long course of UN security training. It was a brilliant opportunity for learning, but also for meeting and sharing information with colleagues, who were mostly country security advisors like me. I learned as much from them as from the New York-based instructional staff.

Still another trip came by way of an invitation from the US Department of Defense's Asia-Pacific Center for Security

Studies at Fort DeRussy in the heart of Waikiki Beach, Honolulu, Hawaii. I was asked to make a speech before a multi-national conference addressing terrorism within the region. I was glad to do so but had to take personal leave to do it. Also, I had to ensure that the participants at that conference understood that I represented personal perspectives in my address, and not the UN.

Shortly after my return, I received an e-mail from Ralph Peters, an old friend. Ralph was at that time one of the best-known soldiers in the US Army. His fame was well-deserved as an author of several terrific military-related books, and as a regular contributor to the commentary pages of the *Army Times* newspaper. He would later go on to become a regular commentator for a major American news channel, and author several award-winning historical novels concerning the US Civil War.

CC on Ralph's message was an unknown e-mail address. The note was essentially an introduction to author Robert Kaplan. Kaplan was already well-known to me. I had already read several of his books over the years, many of which, like Ralph's, were in my personal library. Both Ralph and Robert were well-traveled. I often found much to agree with in their written observations of a seemingly ever-more-complex globe.

It seemed that the two had met at some writer's function. Robert mentioned to Ralph that he was headed to Yemen to do research for an upcoming book. I suppose Ralph told him that if he was going to Yemen he had to spend some time with his friend Bob. I later offered to put up Robert in my apartment in Sana'a in November of 2002. It was no imposition. I had a spare bedroom. Robert gratefully accepted. I was glad to meet him. We had much in common, and he made for an interesting house guest.

For my part, I did what I could to facilitate his activities, to include arranging a meeting with a local sheik, who would help manage his subsequent safe passage through Marib Province. I also arranged a meeting for him with General Ali Muhsen, arguably the second-most powerful man in the country. I even held a social gathering at my apartment, inviting several US Embassy personnel, to further facilitate Robert's research efforts relating to the book he later published under the title *Imperial Grunts*. Robert was more than kind to me in the first chapter of that book. I will not soon forget.

Several of the Western embassies needed to update and practice their evacuation plans. I assisted them on the weekends in my capacity as coordinator for the Forum, and at their request. Because of my previous experience in Sierra Leone, I was considered something of an expert on all matters relating to evacuation. If a terrible experience is the genesis of wisdom, then they might have been marginally correct. I served as both trainer and evaluator on practice evacuations conducted by the British, German, and Italian embassies.

"Be prepared," in addition to serving as the well-known Boy Scout Motto, is also a key element of being a good security advisor.

I met several sheiks in Sana'a. As a result, I also received many invitations to chew khat with them. I sometimes went. It was, essentially, the US equivalent of going drinking with the boys. I took Jamal with me to act as interpreter. We usually sat in a large open area within a home. The floor and walls were strewn with carpets and pillows. Upon entry, the participant, me, would go to each man in turn, shake hands, and greet him in Arabic. Once everyone was greeted properly, I was often given the honored position to the sheik's right. I was also handed a handful of khat.

The best description I can provide is that the activity looked to me like cows chewing their cuds. A man chewing khat for well over an hour would inevitably end up with a huge wad in his cheek that greatly distorted his face. Chewing khat, I was told, released the mild narcotic within the plant's leaves.

I did as they did. No matter how much I chewed, though, I never felt a thing—no buzz at all. At one of these sessions I was asked by the sheik how I enjoyed the khat. I told him via my interpreter, Jamal, that I thought beer was better. Jamal spoke the translation loud enough for everyone to hear. The laughter lasted some time. Yemenis have a well-developed sense of humor.

As earlier mentioned, kidnapping in Yemen is commonplace. In the year 2002, I recall perhaps as many as a dozen hostage-takings. The victims were usually European. In most of these cases, my office was consulted via the mechanism of the Forum by either the ambassador or the chargé d'affaires (the person in charge in the absence of the ambassador). All such assistance had to be cleared first by both James and the Deputy UNSECOORD in New York. To their credit, they always said yes.

During my first year in Yemen I conducted a study of previous hostage-takings going back several decades. What I discovered challenged my understanding of the crime within this context. Kidnapping in Yemen is not kidnapping in the Western sense. In fact, there are significant culturally driven differences.

Surprisingly, kidnapping in the Yemeni context is an unusual means of conflict resolution. The victims of hostage-taking in Yemen, once captured, are often treated with respect and considerable care. The victims are an important means to an end. As every tribal sheik knows, if a victim is not treated well, it is a great shame on the hostage-takers. The cultural component looms large here. Taking a hostage is a means of focusing the central government on their issue. The same used to be true in inter-tribal hostage-takings as well, going back over a thousand years.

Because of my study, and in every instance, I cautioned the embassy involved to avoid placing too much pressure on the central government for a rapid resolution. Tribal negotiations take time. An intermediary must be agreed to and accepted by both sides. Ransom demands must be received and understood. *The ultimate objective is the safe return of the hostage/s.* All other factors are subordinate. I always assured the involved embassy that so long as the kidnapping was "authorized" by a tribal sheik, that man was culturally compelled to care well for the victims, and to ensure their eventual safe return. Although some of the hostage victims were held for as much as a month or more, all were eventually returned safely to their embassies and families. It is a matter of intense personal pride for me that no kidnapping case on which I consulted ended badly. Everyone got to go home.

One instance among many was especially memorable. The kidnapping victim this time was a Chinese engineer walking to work in Sana'a. A group of hostage-takers from the same village and tribal affiliation grabbed him in the street, held a gun on him, and told him that they would shoot him if he gave them any trouble. He complied with their every order. They took him to their village, which was several miles outside the capital. They had been looking for a foreigner for several days—driving about Sana'a—when they just happened to spy the engineer. He was released several weeks later, unharmed. I was not involved in his case. The Chinese Embassy never requested my office's assistance. The Chinese Ambassador callously joked that there were more than a billion of his countrymen; one loss among that staggering number was insignificant.

I asked a UN physician of Chinese origin to contact the victim and ask him if he would permit me to debrief him concerning his experiences in captivity. He readily agreed. I transported him and the Chinese UN physician (who acted as interpreter) to my office for the debriefing. What he subsequently told me confirmed my understanding of kidnapping in Yemen, and a bit more. I eventually shared the information developed in the debriefing with the UN agencies and members of the Forum.

The man told me that for the first few days he was terrified. It became clear to him within hours of the kidnapping that his captors did not know he was Chinese. They merely knew that he was not Yemeni and appeared foreign. He knew, as I did, that Westerners were preferred hostages. He explained that he was terrified that his captors would find out that he was Chinese and would therefore be of no value to them. He feared that he would be killed. His concern mitigated over time, based on his kind treatment at the hands of the villagers.

He was kept under armed guard, but he told me that otherwise he had the freedom of the village. He spoke some basic Arabic and was therefore able to communicate with his captors. The village, he said, was poor, and in return for his safe release, the inhabitants hoped that the central government would provide greater public assistance.

He also mentioned that he was very well fed. In fact, he told me, he had gained weight while in captivity. A different family hosted him each day, so that everyone in the village equally bore the burden of his care and feeding. Each family treated him as an honored guest, and stuffed him full of lamb, rice, and Yemeni flat bread dripping with honey. Once his capture had been conducted successfully, he was never again threatened. His captors assured him on multiple occasions that his release was assured once they had secured promises from the government that their demands would be met. His safe release came on the heels of those governmental promises to the villagers.

The Chinese engineer also mentioned that he held no residual ill will toward his captors. He stated that their poverty was obvious and acute. Finally, he said that he wished the villagers well. In my estimation, this was not a result of the psychological phenomenon called "Stockholm Syndrome." Kidnapping really is different in Yemen.

An additional point of pride for me is that no UN staff member was taken hostage while I served in Yemen. Following the conduct of my study regarding the Yemeni form of hostage-taking, I distributed a list of security recommendations to all UN staff. These avoidance and prevention measures were later hammered home in periodic staff security briefings. Were there no UN kidnap victims because of my efforts, or were we just lucky? This is the ultimate operational dichotomy for every security officer. It is all but impossible to prove a negative.

11

The Rape

Good judgment comes from experience. Experience comes from bad judgment.
—Jim Horning

A call came late in the evening from the Head of the UN High Commissioner for Refugees Office in the southern port city of Aden. He requested that I grab the first available flight the next morning. Somali refugees had detained members of his local staff as well as INGO implementing partners. The reason for the detainment situation was not immediately clear. The Yemini Barracks Commander was reportedly threatening violence against the refugees holding the detainees, and nobody seemed to know why. Radio communications with the camp were spotty.

He told me that one of his drivers would be waiting for me at Aden Airport to pick me up and take me directly to the refugee camp. I had been there several times before. As previously mentioned, and for reasons of its own, the Yemeni government placed the camp in an isolated desert locale. Consequently, there was no landline telephone to the camp.

I called James to let him know why I wouldn't be at my desk in the morning. I took the early flight from Sana'a to Aden, carrying only a black canvas rucksack, issued to me when I was assigned to US Joint Special Operations Command some years earlier. As promised, the driver was waiting for me at Aden Airport. Three hours later, in the mid-morning hours, I entered the UN compound adjacent to the camp. It was already hotter than my grandma's frying pan. I was briefed by a staff member at vehicle-side immediately upon arrival.

What follows below is roughly what the man told me:

> All UN local staff and implementing partners (IN-GOs) were detained—meaning they were not permitted to leave. This no doubt also included me now. I glanced over the way I had come in. There were three Somali males standing just outside the gate with hefty sticks.
>
> The Yemeni Barracks were on full alert—meaning ammunition had been distributed and leaves had been canceled.
>
> Everything had gone sideways late the previous day, when a camp resident made the public accusation that the Yemeni Barracks Commander had raped a teenage Somali girl.
>
> The Elders, the Somali camp leadership, called for immediate action. They apparently wanted the Yemini Commander's head on a spike.
>
> The Yemenis pulled all their troops into their barracks—the commander all the while denying the accusation. The Elders informed the UN and INGOs that they would not be permitted to leave until justice was served.

I had no idea what to do, and time was not on my side. A new report came in that the refugees were in an ugly mood and now headed toward our compound. I glanced over in the direction of the camp proper, where there was a huge dust cloud in the distance, suggesting that most of the camp, and perhaps all, was on the move. Everyone in the UN compound seemed to be looking to me for answers. I had none.

Just then the Yemenis came out of their barracks, which was perhaps a football field distant. All of them were armed. I knew that if the two groups met, it would be a bloodbath. The accusation of rape in both Somali and Yemeni societies, as elsewhere, is highly emotionally charged. Finally, refugee camps in general are tinder boxes of pent-up emotion. I felt the coming danger like static electricity in the air. I saw fear in the eyes of my colleagues. I instructed them to remain within the compound before I headed out in the direction of the Yemenis. I saw the Barracks Commander in the distance. We were acquainted with one another. I adjusted my walking trajectory for a rapid intercept. We met. We did not shake hands. I asked the Commander to immediately return his troops to their barracks. Surprisingly, and after only a few moments of argument, he agreed. I heard him yelling in rapid-fire Arabic. The troops returned to their barracks, with their boss. I hadn't expected to be so successful so quickly.

I was now alone. The troops were off the game board. The UN staff and INGOs remained in their separate compound under guard by the stick-carrying Somalis. For no reason that I could then imagine, those guards did not attempt to impede me when I left the compound on foot to go to the barracks.

I turned toward the refugee camp proper. The huge dust trail created by thousands of angry Somalis was rapidly headed in my direction. Behind me were the barracks. To my right front was the UN compound. I still had no idea what to do. I began walking slowly toward the mob of Somalis. I remember having no special thought in mind. I just started walking. I was afraid, but this was my job. It was my duty to protect UN staff, and by extension INGO implementing partners, and finally, to have a care for the refugees themselves. These words played themselves out over and over in my mind until they were a jumble. Still, I managed to keep my feet moving in what I felt was the appropriate direction, toward the mob of pissed-off camp residents numbering in the thousands.

The distance between the center of the refugee camp and the Yemeni barracks was perhaps a third of a mile. The gap between me and the mob was fast diminishing. When we were perhaps fifty yards apart, I sat down in the dust, legs crossed, while the thousands of Somalis closed fast on my position. They were close enough now that I could hear their voices. Although I did not understand their words, they were clearly yelling in anger and frustration. I bowed my head and waited.

Some time passed. I do not know how much. It could not have been long. I finally found the courage to look up. There was choking dust and heat-upon-heat everywhere. But there were also seated cross-legged to my immediate front and sides several of the Somali Elders—many of whom I had previously met and recognized, even with the much-reduced visibility. The mob consisting of several thousand Somalis had halted. My heart slowed a few beats.

I took a deep ragged breath. I felt rivulets of sweat rolling down my face that I tried to ignore before greeting the Elders in a croaking dry voice in Arabic. They responded in kind. We were surrounded by the mob on all sides. Everyone crowded in closer and closer, trying to hear what was being said. The dust was omnipresent—a physical force.

Fortunately, one of the group spoke some English. Although it may have taken as much as forty-five minutes working the translation from English to Somali and back again, I managed to hammer out an agreement with the Elders that permitted me to investigate the accusation of rape, and once my investigation was complete, to report my findings back to them. The only glitch was that they would permit me only the remainder of that day to interview knowledgeable persons, determine guilt or innocence, and tender my report. What could possibly go wrong?

I asked the Elders to return to their camp and await my

findings. I also asked them to actively protect the lives of the UN staff and INGOs under their detainment. They agreed to my stipulation. So now, in addition to being detained, they were also under Elder promises of protection. The Elders tended to keep their word.

When the Somalis left to return to their camp, following goodbyes in Arabic, I stood up very slowly. I was tired and thirsty, and covered in dust from head to foot. My lower back ached badly from a military parachuting injury that I sustained years earlier. The lesson was, never jump in a chute recently designated "experimental." I never did again. After stretching my back out, I turned and moved at a rapidly increasing pace toward the barracks.

What had I done? For a brief period, several years earlier, I had led a multinational group of military instructors teaching security and conflict resolution in Cambodia. I remembered that one of our teaching points was that a sitting man is seldom considered a threat. Accordingly, I sat down in the dust. It was a desperation move. At several levels it made no sense. But it was all I had. Fortunately, it worked. This is proof positive, yet once again, that it may be better to be lucky than good.

The Yemeni Barracks Commander was waiting for me outside as I arrived. I asked him for water in Arabic. He motioned to one of his subordinates, a sergeant, who handed me a half-full plastic bottle of cloudy water. I drank the entire contents in a few seconds. It tasted fantastic. I then thanked the sergeant, returning the now-drained bottle to his care.

The Commander was clearly curious about what had transpired during the forty-five-minute meeting with the Elders. Although I was at that time unaware of it, the Yemenis were all watching me from their barracks windows. I was evasive and avoided an answer. How could I tell him that my job was now to investigate him? I suspect that such admission would not have gone down well. I requested that he confine his troops to barracks until further notice. He immediately concurred, turned on his heel and gave the order. I think he saw that our interests were at least temporarily aligned.

He then pulled me aside, and in a faint voice, swore to me that he did not violate the Somali girl. I knew nothing of his guilt or innocence. I merely listened. I told him simply that I would require everyone's cooperation and patience. He nodded his assent.

It was now sometime around noon. The sun was directly overhead. The heat at this time of day became a blunt hammer-like force, unyielding and unforgiving, as I returned to the UN compound. The stick-carrying Somalis guarding the front gate once again allowed me to pass unmolested. I headed directly for the classroom, the area where I requested that the camp staff wait for me.

The classroom was large with a blackboard that covered one entire wall. There were perhaps thirty plastic chairs inside occupied by a half-dozen people. Without going into any detail, I informed them that I was immediately beginning an investigation concerning the events of the past twenty-four hours, and the accusation of rape leveled against the Yemeni Barracks Commander. I also assured them that I had secured a promise from the Elders that, although still under detainment, they would not be harmed. I first interviewed them. It did not take long to determine that there was not one among the group that had any direct first-hand knowledge of the alleged rape.

I then asked to interview a group of reportedly knowledgeable Yemeni soldiers. The result was the same. No soldier had any direct first-hand knowledge of the alleged event. This investigative technique of mine was going nowhere fast. However, there was a method to my apparent madness. I knew that I had to put on a good show, even if it took additional time. Essentially, I had to ensure that the Yemenis, UN staff, and implementing partners (the detainees), and most importantly, the refugees themselves, perceived me as acting in the role of an impartial agent of justice.

Finally, I asked to interview all knowledgeable Somalis. A large group came and joined me in the classroom. Working again from English to Somali and back again, I pieced together that a relatively new arrival to the refugee camp, a male, was the one who had made the accusation. The allegedly raped girl was reportedly his daughter. I was also informed that I could not interview the girl. She was being held in the protective custody of a group of Somali women. Interestingly, not one Somali present had direct first-hand knowledge of the sexual assault. The accuser was strangely unavailable. That troubled me.

I demanded to speak with the accuser. I was, after all, investigating this matter for the Elders. My report would go to them. Under these circumstances, I could not be refused. One of the Elders departed, promising to return with the father of the girl. Time passed. The Elder returned, but alone. He reported that the accuser had apparently developed cold feet. He did not wish to be interrogated by me. Moreover, he was now not altogether certain that an actual rape had occurred after all. The cat was out of the bag.

The assembled Elders now knew that there had been no rape, and that the accuser had made a false statement for reasons unknown. They were clearly unhappy to hear that one of their own had lied. The Elders subsequently made a big display of apologies. Each in turn thanked me for my investigation and honest handing of a clearly explosive situation, as they departed to return to their camp. The relief I felt was profound. I would not have wished to be the false accuser at that point, though. I suspect that refugee camp justice is swift, likely painful, and perhaps even permanent.

My return to Sana'a was marked by poor judgment on my part. I had been waiting in a long line for a long time at the airport in Aden to be issued my ticket. I was hot, tired, and dirty from my time spent in the refugee camp. Three men in local garb brushed past me at the front of the line and went straight up to the ticket agent demanding his attention. I immediately spoke up and was subsequently ignored. That tore it for me. I walked forward and placed my hand on the shoulder of the man who appeared to be the senior of the three and spun him around to face me. The other two immediately pulled concealed handguns and pointed them at my head. I came to understand thereafter, and in short order, that the man I had just laid hands on was the son of President Saleh. This was not my finest moment, not by a long shot.

12

A Reluctant Bride

Being deeply loved by someone gives you strength, while loving someone gives you courage.
—Lao Tzu

Surprisingly, I met an extraordinary woman in Yemen. Her name is Naima. She was born in Cairo, Egypt. After completing a BS and MA in her country of birth, she took a job with the UN in Syria. She later quit that position to pursue a doctorate at the University of Wisconsin in Madison. After she attained her goal, she once again went to work for the UN, this time in Yemen, where we met and fell in love. She was at first the chief technical advisor on a multi-million-dollar UN project benefiting poor women in rural areas. Still later, she took a job working for a well-known INGO, again in Yemen.

This is the woman who when we first met—shortly after my arrival in Yemen—verbally assaulted me. All I really remember clearly about the incident was that during her entire harangue, I could not help thinking to myself that she was incredibly cute.

Sometime after our first inauspicious meeting, I noticed Naima outside of my office. I went straight out to greet her. She immediately attempted an apology, which I quickly brushed off. I then told her in my best professional voice that my office offered all UN staff members formal residential security assessments. In other words, I explained that I would come to her villa, conduct an inspection, and then provide her a series of formal recommendations on how she could improve the security of her home. She quickly accepted my offer. Now, this is where I stepped out of bounds.

I subsequently told her that there was only one condition that must be met before we could agree on a date and time for the assessment. The condition was that she had to feed me. I explained that I had been eating my own cooking for many weeks, and that I thought that my health, and perhaps even my life, were at risk. My ridiculous ploy worked. She laughed.

The meal she prepared for me was spectacular. To my everlasting shame, I never conducted that promised residential security assessment. But in my defense, I am compelled to point out that thereafter she became one of the best-protected women in Yemen. I made it my personal mission to ensure that I was henceforth always close by in the evening hours, when thieves stalk the streets, especially around dinnertime.

It was Christmas Eve 2002. I took Naima on a Caribbean cruise, all part of my plan. I had already asked her to marry me on multiple occasions. She was beautiful. She was smart. She was caring. Perhaps more importantly, she seemed all but blind to my personal failings—possessing a seemingly inexhaustible well of tolerance concerning my many faults. What more could a man ask for? I dared not let her escape. Unfortunately, she was not interested in tying the knot. As much as she loved me, and I know that she did, she wanted nothing to do with marriage. She turned me down every time I asked. I was starting to feel unwanted.

How could I be sure that she loved me? She kept feeding me. Although this is a wholly sexist perspective, in my experience, a woman will eventually refuse to feed a man she does not love.

So months earlier, I had begun to work up a scheme to ensure that the next time I popped the question, her response would be in the affirmative. It was planned down to the minutest detail. The Christmas Eve dinner aboard the cruise ship was formal. I wore a tuxedo and military medals. She wore a gown. I roped-in the band, the hostess, our waiter, and the guy working the spotlight. At the appointed moment, the band fell silent. There was a drum roll. The waiter delivered the package. The hostess was ready with a camera. A spotlight lit up our table, with special emphasis on me kneeling at Naima's feet. Roughly five hundred people sat in rapt attention. I remember hearing a collective "aaahhhh" from the hundreds of women observing the incident as they figured out what was happening.

The British have a term for what I saw in Naima's eyes. She was gobsmacked! She was caught totally flat-footed. She never saw it coming. She was completely speechless for several moments. Finally, she broke her silence with a coy smile, a gentle nod of her head, and the fateful word "yes" passed her lips. The crowd broke into thunderous applause. I placed the diamond ring on her finger. The band played a lively tune. The hostess took several photographs. A champagne bottle appeared. The cheering lasted for some time. Many couples came by our table to congratulate me, specifically. Apparently, several in the crowd were impressed with my detailed planning and execution. To be honest, I was more than a little pleased with myself.

Later, back in our stateroom, and when the door was shut, Naima turned and slapped me hard in the face. It hurt too, but I managed to smile through the pain. "Why did you do that?" she yelled. "That's easy," I replied with a huge Cheshire grin. "Because you said *yes*."

How did I know that I would succeed that night when all my other attempts had failed? Naima was born Egyptian. Egyptians generally care what others, even strangers, think of them. I was born an American. For good or ill, Americans often couldn't care less what others, especially strangers, think of them. Essentially, I theorized that Naima would not turn me down in a public arena, because she would never embarrass me in front of so many people. It worked! My cheek hurt for another hour or so, but it was well worth the discomfort.

I learned a very great deal from Naima. She served as my mentor in several key areas, including UN development and humanitarian work, local government and tribal matters, and even security-related issues, of which I was supposed to be the subject matter expert. Her advice and assistance, both personally and professionally, were critically important to my further development as a UN staff member, a security advisor, and not least of all, a person.

Maps by sierrasketches@gmail.com

Figure 3. Map of Iraq

13

The Road to Iraq

Hell is empty and all the devils are here.
—William Shakespeare

The much-anticipated US invasion of Iraq was about to begin the following month. Although I was a trained specialist in Middle Eastern affairs, and had previously lived and worked in Iraq, I never understood why the invasion was considered necessary by my government. Iraq had nothing whatsoever to do with the tragic events of 9/11.

I received the phone call late one evening in mid-February of 2003. The call came from my regional chief in New York. She asked me if I was interested in the senior UN security post in Iraq. It was a fascinating proposal, and no doubt challenging as well. She also mentioned that a promotion would be likely if I accepted.

The mission there was called the UN Office of the Humanitarian Coordinator Iraq (UNOHCI). In large measure, it was the implementing agency for the UN-administered Oil-for-Food Program. It was neither fish nor fowl by way of comparison with my previous assignments. It wasn't peacekeeping, and it wasn't strictly agencies. Essentially, the SG appointed an assistant secretary-general in charge and superimposed that control mechanism over the normally independent agencies. Like Yemen, this was an assignment where I would carry no firearm. This was yet another posting that would stretch me in unanticipated ways, and in this case, near to the breaking point.

Unlike the mission in Sierra Leone, where I worked for the CAO, in Iraq I would work for the Humanitarian Coordinator (HC) in his capacity as the Designated Official for Security (DO). This reflected a policy change in New York. Unlike Sierra Leone, in Iraq and henceforth globally, the senior security officer in a country would work directly for the most senior UN official. Initially, and from my perspective, it was a very welcome change.

I was not surprised to receive the job offer. A friend had called me a few weeks earlier and asked if I might consider accepting the post. I had replied in the affirmative. My friend told me that he could make a recommendation but wanted to check with me first. I gave him the green light, while secretly wondering to myself if my bosses in New York would trust me with another big mission. After all, things in Sierra Leone had not gone well. There could easily be lingering doubts about my capabilities.

I had been in Yemen for over two years. Of necessity, I had grown as a UN Security Advisor. My understanding of both the country and the region had grown as well. In my estimation, the key word to remember in the Arab World is "humiliation." This is because the Arabs have suffered for centuries. The Arabs were once great but are great no more. Their histories of the last five centuries have been written by scholars in the West. Their armies were defeated. They were subsequently colonized. Their predominant religion became reactionary. Their economies are consistently noncompetitive. Finally, there was not one democracy worthy of the title anywhere in the Arab World. Autocrats, royalty, and military dictators ruled everywhere at that time. Unsurprisingly, not much has changed in the ensuing years.

I had learned the art of diplomacy in Yemen. It is a tough, complex, and personally demanding profession. But the facts are that if you are not at least marginally politically astute in the UN, no matter your primary profession, you will not go far. In other words, first be a good diplomat, and then be good at whatever else you might do. The former is the predicate to the latter. American humorist Will Rogers said that, "Diplomacy is the art of saying 'Nice doggie' until you can find a rock." Which brings us to a critical issue.

The notion of many Americans that it is important to "do the right thing" had little resonance with some of my UN colleagues. Doing the "right thing" for them means, as earlier mentioned, to do what is right for themselves and their family, village and tribe. This lesson would be often reinforced throughout my UN service. I eventually came to see it less as a condemnation than merely a fact that must be understood. I could not change the world, but only live and work within it. However, these stark differences created a clash of values that would later come to haunt me.

I called New York the next day. After a perfunctory telephone interview, and the wait of a few weeks, I received a letter signed by the UNSECOORD. That letter directed me to report as the new head of security for Iraq. Our mission headquarters at that time was in Larnaca, Cyprus. All UN staff had been evacuated from Iraq in March, just ahead of the US invasion. The UNSECOORD gave me a mere five days to get to Cyprus. The date was 19 April 2003. Since I could not accomplish all administrative requirements associated with a permanent move in that length of time, I departed Yemen on mission status. That meant that I must later return to Sana'a to complete out-processing that duty station.

I arrived in Larnaca via Amman, Jordan, mid-evening 24 April. I had not conducted an area study prior to that. I thought I already knew something of Iraq. I was wrong. The

Iraq that would emerge following the invasion was nothing like what I had known previously.

I was met by Richard Manlove at the airport. Richard was by now one of the most senior security officers in New York, and an old friend. He was on temporary duty in Cyprus, coordinating the regional dimension of UN security for Iraq.

Richard and I went out to dinner, and then he dropped me at my hotel. Since I had left Yemen after 3:00 AM, I was badly in need of rest. I also anticipated living in Cyprus for a while, because I did not foresee a UN re-entry of Iraq in the near term. I was wrong again.

A few days later, my new boss, the HC, informed Richard and me that the SG had made the decision to re-enter Iraq as soon as possible. Neither of us then understood the need for such haste. Per UN security policy, Iraq had been declared Phase 5. This was the most severe and restrictive declaration—essentially meaning that we could not operate there. Iraq was still in Phase 5 at that time.

Under these circumstances, and consistent with UN security policy then on the books, I suggested to my new boss that I take a small team of security officers into Baghdad and conduct a formal security assessment of a week or two. That team would examine security issues like road safety, communications, office facilities, available secure accommodations, possible Coalition Provisional Authority (CPA) support, status of environment (permissive or non-permissive), and much more.

Why was I concerned? Although the US invasion had been successful in March, there were no functioning police. Armed robberies were common. Looting was ubiquitous. Hospitals were ransacked. There were no emergency services. There was no judiciary. The national electrical power grid had been disabled. Many bridges had been destroyed by American bombing. Violent prisoners had been released from their cells by Saddam. The government had collapsed completely. Moreover, the entire country was awash in arms and ammunition. It just seemed to me that greater caution was warranted.

In most countries, the UN was almost wholly dependent upon national governments for basic safety and security services in support of their deployed staff. In Iraq, there was nothing. The risks were therefore very significant. The UN often counted upon its worldwide reputation for neutrality and humanitarian acts to enhance its security. We later discovered that our reputation held no water in the newly emerging Iraqi context.

I tried to make this case to my new boss. The HC stopped me before I was done. He told me that the SG had made his decision. Discussion, if there had been any on the security front, was over. We were in execution mode. But we were not done quite yet.

I spoke with Richard. He, as the more senior of the two of us, made the phone call to the UNSECOORD. Richard was in full concurrence with the recommendations that I had made to the HC. Our boss in New York had the authority to either approve or disapprove the plan.

Essentially, Richard subsequently made the same case—that I be permitted to conduct a security assessment in Baghdad prior to launching blindly into Iraq with vulnerable UN staff members in tow. Our New York boss told Richard the same thing that the HC told me. The decision was already made.

This "decision" rationale was very difficult for us to accept. We were of similar minds. Richard raised his voice while telling the UNSECOORD that to enter Iraq with UN staff at that time—a dangerous combatant environment—and without a front-end security assessment, was simply "irresponsible." The discussion became heated. Richard was adamant enough to satisfy us both. At times, he was downright rude. Still, it had zero effect. The UNSECOORD would not be moved. We were directed to comply.

That was that. We had exhausted our options. My boss and Richard's were the only courts of appeal available to us. The UNSECOORD by policy reported directly to the SG. The HC was the most senior UN official assigned to Iraq. Both were—by rank—at the very senior level of assistant secretary-general. Now we had to execute our instructions.

Richard was also tasked with accompanying the party into Baghdad. Other agency officers were included in the mix, too. I was very grateful for their presence. Several were a good deal more experienced than I was.

We arrived in Amman, Jordan, in the late afternoon of 31 April via air from Cyprus. We were getting off the transport buses in front of our hotel and entering the lobby when the HC sought me out. He informed me that the briefing for tomorrow's road movement across the Jordanian and Iraqi desert would begin at 9:00 PM in one of the hotel's conference rooms. I thanked him and then asked the obvious question, "Who is briefing?" In a hurried and disinterested voice, he said, "Why, you." He then headed off toward the front desk, leaving me stunned in his wake. It could not be true, but it was. My new boss had apparently forgotten to mention to me that I was to be responsible for <u>all matters</u> relating to the road movement of our convoy from Amman to Baghdad the following morning. This was of course a road I had never traveled.

I recovered myself as rapidly as I could, while beginning to develop a plan in my head. I had a few hours to pull together a briefing for the twenty-two persons identified as the first group of UN staff to re-enter Iraq following the US invasion. We would proceed with eight SUVs and attempt to make it all the way to Baghdad in one day, hopefully arriving before dark. The US military imposed a curfew that began at sunset. This was going to be challenging. We were about to enter a still-unsettled Iraq, and none of us were armed. The assumption was that our UN-marked vehicles would provide all the protection necessary. I was not so sure. It is unwise to assume away potential threats.

I had two advantages in developing a plan for road movement. I had previously been responsible for supervising numerous similar activities while commanding two military intelligence companies in the former West Germany. I had also attended the US Army's Ranger School. As any Ranger School graduate will quickly verify, the five-paragraph field order is drummed into your head. The five-paragraph field order is a superb method for organizing small units for specific missions, like tactical road movements in a non-permissive environment. I went immediately to work preparing one from memory.

Of course, the key assumption on the part of the UN's most senior leadership was that combat in Iraq was over. After all, the Americans with coalition support had won. Peace was therefore expected to become the new normal. President George W. Bush had already taken a regional victory lap. Secretary of Defense Donald Rumsfeld assured all parties concerned that the Iraqis would be thankful to the Americans for the overthrow of Saddam Hussein. Vice President Dick Cheney spoke about the potential new democracy, and business opportunities. None of these pie-in-the-sky expectations came to fruition.

My greatest worry, which I shared with nobody, was the possibility of ambush along our route of march. The area between the border crossing site and Baghdad was largely lawless. To add insult to injury, normal military procedures regarding ambush were non-starters in such an environment because we were unarmed. I only hoped that my concern did not show. Fear and its sibling, panic, are the most dangerous contagions known to humankind.

The evening briefing went surprisingly well. My prior military training had prepared me for unexpected UN tasks of this sort. I was asked the question about ambush, though.

I responded by telling the group to simply follow me and to do whatever my vehicle did. Thankfully, nobody thought to ask the perfectly reasonable follow-on question; what if my vehicle were the first hit, and I was dead or disabled? I didn't have a good answer for that one. There was great risk in this endeavor, and for reasons that could not withstand even casual scrutiny.

I directed that all drivers with their vehicles gather the following morning at 5:00 AM. The road distance between Amman and Baghdad is five hundred fifty-seven miles. Making it in one day, and before dark, was going to be tough. It wasn't just the distance. There was also the matter of the border crossing site at Karameh. Border crossing officials in this part of the world have a well-deserved reputation for sloth.

There was something else troubling me, too. A few months earlier I had been asked to participate in an Iraq re-entry planning session sponsored by UNSECOORD 29-31 October of the previous year in Vienna, Austria. If memory serves, as many as a dozen senior security officers from New York and the Middle East region attended with me. We conducted detailed planning concerning our re-entry into Iraq, even before the actual invasion took place. I thought it would be smart to get ahead of the curve for a change. The planning leader from UNSECOORD in New York returned to his home station on Manhattan Island after we completed the task. He was subsequently reassigned to other duties. All the planning we did was apparently thereafter buried. I never saw nor heard of it ever again. Curious, all that time, money and trouble was seemingly wasted. Why?

The eight blue SUVs appeared on time at the assembly area. UN markings had been placed on the vehicle sides and tops in day-glow orange. Why blue and day-glow orange? US military officials had previously informed us that when the invasion began in March, some American troop formations had been attacked by regime paramilitary units driving stolen

UN vehicles in the traditional white livery with black or blue UN lettering on the sides and top. Understandably, American Commanders directed their troops to consider those driving such vehicles as potential hostiles. We changed our colors to blue and day-glow orange temporarily, out of a keen interest in our own survival.

I announced at the evening briefing that nobody accompanying us into Baghdad should take personal luggage heavier than roughly thirty pounds. We had only eight vehicles. We carried supplies of food, water, fuel, ballistic vests and helmets, communications gear, and more. We even brought our own vehicle fuel in a towed trailer. To fit people, supplies, and equipment into these few vehicles, we had to limit items that were considered personal in nature. Only one person failed to comply: our only woman, the HC's spokesperson. She arrived at the assembly point with no less than eight items of luggage, exceeding my stated weight limit by well over a hundred pounds, and probably a good deal more. It was clear that most of her luggage was personal in nature. She insisted that all her belongings had to go.

The situation was absurd. In other circumstances, it might have been laughable. The woman insisted that every item of her luggage was essential to her in Baghdad. I could not reason with her. I tried. My exasperation with her was shortly in high gear. My boss, although aware of the issue, chose to remain silent on the matter, leaving the decision to me. One of the drivers pulled me aside, suggesting that with a little help, he believed that he could fit her luggage into our convoy, by spreading it out among all our vehicles. We were delayed in our departure while the drivers made it so. UN personnel are not soldiers, and only rarely follow direction.

We were finally on the road. I was in the lead vehicle. It was still dark. Two types of UN security advisors were present in the group: those who worked for the UNSECOORD and those who worked for their respective UN agencies: in this case, the UN Children's Fund and World Food Program. I appointed UNSECOORD Security Officer Marco Smoliner to handle rear security. We stayed in touch via vehicle-mounted and handheld radios. I appointed another UNSECOORD security officer in charge of external communications. His job was to keep American forces regularly abreast of our location using satellite phone, once we entered Iraq.

If we ran into trouble between Karameh and Baghdad, I wanted to be able to call somebody for help. The Americans were the only alternative once we passed the border. Both above-mentioned officers had been temporarily pulled from their duty stations somewhere else on the globe. They would eventually have to return to their home countries. Temporary or not, I was glad to have them on board. Only the UNSECOORD officers worked for me.

The downhill ride (Amman is over 3,000 feet above sea level) to the Karameh Border Crossing site was uneventful. We drove directly into sunrise. A good pair of sunglasses was essential. I had arranged and paid out-of-pocket for pre-prepared breakfast and lunch meals in boxes, and had those meals distributed prior to departure. Except for Karameh, as far I knew, there would be no open restaurants on our route of march. We had no time to stop for a meal in any case, if we were to beat the sun. I was provided no money from my department in New York or the mission. What cash I had in hand was what I had brought with me from Yemen and my personal accounts. I found out later that under UN rules governing such matters, I could not be reimbursed for the box meals—a small disappointment, but hardly my last.

I was essentially entering Iraq all but blind. The HC had a small three-man international security staff who had assisted him in the evacuation of Baghdad just prior to the US invasion. I met two of them in Cyprus. I expected that either one or both would accompany us back into Baghdad. Neither did. The more senior of the two had some pressing family matter that required his presence in New York. The other had sustained a neck injury. That meant none of the security officers in the convoy with me had ever previously lived and worked in Baghdad. We were all novices there. That fact added to my already substantial worries.

The trip to the border crossing was a thoughtful one. I had little idea what to expect when we entered Iraq. We would soon traverse Anbar Province, and then pass by both Ramadi and Fallujah before entering Baghdad, again, hopefully, before darkness fell. We knew little of the security situation along our route of march or, for that matter, in Baghdad.

We negotiated the border crossing point in less than two hours. Our drivers managed the visa process with the Jordanian officials. There was no passport control, as I recall, on the Iraq side of the border to impede our progress. The great western Iraqi desert lay before us. The heat of the day beat down mercilessly. I was grateful for the air conditioning in our vehicles. Years earlier, when I was a major working in the Sinai Desert as a UN Military Observer, our vehicles had no A/C, making patrols in the summer heat brutal.

The highway was all but empty. I pushed our speed up to eighty miles per hour, and more. Was I reckless? I remained concerned about the possibility of arriving in Baghdad after dark. I was attempting to balance risk. We saw occasional vehicles headed in the opposite direction—toward Jordan—but we seemed to be the only ones headed in the direction of Baghdad that day. Ominous... did somebody know something that we didn't?

The desert can be mind-numbingly boring, even at high speed—sand and rock in a near-uniform beige/rust-colored combination mile after mile. I tried not to doze. I had managed only three hours of fitful sleep in Amman before rising early to prepare for the long day ahead.

I kept myself busy by consulting the road map on my lap and speaking with our external communications officer over the radio to ensure that he made regular reports to American forces concerning our current road location. I also checked in regularly with our rear security vehicle. I attempted to maintain roughly fifty yards between vehicles. At higher speeds, we expanded that distance closer to seventy-five yards out of an over-abundance of accident safety concern.

Given the nature of nature, we stopped on one memorable occasion just east of Fallujah. Twenty-one men hurried to the right side of the roadway on top of a small berm, faced south, and relieved themselves, me included. I noted on my return to the vehicles that our spokesperson remained in her vehicle. I opened her door. Her face and body language communicated distress. I asked her to follow me. She followed, perhaps a bit sheepishly, but understanding my intent. I walked her to the opposite side of the small berm, where she could not be observed from the convoy. The men by this time were gone. I pointed out a likely location. She hurried to the chosen spot. I turned my back and waited for several minutes while she obeyed nature's call. She returned no doubt much relieved, smiling, and thanking me in both French and English on the return walk to the vehicles. I responded in both French and English. My French language speaking ability is rudimentary at best, but wholly sufficient for the need on this occasion.

We arrived in Baghdad with daylight to spare. Our driver found the Canal Hotel in short order. We drove up to find that the hotel was occupied by headquarters elements of the US 2nd Armored Cavalry Regiment (ACR). I recognized their shoulder patches. The front gate to the unwalled compound was manned by young soldiers. I got out of my vehicle and walked up to the sergeant on duty. I identified myself and explained that the UN Humanitarian Coordinator was in the second SUV in my convoy. The sergeant, no doubt following his orders, told me that our vehicles would have to be searched prior to permitting us entry. I politely declined, pointing out that the Canal Hotel was a UN Headquarters, and that we were merely re-claiming that which was by rights already ours. I asked the sergeant to call his Commander to come out and greet the senior representative of the UN in Iraq. This explanation seemed to give the soldier pause. He complied. We did not have to wait long. The Commander of the 2nd Armored Cavalry Regiment strode shortly thereafter into view. He welcomed us into the compound without delay.

Why had I been chosen the UN's senior security officer for Iraq? As I discovered later, there were other more experienced officers available for the appointment. I was at that time still at P-3. The post in Iraq was graded for a higher-level P-4. I had, though, one undeniable asset: I was a retired US Army officer. The US Army at that time, for most intents and purposes, was the government of Iraq. There is little doubt that the UN wanted somebody that spoke the language and understood the culture of the American military. I was not the best; I was merely the guy with the advantage of a deep familiarity with the US Armed Forces. Plus, and this is no small matter, I was willing to go. I would soon come to regret that willingness.

14

Frustration

Power does not corrupt. Fear corrupts... perhaps the fear of the loss of power.
—John Steinbeck, *The Short Reign of Pippin IV*

The morning after our arrival in Baghdad, I asked the HC to take me for a tour of the UN compound. He agreed. Before the heat got too bad, perhaps around 9:00 AM, we began. We had both slept in our respective offices the previous night and would continue to do so until my staff security-cleared outside accommodations.

The same evening we arrived, I was told the US Marines had first occupied our headquarters, later followed by the 2nd Armored Cavalry Regiment. Because the Canal Hotel was occupied by the Americans, it had not been looted. So much of what had been left behind was still there when we arrived at dusk the day prior. We were very lucky.

Troops were everywhere as we walked the perimeter of the unimpressive building and compound. There was the three-story rectangular main building, an area for storage, a small vehicular maintenance section, a covered parking lot, and a small elliptically shaped two-story building belonging to security at the front gate that led out onto the Canal Road. The Canal Road was on one side, and there was also a small access way off that road that led to a hotel hospitality school perhaps one hundred fifty yards behind. There was also a large undeveloped area that would later become the site of our Tent City (overflow sleeping accommodations for transient UN staff). There was little fencing and no compound wall. From a security perspective, the Canal Hotel was a potential disaster.

I also noticed an abandoned Iraqi anti-aircraft gun emplacement very close to the back side of the UN compound. My assumption was that Iraqi gunners, fearing being killed by US military aircraft during the invasion, had cozied up to the UN compound to avoid attack. They knew that the Americans adhered to the Law of Land Warfare. The Canal Hotel, as UN Headquarters for Iraq, was therefore no doubt designated by US aerial targeting specialists as a protected area. Of course, the Iraqis violated the law when they moved their gun position into such proximity.

When finished with the tour, I informed my boss categorically that I could not secure the compound, as the Canal Hotel was completely untenable from a security perspective. I also told him that it would be prudent to move to another location that could be secured. He shrugged, saying only, "This is what we have to live with." The shrug said it all. I was stunned by his attitude. On reflection, though, and at that time, there was no "politically correct" alternative. Politically correct in this context meant both separate from occupation forces and secure.

I later met with the 2nd Armored Cavalry Regiment Commander, at his request. He was planning a move to a new headquarters site, now that we had arrived to re-occupy our compound. He informed me that he would be out of the Canal Hotel in a few days and hoped that it was not an inconvenience. I thanked him. It was no inconvenience at all. He also surprised me by offering to leave behind his air defense artillery platoon, consisting of roughly thirty soldiers, to augment our unarmed local security force. There was at that time no air defense threat. I gratefully accepted his generous offer on the spot, and without consultation with my superiors. We were outrageously vulnerable at the Canal Hotel. When I later informed the HC that I had accepted the Commander's offer, he surprisingly did not accuse me of exceeding my authority, as I most certainly had.

Baghdad in those days was quite simply a bloody mess. In a nation awash with oil reserves, there were severe gasoline shortages. Vehicle lines for fuel in some cases were well over a mile long. Businesses were therefore struggling to bring food to market. No public services were functioning. Hundreds of thousands of Iraqis who had worked for the regime were now jobless, and therefore had little money. Essentially, there was no government whatsoever. Those former public-sector employees included the enormous Iraqi Army, which was the only societal glue remaining in the country following the invasion.

The Baghdad International Airport had been looted of anything of value and was initially non-functional for civil air traffic. International commercial airliners would not land there in any case. Insurance underwriters would not cover them. The US Air Force subsequently brought in the necessary equipment to make it work.

Iraqis at that time wanted only two things from their new American rulers. They wanted security for themselves and their families, and they needed jobs. They got neither. The issue of democracy, although much discussed in America's capital city, was in a very distant third place, if even considered. The senior US soldiers I spoke to within the Green Zone were aware of these facts. The people who didn't know it were thousands of miles away to the west inside the comforting confines of the DC Beltway.

Ambassador Paul Bremer arrived in Baghdad shortly after we did, at the beginning of the second week of May. He replaced Lieutenant General (retired) Jay Garner as the senior

US political official in Iraq. Nobody seems to know for sure why Garner was replaced. He and his staff had spent several months pulling together a post-conflict plan for Iraq. He had hardly begun his work when Bremer was appointed, and the retired three-star was brushed aside. Subsequent articles suggested that the White House did not share Garner's desire to hold early Iraqi elections. Reportedly, Garner also failed to express support for a White House plan for early business privatization as well.

Shortly thereafter, Bremer executed the single most catastrophic action of his tenure when he unilaterally disbanded the Iraqi Army. With the stroke of his pen, he turned a goodly portion of approximately 250,000 former regime soldiers into unemployed, armed, and hostile former regime elements that would later lead the attack on US and Coalition forces in Iraq for much of the next decade. Per trusted knowledgeable sources, that decision was in fact made in Washington, DC, and well prior to the invasion. The Iraqi Army at that time would have worked for anyone able to make payroll. Whoever made the actual call in DC — in large measure — kick-started the organized armed opposition.

Put simply, Iraq was a war that did not need to be fought. Other than ridding the world of another dictator, all the rationales provided for the invasion proved to be false. American credibility within the international community took an enormous blow. George Tenet, the former Director of the Central Intelligence Agency, who insisted that it was a "slam dunk" that Saddam Hussein possessed weapons of mass destruction, was wrong. His hubris led to one of the most catastrophic foreign policy blunders in modern US history, enabling President Bush to serve the interests of his "higher father" by invading Iraq. The war tarnished the reputation of one of my personal heroes too, General Colin Powell. In addition, and more importantly, the choice to conduct two wars simultaneously, Iraq and Afghanistan, was always a fool's errand. History has proven it.

On 6 May, at the first formal Security Management Team meeting, I made the following comments:

- Recommend the Security Management Team establish the staff ceiling on a quota basis
- Take deliberate (step-by-step approach) to the re-introduction of UN staff
- 100% Minimum Operational Security Standards compliance

None of the above recommendations came about.

I always had a problem with the UNSECOORD promulgated term, "Minimum Operational Security Standards." It struck me as absurd that the UN as a body was willing to provide only "minimum" funding for staff security. I even went so far as to send a strongly worded suggestion to New York that the term be adjusted to "Operational Security Standards." Of course, nothing happened.

Although it was the HC's decision to make, perhaps my greatest single mistake occurred on this day as well, when I agreed to tender a request to New York asking that the Security Phase be reduced from five to four. If Iraq remained in Phase Five, normally, no UN staff other than security professionals and a few key staff would be permitted to enter.

Essentially, I agreed to put in the request for two reasons. First, there had not yet been any attacks on either international organizations or US forces. Second, I wanted to believe in my chain of command that led all the way up to the SG. I was wrong in the second instance.

By policy, my office prepared the minutes of the security meetings. The HC was supposed to sign these minutes, and then I was tasked to forward them to my desk officer in New York for review. The HC never signed the minutes of any of these meetings. My office did its part. We prepared the document. We sent it to him, and there it languished. Finally, after several frustrating weeks, the Deputy UNSECOORD called and demanded that I send the unsigned versions of the minutes to New York. I was happy to do so. It made no difference from my perspective. To my knowledge, the UNSECOORD took no positive action as a result.

The minutes encapsulated most of my key recommendations to the HC and the heads of UN agencies. Anyone reading them would have noted that there were very real concerns on the part of the UN security community in Iraq. Those concerns went repeatedly unaddressed.

As example:

- Please slow down.
- Instruct your people in the Field to move ahead with deliberate due caution.
- Compliance with guidelines is not 100%.
- Disseminate security-related information to all your staff! Everyone is not getting the word.

UN heads of agency were acting as if it were still Saddam Hussein's Iraq. Two exceptions were the World Food Program and the UN Children's Fund. They were security-conscious, but two agencies among many could not turn the tide.

A brief time later, one of the senior UN humanitarian affairs officers asked me to approve an assessment mission to Fallujah, which I did not want to do. This region of Iraq was wildly unsafe for the UN in my estimation. I gave him my personal threat assessment. However, my job was to facilitate humanitarian activities, and he insisted that I comply with my terms of reference. Of course, the city of Fallujah would later become famous. But then, few Americans had even heard of it. Fortunately, I had an ace up my sleeve.

I made a phone call to an old friend in Jordan, who at that time was still an active duty senior officer in their military.

I asked my friend to arrange security in Fallujah for the UN staff I would shortly send that way. I was aware that the Jordanian military had placed some of their people in the area. It was done. The assessment team made their visit, accompanied by three UN agency security officers. They were met by the Jordanians. A local sheik provided security.

To my knowledge, we did not return after that. All indications were that the UN could not safely work in and around Fallujah at that time. One of the participants of this mission said that Fallujah "scared him shitless." Reportedly, they were shadowed by hard-looking armed men everywhere they went. For once, the humanitarians came to agree with me, but only after they saw for themselves.

One of a very few positive moments in my early days in Baghdad came when I paid a visit to the Palestine Hotel, which at that time hosted most of the foreign journalists working in Iraq. I was both surprised and pleased to run into Richard "Mitch" Mitchelson, who had left Eritrea and was now managing security matters for CNN. We shared a quick lunch together, and only rarely saw one another thereafter. His schedule and mine were both brutal. Mitch would go on to later establish a large and successful international security company.

Between 16 and 25 May, I made two long and difficult road trips to Basra in the south, and then, later, Mosul and Irbil in the north. My boss, who preferred to keep me nearby, did not want me to go. I made the point that I had to go as the senior security officer for Iraq and not just Baghdad. He finally relented.

The trip to Basra of two hundred eighty miles sparked memories that I had successfully suppressed for several years. This was not my first time visiting the south of Iraq.

Some years earlier, I had served in my last volunteer peacekeeping tour with the United Nations Iraq-Kuwait Observer mission, and just prior to my retirement from active US military service. This mission was established at the end of Operation Desert Storm in 1991 to monitor the Demilitarized Zone (DMZ) between Kuwait and Iraq. The DMZ was well over one hundred twenty-five miles long and nine miles wide starting at the Iraqi port city of Umm Qasr and ending near the tri-border area of Saudi Arabia, Iraq, and Kuwait. Our headquarters was in Umm Qasr. Most of our funding came from the Kuwaitis, who wanted to place tripwires between themselves and the brutal dictator to their north. They were also at that time building an electrified border fence the entire length of the DMZ.

In the last half of my assignment, I served as the senior duty officer within the headquarters. This post is essentially the Chief of Current Operations in American military parlance. In that capacity, the Commanders of both sectors reported to me. I also maintained operational control of our helicopters. This meant that I could mission-task these airframes, and then launch them on my own authority. One of their missions was aerial casualty evacuation (CASEVAC).

One evening I received a call in my small sleeping accommodations at the headquarters. It was reported that one of our patrols in Sector South had run across a badly wounded Bedouin boy. His parents begged the patrol to medically evacuate him. The youngster apparently stepped on a piece of ordnance left on the former battlefield, on the Iraqi side of the border. That ordnance exploded.

I put in a call to the pilots and directed them to go to Sector South and CASEVAC the boy to our German Medical Detachment at Umm Qasr. Sadly, such incidents were not uncommon. This was not my first or last such authorization. But this time it was different for reasons that I cannot explain. By policy we evacuated only the victim, based on the humanitarian imperative—help when you can to preserve life and alleviate suffering. However, the UN did not wish to be responsible for the relatives of the wounded as well.

It was my habit to meet the helicopter when it landed. I did so this time as well. The boy had been stabilized in route. His leg and foot wounds were field-bandaged, rough but serviceable. He was alert, but clearly in pain. He was acting very brave, while no doubt badly frightened. He fought back tears as they moved him on a stretcher from the helicopter to the ambulance. I admired his pluck. I escorted him with the German physician to the medical clinic, where he was to be treated. In the next few hours the doctors and nurses fought hard to stabilize him further, close the boy's wounds, keep him sedated, and pump him full of broad-spectrum antibiotics. It worked; the boy got better. I do not know why I stayed, as my presence there would not change the outcome. I was still there when he woke up the following morning.

I was sitting next to his bed when he opened his eyes. He was groggy at first, but as his mind cleared, I saw fear again in his eyes. He reached out for my forearm and held it tightly. I placed my hand over his. I have no idea why he felt safe with me. He smiled. I smiled back. We were instantly buddies. He told me that his name was Karim in Arabic. I shared my name in Arabic as well.

He was young, perhaps ten or eleven years old, and painfully thin. His thick black hair was matted with desert dust. One of the nurses had given him a thorough sponge bath while he recovered from anesthesia, so he was otherwise clean. He had big dark eyes that darted about his surroundings, looking at the medical personnel and machines, and then settling back on me. I tried to appear upbeat, but I was troubled.

By policy, I was required to turn over casualties of this type within twenty-four hours to the Iraqi Liaison Officers in Umm Qasr. I had done so previously. The Iraqi side of the border had never been cleared of the detritus of battle. Burned-out tanks, vehicles, landmines, bomblets, and much more were strewn all over the desert. It was common for some of the poorest Basra residents to scour the former battlefield for usable scrap metals. Sometimes they were lucky. Sometimes they were not. When their luck ran out, I sometimes received a call for CASEVAC. The Bedouins also transited this area during their seasonal migrations.

The nearest minimally capable Iraqi hospital was forty miles away in Basra. There was no ambulance service for Bedouin. Given the realities of Iraq at that time, there were shortages of just about everything. It wasn't uncommon for Iraqi officials to simply remove the badly injured from all medical life support, thereby condemning them to a painful lingering death.

I called the Commander of Sector South and asked him to give the parents the good news that their son had stabilized. I also asked him to provide them assistance in getting from the tri-border area to Umm Qasr. It is contrary to policy for any but UN civil or military staff to ride in UN vehicles, but we agreed that, given the situation, alleviating family suffering outweighed policy concerns.

I requested a meeting later in the day with the Iraqi colonel in charge of liaison functions. I had spoken with the German doctor earlier. The physician informed me that the boy's chances of survival would be greatly improved if he could remain in his care for another twenty-four hours. I asked to see the Iraqi colonel to request the additional time. At the meeting later that day, the Iraqi officer demanded that Karim be turned over immediately, and would not relent, despite my pleas for more time. He said that the boy was a citizen, and that I had no right to keep him. The colonel also stated that Karim, given the extent of his injuries, would be better off dead. The bastard was of course legally correct, even if his position was morally bankrupt. He pissed me off! I was going to give this kid every possible chance for survival.

I told the colonel that I was going to keep the boy for the additional twenty-four hours, and if he wanted to lodge a protest with the UN Security Council, I would gladly put him in touch with the right people in New York. Now it was the Iraqi colonel's turn to be pissed off. He stormed out of the meeting. For my part, I left in a far better mood than when I had arrived.

My pleasure with myself was short-lived. I returned to the medical detachment and spoke with the doctor. He was pleased that they would have Karim for another twenty-four hours. He assured me that they would do all they could in the limited time available, but that even so, and on the Iraqi side of the border, there were extreme shortages of both qualified medical personnel and supplies. Moreover, he was aware, as I was, that seriously wounded persons were sometimes just left to die. This of course happened far more commonly among the poor and disenfranchised, like the Bedouin. The doctor lastly informed me that if the wounds Karim sustained were not properly treated in the weeks ahead he could easily lose his leg to gangrene, followed by a slow agonizing death.

I received a report from my operations staff that Karim's parents were proceeding northward. However, they would not be allowed by Iraqi authorities to cross to the Kuwaiti side of the border, where our HQ was located. They would be required to wait on the Iraqi side of the border. I spent much of the next twenty-four hours with Karim. I spoke very poor Arabic. He spoke no English. Somehow, though, we managed.

I was called on the carpet later that day and verbally disciplined by my UN military superior. The Iraqi colonel had submitted a formal complaint. There was no question that I had exceeded my authority. I took my ass-chewing in stride. My UN boss, a French colonel, did not order me to turn over Karim.

I was present when the turn-over took place the following day. Karim held my hand until the time the Iraqis took him. There were tears in his big dark eyes as he was carried away on a stretcher. He locked those eyes with me until he was out of sight. My emotions overwhelmed me. I shook. I returned to my quarters, closed and locked the door, sat on the edge of my bed, and wept.

I cried for all the tomorrows that Karim would likely never see. I cried for his parents. I cried for all the suffering Iraqi children to come. Lastly, I shed tears for myself, because there was nothing that I could do to change the outcome. I was no stranger to the never-ending tragedy of Iraq. My arrival in Basra terminated this sad walk down memory lane.

Following consultations with the UN Area Security Coordinator, I made a call. I appointed a former Belgian Army colonel to Basra. The two turned out to be a superb pairing, and did an excellent job managing UN security in the south.

It was during the trip to Basra that I asked my driver, Mazzin, if he would accept an immediate promotion and appointment as my security assistant. He enthusiastically agreed. Although I had known him only a brief time, Mazzin impressed me with his work ethic and intelligence. He held a master's degree in civil engineering from a prestigious Iraqi university but could make more money working as a driver for the UN. I would have to train him as we went along. He was a very good man; although inexperienced, he sucked up knowledge like a vacuum. He also accepted the post based on my promise that he would eventually be paid. At that time, and despite multiple requests of my department in New York, I was without a budget.

The trips south and north were instructive. There was no good news anywhere. Nothing worked. Iraq was broken. Nobody seemed to know how to fix it, least of all the folks in DC. My maternal grandfather, Alfred Cormier, a very smart man, told me once, "Bobby, the fish stinks from the head down." What he meant is that bad decisions at the top (the head) always result in confusion and negative outcomes at the implementing level (the tail). Policies made inside the White House or Pentagon and then subsequently implemented in Baghdad clearly had little relationship to ground truth. The stench in

Baghdad started many thousands of miles to the west, and on the Potomac River. My grandfather was brilliant.

Shortly after my return from the north, I invited several heads of UN agencies and senior mission personnel to lunch at the Canal Hotel. I had a personal agenda. Ever since my arrival in Baghdad, I heard complaints by senior UN staff members about the American Army's failure to stop the mass looting that took place in the wake of the US invasion. I was personally fed up with their commentary. In addition to the senior UN staff, I also invited a young American private of the 2nd Armored Cavalry Regiment. I could easily lure him into attendance with the simple promise of ice cream. At that time, we had it, while the soldiers didn't. It was a no-brainer in the one hundred-ten-degree heat.

When everyone was seated, I presented the young private to the assembled senior UN staff from both the mission and the agencies. I suggested to them that they ask him their questions. I knew what his answers would be, even though I did nothing to prep him. One of the senior staff took the bait and asked the most pressing question. The private regretfully put down his bowl of ice cream and responded in a clear and respectful voice, "Sir, we are American soldiers. We would never shoot unarmed civilians, even if they are looting." The silence at the table was deafening. That soldier in a few words had accomplished more than I could have hoped for. I could have told them, but from me the response might have seemed self-serving. The young soldier was absolutely without guile. His simple truthful response was accepted as fact by all present. I heard no more about this matter.

However, in fairness, I am compelled to point out that US occupation forces, which included coalition partners, and under international law, were responsible for law and order in Iraq in the wake of the invasion. I heard much later that Secretary of Defense Donald Rumsfeld personally took the decision to eliminate several military police units from the force list that was scheduled for deployment to Iraq. The maintenance of law and order is the mission of the military police in occupation operations.

Even though we had been in-country less than a month, the stress was building. I was tired. Lack of sleep, driven by an endless multitude of taskings, was starting to tell. In an e-mail note to New York, I shared the following:

> I am swamped with coordinative work, writing requirements and meeting obligations… I have to pace myself better. I can feel the fatigue in my bones.

But the situation was about to become even worse. On 27 May, the SG announced the appointment of the special representative of the secretary general for Iraq (SRSG). This appointment was widely heralded in the press as a positive development at the time. The SRSG was known to be a tough negotiator, who was intelligent, dedicated, and charismatic. I met him plane-side upon his arrival at Baghdad International Airport, and then personally provided the security briefing to him and his staff. I made it clear that the security situation was uncertain and likely soon to worsen.

The SRSG had been a prominent naysayer concerning the US invasion of Iraq. He felt that the justification for the invasion was grossly insufficient. I respected his analysis and his willingness to state contrary opinions in public forums. And of course, I agreed with him.

As an under-secretary general in rank, he immediately became the senior UN official in Iraq. Under our security policy rules of that day, he should have accepted the mantle of Designated Official for Security. He declined this task, leaving it to the Humanitarian Coordinator. "After all," he told me grinning, "I am only going to be here for four months." It may have been his intention to return to his desk in Geneva as the UN High Commissioner for Human Rights in four months, but it was not in the cards.

I shared my security concerns privately with the SRSG, but he believed that the UN's reputation for independence would serve as its best protection from possible attack. This belief, perhaps understandable given his previous service, could not withstand serious scrutiny in the developing context of Iraq. However, the fact was that, upon his arrival in Baghdad, the threat to the mission dramatically increased. With the SRSG's entrance into Baghdad, the UN role in Iraq broadened significantly from humanitarian action to engagement in contentious sectarian politics that would soon tear Iraq apart.

Also, and previously, Osama Bin Laden—in a taped message—had identified the UN as a future target of Al Qaeda. The reason given was the UN's support of the breakaway province of Timor at the eastern end of the Indonesian archipelago. Indonesia is the world's largest Muslim nation. Bin Laden viewed the UN's activities in Timor, then led by our new SRSG, creating a new and independent non-Islamic nation-state, as a direct attack on Islam. The stage was set.

The mission's CAO was preparing expanded offices on the third floor of the Canal Hotel for me. I badly needed additional office space for what little staff I did have. With the announcement of the SRSG's appointment, I was notified that I would have to remain in my small offices on the back side of the building. The SRSG and his staff were to occupy the space formerly designated for me and mine.

On 28 May, a nearby explosion shattered some of the Canal Hotel's windows and scared the hell out of me. I immediately feared the worse. I walked rapidly outside from my office to see what had happened. Several other staff members had the same idea. I ordered all of them to remain inside until I had the opportunity to assess the situation. Mazzin accompanied me in case I needed an interpreter. I proceeded in the direction of the dust cloud thrown up by the explosion outside the compound and behind the tent city.

I noted some American soldiers near the blast. I was angry. If there were to be scheduled explosions in this vicinity, I should have been informed. I asked Mazzin to stay behind. There was no reason to endanger anybody else, and I needed no interpreter with the Americans. I headed straight toward what appeared to be the man in charge. As I closed the distance, I noted the black single bar of a first lieutenant with the collar insignia of a US Army Engineer.

When I was within a few yards, I shouted, "What the hell are you doing, lieutenant?" I did not identify myself, but the young officer was immediately cowed. I had chewed out my fair share of young officers over the years. There is an art to it. The engineer immediately apologized, "I am terribly sorry, sir. We didn't know that there was more underneath." I took a slow steadying breath, lowered my voice an octave, and demanded greater detail.

The lieutenant explained that he and his small team of engineers were tasked with Explosive Ordnance Disposal in the area. They were performing this mission when they came across what appeared to be some old mortar rounds partially buried in a mound of earth. Their orders were to destroy all such "in place." This meant that they would place perhaps a quarter-pound block of plastic explosive adjacent to the ordnance, back off a safe distance, and then explode the plastic explosive. The explosive was supposed to "sympathetically" detonate the mortar rounds.

What the lieutenant apparently did not know was that there were other devices with explosive potential underneath the mortar rounds that he could not see, perhaps more of the same. He had anticipated a much smaller explosion than occurred. The larger blast, which took out some of the windows in our headquarters, was completely unanticipated. The lieutenant was clearly embarrassed. My initial anger lost some of its steam.

I told the lieutenant that in future he was to inform my compound security officer any time he anticipated conducting further ordnance disposal near our headquarters. The young officer agreed and apologized once again. I took his hand in mine, shook it firmly, and told him that I had learned more from my mistakes over the years than from my successes. I wished him well and turned on my heel to return to my office.

By this time, an agency security advisor had arrived. He and I began walking back to the Canal Hotel together. I explained to him what had happened as we walked. I saw that Mazzin was coming toward me carrying something in his hands. I paid little notice. I was focused instead on the conversation with my colleague. I was still looking and speaking to him when Mazzin arrived with a big grin on his face, while handing me something. I unconsciously held out my hands to receive whatever he wanted me to have. It was heavy and very warm, almost hot. I looked down.

A racing heart and burst of sweat was my immediate response. I remember also watching the hair on my arms rise. What I was now holding in my hands looked like a Russian 82mm mortar round. Apparently, the round had been blown into our compound, fifty yards distant. After the beating it had taken, I had no idea how volatile it might be now. I looked hard into Mazzin's eyes. It was not until that very moment that he realized what he had done, first endangering himself, and now me and others. I saw it dawn on him. Several negative emotions played out across his face in a second. He spit out an apology. But I wasn't paying attention. There were more immediate concerns.

I suggested to my agency colleague and Mazzin that they should immediately return to the compound. They moved off quickly, Mazzin looking over his shoulder as he walked away, his face contorted with shame and guilt. I looked about for some safe place to relieve myself of the unwanted package. At that moment, I would have preferred to be holding a rattlesnake by the throat. I saw a depression perhaps ten yards distant and away from the compound populated by UN staff.

I began walking slowly and carefully. The mortar round was hot against the skin of my palms, and I was perspiring profusely from every pore. The ground was uneven. The sweat streamed down my face and into my eyes. A shiver went up my spine. At least, if I go, it will be fast, and I will feel no pain, I thought gratefully. It felt like an eternity, but I know it was less than a minute. I was acutely aware that every step was potentially my last. I knelt in the depression, and as gently as I could, laid the mortar round down in its center. I do not remember breathing, though I must have. I wiped my eyes free of moisture with my shirt sleeve as I stood.

I backed slowly away, turned, and then walked rapidly to get as much distance as possible between me and the round. I do not know why I did not run... perhaps because others were watching? My sense of relief when I cleared the "kill zone" behind me was enormous. I remember taking a huge ragged breath of air when I got about ten yards away.

Mazzin ran to my side while still apologizing. I remember laughing out loud. He looked at me quizzically because he had not expected that response. I was alive. I was happy. The laughter was real. I smiled at him. I hugged him and forgave him on the spot. I had seldom felt more alive than at that moment, despite the weakness in my knees.

The lieutenant and his soldiers were watching my predicament from afar. I called out and asked him to please take care of the errant mortar round I had just left in the depression. I only hoped that my voice did not betray the fear I had so recently felt. He saluted his agreement.

I returned immediately to my office alone, closed the door, and guzzled a large glass full of some truly awful Iraqi-made whiskey. It was wonderful.

Every day was a whirlwind of activity. As the security situation in Baghdad and elsewhere in Iraq deteriorated, the numbers of UN staff increased dramatically. All attempts by my office to stem the tide failed. Perhaps the SG wanted to ensure UN political relevancy in Iraq. There might soon be available millions of dollars for humanitarian and development projects via the Coalition Provisional Authority. Moreover, the UN-administered Iraq Oil-for-Food Program had to be shut down and turned over to the Americans no later than 21 November 2003.

I had no argument with the desires of the UN's most senior leadership. It is true that to be relevant, the UN had to be in Iraq. Droves of political, humanitarian, and developmental cadres were all on hand to perform their mandated functions. My issues were simple; these people were all extraordinarily vulnerable to potential bad actors. We needed more security personnel. We needed additional money to perform crucial functions. We needed the wholehearted support of our leadership in both Iraq and New York in the attempt to create a more survivable environment. Other than the HC's agreement to build a perimeter wall and install shatter-resistant film on the Canal Hotel's windows, which were significant concessions, it seemed that most of our other security recommendations were to go largely unaddressed.

Route Irish, the roadway used by just about everyone to get to Baghdad International Airport, was slowly becoming one of the most hazardous highways in Iraq. Improvised explosive devices were coming into vogue by hostile, unemployed former regime elements. US military HUMVEEs, yet to be up-armored, were easy prey. UN convoys were even more vulnerable.

It was about this time that I noticed several UN security officers were carrying unauthorized concealed side arms. Most carried them in what looked like fanny packs. Although I knew that such carriage was contrary to UN policy, I chose to say nothing about it. Iraq was becoming more dangerous every day. The only people that did not seem to know it were our bosses. On most occasions, I was fine with going unarmed. But in a small percentage of cases, and Iraq might have been one, a side arm made perfectly good sense. Despite UN policy to the contrary, I acquired a 9mm Beretta pistol with ammunition that I kept in my hotel room, just in case. It is an American axiom that it is better to be judged by twelve than carried by six.

I acquired a long-term rental apartment on the top floor of one of the local hotels in Baghdad. UN staff were pouring in. We had to go somewhere, so we scouted some of the hotels in the area. We found a few that met our criteria—some security, running water, and on-site power generation. My hotel was one of these. The drive to work every day took about ten minutes. We established a curfew for UN staff during the hours of darkness. Movement at night was becoming more dangerous, as some locals were settling old scores. In the early days in Baghdad, it was not unusual to find fresh bullet-riddled corpses of Iraqi citizens in the streets.

In early June, I established a UN Security Cell. I had never done this, and therefore had no experience managing one. Essentially, a Security Cell is composed of all UN security officers in-country. As the senior officer, I was responsible for holding meetings, collecting and disseminating security-related information, and requesting the support and advice of the membership. The UNSECOORD and mission officers worked for me. As earlier mentioned, agency officers worked for their respective agencies—UN Children's Fund, World Food Program, World Health Organization, etc.

Frankly, I had no idea how to go about creating a Security Cell. As I discovered later, it largely depends on the person running it, and their ability to gain and maintain the cooperation of these officers outside of a formal chain of command. As a former military officer, I was dubious of the added value of creating one. I was wrong.

The idea to create the cell belonged to the senior security officer of the International Organization for Migration. In brief, this officer entered my office in a rage, calling me a "bloody idiot," and then proceeded to explain in minute detail why I was a "bloody idiot"—because I had not created a Security Cell for Iraq. When he had finished, out of breath and red-faced, I admitted that I was a "bloody idiot" and immediately sent an apology to all UN security officers in Baghdad via e-mail, along with an invitation to attend the first Security Cell meeting the following morning. I learned a long time ago to never let your ego get in the way of learning new things; in fact, it became one of my "laws." The Security Cell worked beautifully. In any other country, its creation might have made all the difference.

We held Security Cell meetings every morning at 7:30 AM in a private dining area adjacent to the UN cafeteria in the Canal Hotel. It was a testament to the value of these meetings that no UN security officer in Iraq, and then present in Baghdad, dared miss one. My staff started by providing updates on the security situation based on daily coordination with the Americans, and then the free-for-all began. These meetings became more and more tumultuous as time progressed, and with the degrading security situation. I often felt less like the senior officer present than a referee in a no-holds-barred barroom brawl. Nerves were on edge. Tempers flared. On one occasion, I had to physically place my body between two potential brawlers. Everyone's intentions were good. Many simply disagreed about solutions. Some agencies were accustomed to spending money on security. Others, not at all. But everyone within the Security Cell feared the future.

There was something else, too, and very important. I made lots of security recommendations within the context of the Security Management Team. Because of the positive influence of the Security Cell, I soon changed my slide presentations—removing the word "I" from those presentations and began replacing it with the plural pronoun "we." A genuine team spirit was developing among we security officers in Baghdad because of the existence of the Security Cell.

By policy, I was the one who spoke for the entire UN security community in Iraq. I was not shy. In the capacity of senior officer, time and again I spoke truth to power, both orally and in writing, in New York and Baghdad. I did so when alone with my leadership and in meetings with several others in attendance. Nothing I said or did seemed to positively impact our superiors. In fact, and on more than one occasion, I was accused of overstating the threat by some members of the Security Management Team. At the same time, Security Cell members pushed me to be harder on our bosses. I lived every day with enormous and growing frustration. I felt the pain of daily existing between a rock and a very hard place.

The issues were legion. First, as mentioned, we within the security community sensed the growing danger, particularly in Baghdad. Fear is powerful. It affected all of us in diverse ways. The mushrooming dissatisfaction of the Security Cell was palpable.

Second, each agency had a different appetite for risk. Some, like the World Food Program and United Nations Children's Fund, often operated successfully in questionable security circumstances. Their staff was trained and equipped for it. Others, like the UN Educational, Scientific, and Cultural Organization and the UN Food and Agricultural Organization, had no idea how to cope in a hazardous environment. The latter category placed enormous strains on me and my small headquarters staff.

Third, many agencies had no security professionals on staff. In these cases, I asked the head of agency to appoint a security focal point. This was often a person, assuming they had time to attend meetings, who was either untrained or unhappy to have been thusly tasked, sometimes both. Some security focal points were switched on. Others were not. They were simply a mixed bag.

Fourth, arriving staff members would skip mandatory entry briefings, and many more would fail to comply with what we called minimum operating security standards. These mandatory minimum standards included ballistic vests, helmets, radios, vehicles, and more. Tragically, there was no enforcement mechanism.

Fifth, my boss maintained one hundred percent control over the security clearance process. Under rules in force, then and now, if any UN staffer wanted to come to Iraq, first they had to apply for security clearance to do so. This process is nearly always managed directly by the country security office, and under guidelines approved by someone like the HC in his role as Designated Official for Security. I did not then understand why he kept personal control of this process.

On 21 June I sent the following e-mail to the HC's acting deputy, who was also the acting Designated Official for Security. The HC was not in Baghdad at that time.

Soldiers of the 2nd ACR came to my office this morning. They had been formally tasked by their headquarters to "secure" this facility. In order to accomplish this, they feel compelled to violate normal rules concerning weapons in UN facilities. In other words, they are going to "secure" this facility. That means putting spotters on our rooftops and soldiers with weapons inside our compound. Frankly, and given our current security circumstances, I am inclined to agree without comment until a more acceptable and politically correct solution is found.

At that time, senior UN staff near-universally disliked being protected by US soldiers. Their reasoning was solid enough. The Americans with their coalition partners were the occupying force. As the UN, we needed to gain and maintain some distance, so as not to become too closely associated politically. In any case, I was later disappointed when the much-anticipated additional US military security failed to materialize.

A UN security officer from a Scandinavian country came to my office shortly afterward. He told me confidentially that he represented his government regarding what he was about to propose. I was intrigued. He told me that his country was ready to offer the UN in Iraq an infantry battalion to secure our headquarters. I was immediately excited by the possibility. It seemed a near-perfect solution. This Scandinavian country was well known for both its neutrality and military competence. Also, the roughly thirty soldier platoon left behind by the US 2nd Armored Calvary Regiment Commander, although welcome, were grossly insufficient to cover the entire perimeter of the Canal Hotel compound 24/7.

I took that offer immediately and directly to the HC. He declined, saying that the timing was wrong, and that he preferred using an Iraqi Police Unit instead. I was deeply disappointed. Although requested, there were no Iraqi police units then available for this purpose.

On 28 June, I sent a message to New York. A portion of that communication is provided immediately below:

> ...we are in a degrading security circumstance. At the same time, we are increasing the numbers of UN missions and staff. Although we have managed adequately to date, this situation should not be permitted to continue. Corrective action is required.

I asked one of my officers to create a daily security update that could be sent out over the Internet to UN offices countrywide. We soon received a plethora of requests for these updates to be sent directly to UN Headquarters offices in New York, Geneva, Paris, Rome, and Vienna. We also started receiving requests from the humanitarian INGO community for the updates. I always approved those requests. Consumers of this report were soon over 1,000 strong.

On 29 June, we set up a Security Information and Operations Center in the small, elliptically shaped security building by the front gate to the compound. Such operations centers cost money and require personnel and equipment. But at that time, we had no funding to create it. Still, the need was paramount. We did it anyway, even without money. We spent the better part of three weeks of June setting it up.

At New York's direction, I wrote a formal request for donor support to fund this function. It struck me as absurd that the security of our staff was held hostage to donor funding. In any case, that funding, even if approved, would not be forthcoming until 2004—six months away. In the meantime, staff would remain at significant risk, so we created the Security Information and Operations Center on a shoestring, which in some cases was funded out-of-pocket with the personal funds of security officers.

The idea to establish this function was the brainchild of the UN Children's Fund Security Advisor. He offered the suggestion, and then provided the organizational skills behind the initiative. All members of the Security Cell then in Baghdad volunteered to take turns manning the Security Information and Operations Center. My office provided the computers, radios with operators, and office space.

Prior to my departure for R&R, my boss held a Security Management Team meeting. My concern was growing daily regarding the too-rapid influx of staffers who were not prepared to deal with the security context, and the fact that the number of incidents involving violence was rising simultaneously.

To make my point, I included on one of my many Power-Point slides the following bolded and purposefully provocative statement: **"It is only a matter of time..."**

One of the agency heads looked up quizzically at me while asking, "What does that mean?" I responded, "It is only a matter of time until *we are attacked*." He shook his head in disbelief saying, "How could you possibly know that?" I then pointed out, "It's not just my opinion; it is the opinion of the entire Security Cell—our collective assessment, with no one dissenting." That answer gave him pause. I was telling him that every UN security officer in Iraq at that time, including all agency officers, agreed that the UN would come under attack. We simply had no way of knowing when, where, or how.

I also included several recommendations during that meeting. Below are a few:

- Immediately cease influx of incoming UN staff to Baghdad.
- Reduce the numbers of staff in Baghdad.
- A new staff ceiling should be implemented and strictly enforced... recommend 200.
- Establish a deadline for 100% MOSS compliance of 12 July.
- Curtail developmental, cultural, and political activities to the degree possible.

None of these common-sense recommendations were implemented. I did not understand why. The truth, though, did eventually come out.

15

Death Watch

The sun was shining on the sea,
Shining with all his might.
He did his very best to make
The billows smooth and bright—
And this was odd because it was
The middle of the night.
—Lewis Carroll, *The Walrus and the Carpenter*

Naima met me in Amman after flying over from Cairo for my R&R. Then we flew together to the Egyptian Red Sea resort of Sharm Al Sheik at the southernmost tip of the Sinai Peninsula. She was shocked at my appearance. I had lost twenty pounds in the two months that I was in Iraq. The combination of unrelenting heat, poor food, and merciless work schedule had done the trick.

The UN had authorized five days R&R every two months for staff members working in Iraq. I was grateful for it. I was going on four to five hours sleep a night while in Iraq, and days off were impossible. My primary activities on R&R were to eat and sleep. The stress I felt was not a consequence of a worsening security situation. The stress was the result of consistent lack of support from our superiors. The five days went by all too quickly.

Naima returned to Cairo, and I departed for Sana'a, Yemen, to administratively out-process my former duty station. While there, I was directed to report to UN Headquarters in New York for consultations with the UNSECOORD.

I met with him in his office on 45th Street in Manhattan, between First and Second Avenues, just up the street from the US Mission. His first question was, "How many UN staff are currently in Iraq?" My response was quick and sure, "I have no idea. Agencies are failing to report their numbers. And the Humanitarian Coordinator is personally managing security clearance approvals." I then handed him a document I had written, entitled "Draft Iraq Lessons Learned." In that document, I enumerated many of the failures of the UN security system, which were substantial. I hit each point as diplomatically as possible. In fact, though, many of those failures reflected badly on both him and his staff in New York.

What follows below is just one quote from that document:

There is no kind or gentle way to say this... so I will just spit-it-out. The level of administrative and budgetary support to the field is abysmal.

I did not intend to attack him personally, but it had always been clear to me that to fix a problem, one had to first know of its existence. I wanted to let him know, in writing, just how dysfunctional UN security policies and procedures really were in terms of field support in Iraq. My observations were perhaps taken as threatening. We did not have enough money. We did not have enough staff. My many requests for assistance to New York went unanswered.

The UNSECOORD was also the former HC in Iraq, the post that my current boss now occupied. He no doubt felt that he knew a great deal about the situation there. But unfortunately, those circumstances no longer existed. The former security of Iraq, imposed by Saddam Hussein through brutal repression, had vanished. The new Iraq was teetering on the edge of an abyss.

One good thing came out of my trip to New York. I personally followed up on my multiple requests to headquarters to provide me with a budget. During my two months in Iraq, I had exhausted all my personal funds. I had to pay for gas, food, accommodations, and office-related expenses out of pocket. Moreover, and as mentioned earlier, I was in the process of hiring local staff on the promise of a contract. We were in dire need of funds. Multiple e-mail and telephone requests for budgetary assistance had gone unaddressed. I was beyond frustrated.

After fulfilling the primary requirement — consultations — I made a beeline for the UN Development Program office nearby. They were responsible for providing administrative and budgetary support to our field offices. One of the clerks there informed me that the money was available, but that they were waiting for the signature of my department's administrative officer. My next stop was there. I acquired the necessary signature on the spot, and then walked it back to the UN Development Program office. *Et voilà!* I had a budget. I could now at least pay for office needs, purchase vehicles, and formally hire local staff. I never received a satisfactory explanation why it took this level of personal intervention to acquire something as straightforward as a budget authorization.

I was not looking forward to my return to Iraq. UN staff members, particularly those lacking humanitarian or peacekeeping experience, had no idea how to live and work in what was soon to become a combat environment. They placed enormous strains on my office. Many refused to attend what were supposed to be mandatory security briefings on arrival. Many ignored the evening curfew. Many failed to acquire security clearance to enter Iraq. Many did not meet minimum operational security standards for operating in Iraq. And sadly, there were seemingly no consequences for those who failed to comply.

We had to do a better job of adapting to the increasing threat. Prior to my departure from Iraq on R&R, I had received approval from the HC to conduct a Security Stand-down Day on 8 July in Baghdad, and 12 July in all other UN locations within the country. These other locations included Basra, Al Hillah, Mosul, and Irbil. I had appointed security officers in charge of each. The Security Cell, composed of all UN security personnel in Iraq, would assist in teaching an entire day's worth of security-related classes to international as well as local staff. It was an attempt on my part to try to catch up, and to impress upon those UN staff now spreading out all over the country that the security situation was deteriorating.

These two stand-down days were abject failures. Attendance was poor countrywide. It became clear that many of the most senior UN managers in Iraq could not be bothered with matters relating to security. The officer I had appointed my interim deputy in Baghdad, and in charge of security matters in my absence, Marco Smoliner, reported to me via phone the negative results of the initiative.

I asked Marco to formally highlight all the areas where we had made recommendations, where the Security Management Team had failed to institute appropriate corrective action. Marco did as I requested. The list of failures was long. The impact, once again, was negligible.

I returned to Baghdad on 19 July by the UN aircraft via Amman, Jordan. There was no good news anywhere. I was in a foul mood when I wrote these words to New York in an e-mail on 22 July:

My fear is that we will continue to drag our feet. The agencies in general are too complacent. I know that we have made all the right recommendations. I know that we have stood-up the Security Information and Operations Center without support from our own UN community. I know that we have to live within our limitations with regards to manning. I know that the UN system is ponderous and slow moving. The problem is that the security situation is dynamic and fast moving.

It is probably important to mention at this point in the story that it was our collective job as security officers to enable the missions of those UN agencies we supported, to find a way to say yes. Tragically, lacking increased security personnel levels, additional funding, and critical equipment and vehicles, saying yes was often all but impossible.

On my first day on the job after returning, I mentioned to the HC that our UN unarmed Iraqi guard force had been hired at a time when Saddam Hussein and his intelligence services might have had a hand in their selection. I suggested that we should consider a vetting process. He reacted as if personally affronted. He accused me of being "unfair and biased" and stated that there would be no vetting process of our Iraqi unarmed guard force.

In the evening hours of 22 July, while I was in my hotel room, gunfire seemed to spontaneously erupt everywhere in the city. Naima had joined me by this time, having secured a consultancy with the World Food Program. I immediately placed her in the bathroom (safe room) and went outside on the roof to see if the fire was directed at any specific point. It wasn't. The sky was lit up three hundred sixty degrees with tracer fire.

I called our radio operators on the handheld radio that I carried with me everywhere. I asked the obvious question. It took a moment, but I came to understand that it was celebratory fire. It had just been reported that the much-hated sons of Saddam Hussein, Uday and Qusay, had both died in a gunfight with US Forces in Mosul. This apparently happy news resulted in what I was witnessing now. The problem was that all things that go up eventually must come down. Gravity is a bitch that way. Rounds were landing on our thin plywood rooftop. We could hear the bullet strikes. I returned to Naima in the bathroom. We remained there together until the celebratory fire subsided.

Naima and I had a tremendous fight before her arrival in Baghdad. Knowing what I knew about the deteriorating security circumstances in Iraq, I asked her to return to Cairo and to give up any thoughts of a job in Baghdad. Long story short, she refused all my entreaties. She was a professional. She was an adult. She would make her own decisions about where she went and when and for what purposes. Our interpersonal status did not give me veto power concerning her job choices. She was going to Baghdad, and that was the end of it. She intended to share the risk with me. I relented because she gave me no other choice. She was correct in all that she said. That, of course, never changed the fact that I remained afraid for her safety every day she was in country.

On 25 July, I tendered the Iraq Threat Assessment, which had been unanimously endorsed by the Security Cell, to my masters in Baghdad and New York. A few key points from that document follow:

- Iraq, and particularly Baghdad, is extraordinarily hazardous.
- Direct assaults on clearly identified UN staff and facilities are all but a certainty... this is the consensus of the Security Cell.
- ...we would be prudent to institute more restrictive security measures, such as: reducing staff levels; restricting movement; hardening our facilities; and redoubling preparations for possible relocation.

None of these recommendations were implemented. My level of frustration, and that of my security colleagues, was skyrocketing. UN-Baghdad was taking on a fanciful Alice-in-Wonderland quality.

At the following day's Security Management Team meeting, I highlighted that the International Committee for the Red Cross and the International Organization for Migration had both suffered attacks. Each resulted in staff deaths near Al Hillah, more than an hour's drive south of Baghdad. The negative assessments of the Security Cell were coming to fruition. Unfortunately, nothing changed.

It was about this time that I had a serious discussion with two of my senior security colleagues behind a closed door. I told them that I was considering resigning in protest because of the egregious lack of support we in the UN security community had received. My colleagues, both of whom were more experienced in the UN than I, seemed amused. They explained to me that, unlike the American military, there was little UN history of individual officers resigning their posts to highlight systemic deficiencies in something like security matters. They went on to tell me that if I did indeed quit, someone would be found to replace me, and that he or she might not be half as familiar with the critical issues. Essentially, they argued convincingly that we were nominally better off with me than without me.

I was promoted to the rank of P-4 in the month of July. P-4 is the second-highest professional grade in the UN. It was an important event in my professional life. There was no celebration. There was no time.

On 30 July, in a document to New York, I stated the following:

> As the UN's footprint has spread geographically, the day-to-day security situation in Iraq has come to overwhelm the capabilities of the currently deployed UNSECOORD officers. More assets are badly needed, and most urgently.
>
> The security situation in Iraq is dynamic. The current threat is real. My office… is undermanned and under-funded.

My exasperation continued to grow.

On 30 July, and in a separate e-mail to New York, I vented some more:

> The demands are too great. Nearly daily security incidents require full time attention... leaving critical nationwide mission tracking and security planning functions wanting.

The e-mail messages and documents I have previously mentioned reflect only a small percentage of the many reports I dispatched to New York that clearly expressed my ever-growing concerns that Baghdad was becoming more dangerous by the day. Those concerns, as best I could tell, were ignored.

The officer in charge of compound security—mission impossible—came into my office asking for one hundred dollars. Understandably, I asked, "What for?" In response, he stated that he had conducted some research and discovered that we could install steel-plate blast shields over the windows in the Security Information and Operations Center building at the front gate, but money was required. He knew that we had no UN funds for items like this, so he took it upon himself to collect the cash from the members of the Security Cell. He figured we could do the job if every one of us voluntarily donated one hundred dollars out-of-pocket. I gave him the money on the spot. It was good initiative on his part. He knew from previous discussions that my approval was assured. We had already sandbagged the ground floor of our building with money provided by a representative of the World Food Program.

Almost immediately, complaints came in from senior members of the mission that we were "militarizing" the appearance of our compound. I deflected all such commentary as diplomatically as possible. They weren't paying for it, and they had no standing to criticize how we went about modifying a building for which I was personally responsible.

I subsequently invited the HC to attend a special meeting of the Security Cell. I often wondered if his problem was with me, personally. The purpose, I told him, was to give him the benefit of the collective wisdom of all those present. The real purpose was to demonstrate to him that the threat was very real and perceived by security professionals, other than me. Every officer spoke their mind, which I encouraged. Although their words differed from one another, their assessment was substantially the same: That Iraq, and particularly Baghdad, was becoming extraordinarily hazardous for the UN. Essentially, every officer present echoed my warnings. The net effect appeared to be zero. So perhaps it was not me after all.

Years later, I discovered from a knowledgeable source that in broad brush strokes the HC agreed with some of the Security Cell's recommendations. New York, via predominantly the cabinet chief's office, pressured him to allow more staff into Iraq. If the HC had implemented the recommendations of the Security Cell, the pace of staff entry would have been slowed to a trickle. Moreover, everyone knew that the cabinet chief spoke for the SG. The SG is the most senior security official in the UN.

I next arranged a meeting for the HC to meet with the senior US Army intelligence officer in Iraq, Brigadier General Barbara Fast. We had been classmates in the Military Intelligence Officer Advanced Course. Following a friendly greeting and hug (I had not seen her in nearly twenty years), we got down to cases. Barbara provided him what amounted to an unclassified threat briefing. As expected, she provided no good news.

If memory serves, it was sometime in early August when an under-secretary general arrived in Baghdad. He was the executive director of the UN-administered Iraq Oil-for-Food Program. I remember questioning myself at the time, what was someone so senior doing in Iraq at this juncture, when the security situation was degrading nearly every day? What made his mission so damned important?

Naima of course was a native Arabic speaker. Because of her job with the World Food Program, she was immediately placed in close quarters with UN-Iraqi staff members. A few told her—in confidence—that it was common knowledge among them that the Oil-for-Food Program was corrupt. So as far as the local staff were concerned, the UN itself was in league with Saddam Hussein in stealing the money generated by the program—funds that were supposed to buy food and medical supplies for the long-suffering people of Iraq. They had remained silent concerning these matters prior to the war because they feared Saddam Hussein's Mohabarrat (Secret Police & Intelligence Service). After the war, they feared losing their jobs with the UN, and therefore, again, remained silent. Of course, Naima told me. I had to wonder, just how high up did this corruption go?

At the 2 August Security Management Team meeting, the HC told the attendees—based on a query from the head of the UN Children's Fund—that a staff ceiling of two hundred fifty was insufficient due to the requirements of the UN Oil-for-Food Program. I had no idea where this number came from. I recommended a staff ceiling of no more than two hundred. Still more unprepared and vulnerable UN staff were permitted to enter Iraq. Again, I only found out subsequently that it was New York that was pushing staff into Iraq, and against both the HC's, as well as my own, recommendations. New York gave the mission only until 21 November to complete its tasks and turn over the program to the Americans. It was now becoming clearer to me. The SG's priority was seemingly binary—the Oil-for-Food Program and the SRSG's political mission. All other considerations, including security, were subordinate.

On 7 August, a large vehicular bomb exploded in front of the Jordanian Embassy in Baghdad. The extremists simply parked their truck nearby and left. Seventeen died, and many more were wounded. I sent an investigation team composed of two officers as soon as I heard the initial report. They returned with a description of the carnage. As best they could tell, no Jordanians had been killed. Most of the dead were innocent Iraqi passersby. Unfortunately, one victim was a World Health Organization local staff member.

Shortly thereafter, Marco was told by New York that he was soon to be reassigned as the UN Security Advisor for the Philippines. It was my own fault. I had made the mistake of mentioning his outstanding performance in messages to New York. Marco departed a few days later. I missed his presence immediately, and there was no replacement.

On 14 August, I was stunned to hear a New York-based UN agency had decided to hold a conference in Baghdad. They apparently made this decision without consulting my office. I sent a message immediately to Manhattan, recommending against holding their conference in Baghdad. As far as I can remember, they chose to ignore that recommendation and continued to plan to hold their conference despite the clearly deteriorating security circumstances.

On 15 August, the security officer directly responsible for compound security came to my office with the lieutenant in charge of our platoon from the 2nd Armored Cavalry Regiment. The two of them recommended to me that the Americans capitalize on their access to HESCO bastions (large earthen-filled barriers) and place them at key spots around our perimeter by the following day. The recommended placement of these bastions would result in the closure of the roadway adjacent to the Canal Hotel. They were fully aware of my concerns. This is the roadway that the mission's CAO had previously told me could not be closed because it was a public access road. Public access or not, it was a vulnerability that I knew required mitigation.

I agreed with them immediately and took the proposal directly to the HC. He refused the plan, not because of the public access issue, but because the HESCO bastions were "ugly." He added that he preferred a solution that involved the use of large painted concrete flowerpots, perhaps planted with palms—clearly a more decorative approach. I was quite willing to try the more decorative approach, except we did not have ready access to large concrete flowerpots, and I had no idea where to procure them. "Frustrated" does not begin to describe what I felt.

On 18 August, I met with the director of administration for the SRSG. As such, he sat on the Security Management Team. I personally gave him the latest update concerning security matters. My hope was that he might influence the SRSG to pay greater attention to the worsening security situation. His response was troubling. He said he believed that I was "overstating the threat." My warnings once again fell flat. I left his office feeling like ten miles of bad road.

Later that afternoon, I met informally with Nadia Younes, the SRSG's chief of staff. I liked her very much. She was smart, and good company. In other circumstances, and given time, I think we would have become friends. During a brief lull in our conversation, and in her trademark gravelly voice, she asked me, "Bob, it's getting bad isn't it?" I nodded my head in the affirmative, further words being unnecessary. Somebody outside the security community thankfully saw it too I remember thinking. I left her with a weak smile, and "see ya tomorrow."

Tragically, and in less than twenty-four hours, all of Nadia's tomorrows would be stripped away.

16

The Attack

19 August 2003

*I have love in me the likes of which you can scarcely imagine
and rage the likes of which you would not believe, if I cannot
satisfy one, I will indulge the other.*
—Mary Shelley, *Frankenstein*

The sound was an indescribably low-pitched yet outrageously loud multi-tiered rumbling. I have never or since
heard anything quite like it. I could not tell initially what it
was, only that it seemed to last for several seconds. I felt the
air move inside my lungs and then all around me. For the
briefest of moments, there was no air to breathe. My next conscious sensations were both visual and physical. I saw and
felt the building shake violently. Simultaneously, the chair
vibrated hard beneath me. Then the windows of my office
seemed to explode inwards. I did not clearly see—but it could
only have been—flying glass and bits of mortar from around
the windowsill blowing by me at speeds so great I could only
just make out what it was, or perhaps more correctly, what
it had to be. The transparent glass divider between my inner
and outer offices disappeared in an instant.

I glanced to my right. The door to my office was no longer
where it belonged. It was now partially knocked off its hinges

and lay half out and half in the outer office, where my administrative and security assistants normally worked. It was perhaps at this moment that I realized what had happened. My initial confusion stemmed from the fact that there was no sharp report, which was common in a single-explosive detonation. It was a bomb—a very big bomb—and we were the intended target. There was nothing in the immediate vicinity capable of creating a blast so large unless it was intentional. We had been hit. These few thoughts went through my mind in virtual nanoseconds.

I had one very immediate concern. Naima was in the outer office, only a few yards away. She had been using a spare computer terminal to accomplish preparatory work for a consultancy in support of the UN's World Food Program in Irbil. The work schedule called for her to depart for the northern Iraqi city the following day. She would not make it.

I yelled out to her as I was getting to my feet, unconsciously grabbing my handheld radio from the desktop charger out of long habit and placing it on my belt while in motion. There was no response to my call. My heart sank. I remember conducting a cursory visual self-examination as I stood. It appeared that I was unharmed. I observed no blood leakage. I was aware that some wounds, even when serious, are not initially felt.

As chance would have it, there was a wooden cabinet between me and the window that blocked the shards of flying glass. Had I been standing in the middle of my office when the explosion occurred, I would have been peppered with glass and mortar fragments, and my survival would have been questionable. My ears must have been ringing too, but I was not yet conscious of it. I remember feeling some dizziness, but that soon passed.

There was debris everywhere on the floor. Dozens of ceiling tiles had been blown off their mountings and were now littering my office floor. As I proceeded around the desk, I noted in my right peripheral vision that the satellite phone and FAX machine, formerly on the windowsill, were now both lying on the floor in fragments. I walked quickly toward the door, and then kicked it aside. I stumbled through and found her near the far wall lying on the ground face upward and bleeding profusely from a nasty gash over her right eye. She looked terrible. Her condition frightened me. My stomach immediately tied itself into a knot. Not surprisingly, she appeared dazed. The large glass divider between the outer office and mine had produced added shattered glass that covered the floor and desktops.

I leaned over, grabbed Naima by her arms, and pulled her gently erect, while asking if she was all right in a no doubt unsteady voice. The concern must have been all too evident in my tone. I conducted a quick survey of her condition, while lightly brushing her long dark hair behind her head and away from the wound above her eye, so that I could get a better look. Her outward appearance, and the blood flow, made it look bad. Surprisingly, she managed a weak smile and assured me that she was okay. My stomach unknotted a bit.

But that feeling of relief was not long-lived. I observed with rising alarm that a glass shard had pierced her left eye. The shard's jagged edge could be seen easily. Thankfully, she seemed totally unaware of it. And I was not going to tell her. If she thought she was OK, I knew it was best medical policy to reinforce that opinion. The gash over her right eye continued to bleed, but I knew that head wounds often do so without being life-threatening. She was clearly conscious, and with my assistance, I meant to get her the hell out of there, and fast.

I took her by the right arm, placing her on my left as we began making our way out of the building by common and unspoken assent. She was wobbly on her feet. No words were necessary. She knew where I was headed.

We took a right outside of the office, then began to negotiate the stairs that would take us down to the first floor.

Fluorescent lighting fixtures on the ceiling of the hallway had been knocked loose from their mountings. I hit my head on one of these.

We could not see the stairs. A great cloud of gray-white dust descended upon us. The corridors inside the building and stairwell quickly filled with it, effectively blotting out all vision. It made breathing very difficult as well. There was little choice, though. We had to get out. The dust was so thick that we had to feel our way out along the wall; first down the flight of stairs, and then through the recreation area and out the main entrance of the building. I was reminded of the 9/11 attack in New York and the video news coverage showing the massive clouds of dust that arose as the towers fell. This was no doubt a similar phenomenon. It was very tough going.

The ground was covered everywhere with debris, which often tripped us up. The mere fifty yards that we had to traverse felt much greater. We both fell more than once. Naima hung on to me like a bull terrier. The fingernails of her right hand dug unknowingly into my flesh. At that moment, all we had was one another. We were hanging on as much for emotional support as practicality. I placed my right hand on the wall and followed it toward what I hoped would be safety. I was by no means sure that there would be only one bomb, but I did not share that thought with her. She did not need anything else to worry about.

I know that I tried to speak some comforting words as we moved along the wall sightless, though I cannot remember now what they were. Every time I attempted speech it was followed with an immediate coughing jag. I decided to save my breath. The dust was too thick, like an impossibly dry and tasteless soup. We could hear others around us beginning to move—the disembodied moans, sobbing, and occasional muted screams of people in our vicinity, but we could not see anyone: The ubiquitous dust was that thick. The bright afternoon light from outside barely penetrated the gloom.

Naima leaned heavily into me, trusting that I could find my way out. Once we were beyond the recreation area and through the no-longer-existing glass doors that marked the entrance to that area, I managed to barely discern some diffused sunlight in the direction of what must have been the front entrance.

My vision was further worsened by the fact that my eyeglasses were no doubt covered in that thick dust. I sensed more than I knew that we were almost there. I headed for the dim light, abandoning the wall, taking the direct path. More debris on the ground tripped us. Large chunks of concrete had been blown off the walls and support columns, further impeding our progress. We fell and recovered... fell and recovered... until we were finally outside.

The whole journey might have taken five minutes, but it felt much longer. The late afternoon heat had not yet begun to wane. It was over one hundred-ten degrees Fahrenheit. Still, the air was cleaner as we stepped outside and into bright sunlight—it tasted good.

We were apparently two of the first persons to make it out of the main entrance. Only a very few people were immediately in evidence outside. They looked dazed and unbelieving and were uniformly covered with the thick gray-white dust that was still settling everywhere. Many were bleeding, although I could not see it clearly. The dust covered everything... even the crimson of blood. I locked eyes with some of the persons outside. I knew them. Their eyes reflected no recognition in return. The shock would take time to wear off.

We were moving better now. There was less debris outside. I brought us to a halt and took another look at Naima in daylight. The glass shard clearly pierced her left eye to some depth impossible to discern. Still, she remained blissfully unaware of the damage. The gash over her right eye had bled copiously. I was concerned, but less so than before. The unknown always frightens us the worst. In the full light, the wound did not appear as bad. Her blood had spread over the left sleeve of my shirt, but it was slowing. The thick dust in the building might have served to staunch the flow. I was heartened by the fact that there was no apparent arterial bleeding. I had checked for this when I first picked her up off the floor of my outer office. Had a shard of glass severed a major artery, I knew that she could have bled to death in a mere four minutes. We were very lucky.

Somehow both my Iraqi security and administrative assistants, Mazzin and Fatin, found us. I only discovered later that Fatin had gone to an adjacent room to photocopy a document, and this was why she was not in her work area at the time of the explosion. That mundane chore saved her from harm. Mazzin was on the road performing an errand for me. He arrived at the front gate within minutes of the attack. I was immediately grateful that both were unharmed, and by our side.

Fatin noticed the glass shard protruding from Naima's eye. Unfortunately, lacking medical training, she pointed this fact out to her. Naima's face contorted, and she promptly collapsed in my arms. Together, we moved her to the nearby grassy area adjacent to the Security Information and Operations Building at the front gate, and laid her down, while elevating her feet. She recovered consciousness quickly, but now was very concerned about the possibility of losing her eye, and understandably so. But I had another pressing problem that nagged at me. I was about to do something that I desperately did not wish to do, and yet felt that I must.

I remember telling Naima that I had to leave her now, and in the care of my two assistants. The words had a bitter taste. I was torn. I did not want to abandon her, but I had no choice. I had critical duties to perform that would not wait. At that moment, I hated myself. Naima's eyes, even the wounded one, pleaded with me to remain. But even she knew that I could not, and very slowly released her grip on my arm. I stood, turned, and left, going immediately to task. I did not turn

back for a look. I could not. I might have lost my already ten-
uous resolve. Leaving Naima at that moment was the hardest
thing I have ever had to do.

My first chore was to determine the condition of our communications. I walked quickly to the Security Information
and Operations Center in the small elliptically shaped building at the front gate of our compound. From the outside, I saw
that every pane of glass was shattered. I wondered about the
condition of those inside. This was the only building within
the compound that was my direct responsibility. The structure also served as guard shed and security offices for some
of my staff.

Luckily, the building was close by and it only took me
moments to cover the distance. I entered the side door, and
despite the debris, took the stairs two at a time to the second
floor, where we had placed the radio room. I opened the door
to find that the radio operators were alive and unharmed, and
their radios were still functional. The reason for this fortunate
circumstance was immediately clear. The large steel-plate
blast shields that I had approved some weeks earlier had been
installed over the interior windowsills. Although these blast
shields had been knocked off their wall mountings, they had
blocked the worst of the concussion wave, flying glass and
shrapnel. A representative of the World Food Program had
given us money to sandbag the ground floor offices too. These
two precautions, the steel-plate blast shields and sandbags
saved the lives of many in the UN security community that
day.

I instructed the radio operators to direct all security personnel to immediately report to me near the grassy area where
I had just left Naima. I also instructed them to contact all UN
agencies in Baghdad, and to direct them not to come to the
headquarters. I knew that bombs could be used as lures: that
extremists could set off a bomb, wait for help to arrive, and
then set off a second bomb—killing even more. I hoped to

avoid that scenario, if it was indeed the tactic of choice. There was no need to endanger additional staff.

Alerting the Americans was unnecessary. The platoon of the 2nd Armored Cavalry Regiment that had been assigned to assist with perimeter security would do this without being told. As a US Army veteran, I knew that medical help was already on the way. Finally, I directed the radio operators to inform all staff that the grassy area was designated as the triage point, where all wounded were to be brought.

I began to retrace my steps down the stairs while glancing outside through a now non-existent windowpane. The first thing I noticed was the condition of the five newly delivered security vehicles. The over-pressure from the concussion wave of the blast had crushed them like beer cans. I returned to the unyielding heat outside.

I made my way to the medical clinic on the first floor of the Canal Hotel, covering the distance outside the headquarters in less than twenty seconds. This is the same distance it had just taken me five minutes to negotiate with Naima. I re-entered the building by way of a side door. The corridor was mostly undamaged. The thick gray-white dust still hung heavy in the air.

Upon entering the clinic, I directed the staff to take all emergency medical supplies to the triage point. They did not immediately respond. Clearly, they were still dazed and confused. I spoke more harshly than I had intended and got their full attention. They nodded their understanding while beginning to move in the direction of the medical stores room. I could not wait to see if they complied with my direction but turned on my heel to return to the triage point.

While making the return trip, I made the call to UN Headquarters in New York using the cell phone on my right hip. I punched the speed dial. Moments later, the desk officer responsible for monitoring Iraq answered. I informed him that we had been attacked with a very large bomb. I tried, and no doubt failed, to keep my voice calm and even.

He somehow already knew of the attack and had been waiting for my call, assuming I was still alive and able. I informed him that we likely had many dead and wounded, but it would take time to determine who and how many. He was clearly taking notes as I spoke. He would report to the UNSE-COORD, who would then report to the SG. I excused myself from that call, telling him that I would be back in touch when we discovered more concerning our circumstances. I hit the red button and replaced the phone on my belt.

Perhaps ten minutes had elapsed since the blast. It is difficult to quantify accurately. I noted that a few walking wounded were beginning to arrive at the triage point. I also noticed that security personnel were congregating nearby. A couple of these had sustained what appeared to be minor wounds, but at that time, all seemed anxious for a job to do. I gathered them together and created three search teams, assigning one team per floor. I told them to check every room thoroughly. We could not afford to miss anyone. Essentially, I told the officers that I wanted a very careful search for the wounded. "The dead," I said, "can wait. We will collect them later." The search teams departed to perform their grisly but necessary task. I didn't want to appear uncaring of the recently deceased. But the priority must be those still living, and in need of immediate medical assistance.

I also assigned one officer to herd the uninjured to the back side of the compound, where our tent city (overflow sleeping accommodations) was located. The area near the front entrance to the compound needed to be kept clear for medical evacuation. Tent City would be our muster point. It was there we could begin reorganizing ourselves. A crowd of half-dazed persons was already gathering near the entrance to our headquarters.

It was about this time that I saw the first US Army ambulances arriving through the front gate. I knew that they would be coming. I did not know how they arrived so quickly. I found out why later. The soldiers took charge of the triage point upon their arrival. I knew that our injured staff were in good hands. I could have assisted. I had emergency trauma training, but the arrival of the US Army medical teams relieved me of the notion.

I took a moment to think another matter through. I knew that families would soon be deluging UN Headquarters in New York with desperate queries concerning the status of their loved ones in Baghdad. I also knew that the task of providing an accurate tally of the dead and wounded would fall to my office. I considered taking an officer from a search team to start the tracking process of the wounded that would soon be medically evacuated. I did not think long, dispensing with the idea. At that moment, I was surveying the triage point. Blood and exposed flesh were everywhere evident.

If I had assigned an officer to tracking, the medical personnel would probably respect my authority and slow the process to accommodate the requirement. But I could permit nothing to impede the evacuation of the wounded. Too many lives were potentially at risk. Seconds mattered for them. Families at home would have to wait for word of their loved ones. Better they wait than the alternative. My decision would be questioned by many senior UN officials in the months that followed. I never doubted, and still stand by, the rightness of the call.

As I surveyed the carnage before me, I remember shaking my head in disgust. I had formally recommended the installation of shatter-resistant film on all the windows at our headquarters in Baghdad. Had that recommendation been acted upon with greater dispatch, many injuries could have been avoided. I also remember wondering to myself why I hadn't resigned in protest. So many of our security recommendations had been ignored, both in Baghdad and in New York.

I already knew the answer. Had I resigned it would have changed nothing. The dead would still be dead. Those seriously wounded might be able to piece their lives back together again. I shook myself from my brief reverie with a self-reprimand. I had no time for regrets and recriminations now. That would come later. At that moment, we had work to do.

There would be little respite for me and the Security Cell. There was much to be done. And what about my bosses... would they approve my recommendation that all UN staff be immediately evacuated from Iraq? They must approve, I thought, they must!

I was considering re-entering the building to help in the search for wounded when someone I did not know grabbed me by the arm, while pointing in the direction of Tent City. "There is a fire," he shouted in a quavering, too-loud voice, "Come, quickly." I looked in the direction of his trembling finger. The smoke billowed upward... thick and dark near the vehicle maintenance building. I hadn't noticed it earlier. We ran there to get a better look.

When I reached the Tent City area, which was perhaps a distance of seventy-five yards, I could see that the fire was inside one of the large metal shipping containers. I had no idea what was in the container, but I also could take no chances. The fire could have been dangerous. Some of the contents were obviously combustible. Were any explosive? The first group that I had sent to the tent city was already there, maybe thirty to forty people. They were watching. I thought I was doing the right thing by distancing them from the blast site, but as it turned out, I placed them unknowingly in harm's way.

I took the man by the shoulders. Once I established eye contact, I instructed him to move all of those who were uninjured outside of the compound, and behind the makeshift barracks used by the 2nd Armored Cavalry Regiment soldiers. He nodded in assent and went to work herding survivors to the area I had designated. It was a potentially bad move, because that area was outside of the compound proper, but there was little choice. At that moment, I could think of nowhere else for them to go. I needed to distance them from both the blast site and the fire.

After launching the man to his task, I noticed a senior Iraqi staffer nearby. I called him to me. He came at a trot. I asked him to contact the recently reconstituted Iraqi Fire Brigade to address the blaze that was still developing in the shipping container. After a moment's hesitation, as if thinking how he might go about it, he responded, "Aiewya (yes), Bob." I responded with a totally automatic, "Shukran, awi (thanks much)." He ran off in the direction of the small building used by the soldiers for sleeping accommodations. There was a landline telephone there that, for all we knew, might still be functioning.

I began heading back toward the triage point. By now dozens of people were streaming out of the building. Those who were ambulatory and not wounded were being redirected to outside of the compound, hopefully to safety. I saw colleagues whom I knew well. Some wanted to stop and speak to me. I had no time, and politely and as firmly as possible sent them on their way.

I remember seeing a man being carried out of the main entrance on a stretcher. Incredibly, a portion of aluminum windowsill almost two feet long was protruding from the side of his face. I took a second look to ensure I was seeing correctly. Apparently, that portion of sill had been blown off its mountings with sufficient force that it had been turned into a kind of javelin. That unlikely spear had lodged itself in his jaw. The loose end was being held gently by one of the security search team members I had established several minutes earlier.

I also remember seeing the HC's operations officer, Robert Turner (more on Robert later). His shirt and trousers were covered nearly completely with fresh blood that was clearly not his own, almost like he had bathed in it. Whoever had lost that much fluid was probably long gone, I thought.

Although I cannot recall precisely when, a bit later, I saw my boss, the HC, on his back and plugged into an IV halfway between the Canal Hotel main entrance and Tent City. He had reportedly passed out. I took a moment with him, as he was semiconscious—assuring him that I was doing all that I could under the circumstances. He was obviously suffering from shock. His relatively minor cuts and bruises had been treated. His office was nearer the detonation site than my own. I also remember seeing the under-secretary general, who was the Executive Director of the UN Oil-for-Food Program. He was apparently unharmed.

I noted that there were still people coming out of the main building's entrance. From a distance, I thought that I recognized one. It was the World Bank security officer. I went to him. His head was dripping blood at multiple points. Nearly half of his face was exposed flesh. Much surface area had been carved away by what I assumed to be flying glass. A flap of skin held a portion of his nose dangling almost to his upper lip. He gazed straight ahead even as I grasped his arm gently. His eyes were fixed on some faraway point. He did not look at me. I speculated that moving his neck might have been painful. "How are you doing?" I asked stupidly. His response would have been funny at any other time. "Bob," he said slowly and deliberately in his upper-crust British accent, "I have had better days." I escorted him to the triage point and turned him over to the medics. He would require much facial plastic surgery in future, but he would survive.

I also noticed one of the senior UN staff members. He was ambulatory. Only the day prior, he had suggested to me that I was "overstating the threat" in Baghdad. His sad eyes told me that he remembered his ill-chosen words of the previous twenty-four hours. He apologized for his comment. I asked him to proceed to Tent City. There was no time.

More wounded were streaming out of the building. Some could walk under their own power. Others had to be carried. Blood and tortured flesh were everywhere evident. I felt strangely guilty that I was whole and uninjured. I would learn a great deal about survivor's guilt in the years that followed.

I entered the building for no reason I can remember, other than the need to do something, and proceeded to the second floor. In the first hallway, I nearly collided with a physician from the World Health Organization. I recognized him. I took him by the shoulders. "Are you all right?" I said, in what I hoped was an even voice. He responded over-loudly, "There is no need to shout... calm down, will you!" I was momentarily stunned to silence. It was he who was shouting. Then it struck me. His hearing had been affected. He had obviously been closer to the blast. Although shaken, he seemed well enough to work. Like everyone else, he was covered by the thick gray-white dust.

"Follow me," I stated as matter-of-factly as I could. Then I took him by the arm while pulling him back toward the stairs I had just ascended. "I have established a triage point. You are badly needed there." With difficulty, we made it back outside. I led him to the triage point. It was now filled to overflowing with wounded. The uniformed medical personnel were already fully engaged. To his credit, the doctor went right to task with the medics.

I had earlier directed that the bodies of those killed be placed nearby. We had no body bags. We covered the corpses with whatever was at hand. Some I could no longer recognize — their bodies crushed by rebar and falling concrete, and their faces utterly obliterated. But I had no time to focus my attentions on the dead. My emotions were nearly overwhelming. I was angry, but I had to shake it off. There was no time for emotion.

I re-entered our headquarters by the front entrance. The thick fog of dust had begun to clear. From the entrance, I could see through to daylight on the opposite side of the building, perhaps forty yards away. This meant that the bomb had detonated on that side of the building, but I did not know the extent of the damage yet. I moved straight ahead toward daylight.

Off to my left, I noticed a male body. I angled in that direction. He was face-up and spread-eagle over a pile of shattered concrete. I leaned forward at the waist and checked for a pulse at his neck with the extended index and middle fingers of my right hand while peeling an eyelid back with my left. His body was still warm... not surprising in this heat. There was no pulse and no pupil response. He was dead.

His right arm was severed below the shoulder. Flies were already circling with the intention of laying their eggs that would lead to the inevitable maggots. My stomach somersaulted, and my heart began to race. This easily could have been Naima. The arm had been torn from his body, leaving an extraordinarily jagged wound. The severed limb was nowhere in evidence. Apparently, he had bled out before any assistance could get to him.

To this day, I do not know who the man was. Because of the gray-white dust now covering everyone and everything, everybody looked pretty much alike. I forced myself to calm down. I took a deep, steadying breath while standing erect. I felt my stomach settle and my heart rate slow.

I continued again toward daylight and out the opposite side of the building, where a wall once stood, with great difficulty. I worked my way over and beyond the rubble to get some perspective. I turned in the roadway. The sight was stunning. The entire corner of the building on this side of the hotel had been blown away. Huge concrete chunks were hanging precariously from iron rebar on the second and third floors. The third-floor offices belonging to the SRSG were completely exposed. If he was in that office at the time of the explosion, I doubted his survival.

I also remembered that those offices on the third floor were originally meant to house my offices and the Security

Information and Operations Center. Had Naima and I been there at the time of the attack, we would probably have been killed. Lucky.

I heard the first of many US Army CASEVAC helicopters in-bound. Over one hundred fifty people were eventually evacuated in this manner, as well as in ambulances and trucks. The Black Hawk helicopter landed on the Canal Road, usually a very busy thoroughfare. Coalition Forces must have shut down public access, I speculated.

I surveyed the whole nightmarish panorama. The still-incomplete perimeter wall that was being constructed on my recommendation had been all but vaporized by the explosion for approximately twenty-five yards in both directions from the point of detonation. Later FBI estimates suggested that as much as 2,000 pounds of explosive material had been used in the attack. The FBI also suggested that it was a multiple improvised explosive device. This meant that the bomb was perhaps not one device at all, but many. Extremists were just beginning to learn how to use mortars, explosives, and artillery shells with horrible and deadly effect.

Although I did not know it at the time, it was a vehicular suicide attack. As a potential matter of historical significance, it is my belief that this was the first suicide bombing of the war in Iraq—directed not against armed and ready US Armed Forces, but against unarmed noncombatant staff members of the UN. Apparently, the extremists had packed a large flat-bed truck with several types of devices with explosive potential. These devices were daisy-chained to explode as one, or they could merely have counted on the sympathetic detonation of the devices when the largest of these exploded.

It was also apparent that the bomb was initiated on the side road leading to the Iraqi Hospitality School behind the UN compound. This was the roadway that I had twice recommended be closed on security grounds. This was an entirely preventable horror show.

There was still smoldering debris evident everywhere. Everything that was combustible within a radius of forty yards was aflame or had already burned out. The over-pressure created by the enormous blast wave had crushed nearby vehicles. Black acrid smoke spiraled upward from still-burning tires. There was a hole in the ground a few yards in width and perhaps more than a yard deep at the point of detonation.

I returned to the triage point, this time walking around the outside of the building by the parking lot filled with crushed vehicles. Once having seen the blast site, I felt better for the knowledge. I do not know why. I saw Mazzin at a distance and motioned him to me with my hand.

Before he reached me, the leader of the SRSG's Close Protection Team found me. He asked that I immediately accompany him back to the incident site. I was about to refuse, but his eyes locked pleadingly on mine, permitting no further discussion. Mazzin arrived out of breath with an expectant look on his face, awaiting my instruction.

We all started together—back to the blast site—while I simultaneously instructed my assistant to select a tent for the establishment of an alternate Security Information and Operations Center. He nodded in the affirmative while tugging at my elbow and informed me as we went that Naima had been evacuated by the Americans. I was mortified for not asking about her. But I had no time to further reprimand myself. I could not permit thoughts of Naima to enter my mind. If I did, I would be unable to function. Mazzin ran off to accomplish the task that I had assigned to him.

None of the tents in what we called Tent City belonged to me; that is, I did not have the authority to commandeer them. But since literally everyone seemed inclined to accept my directives now, I meant to capitalize on it. We needed an alternate operations center. Although our radio room was still functional, the building itself had suffered major damage. We needed to move. I glanced toward the wounded. US Army uniforms were everywhere. IV bags were hanging. Bandages were being applied. Stretchers with occupants were being carried gingerly to waiting ambulances. More CASEVAC helicopters could be heard in the distance. Naima was in good hands, I told myself, repeatedly.

While walking back to the blast site, the team leader explained to me that the SRSG's voice had been heard from underneath the rubble. He meant to show me where. He led me to an area not far from the detonation point, where the corner of the building had stood. There was nothing left but a huge pile of concrete chunks and bare rebar. He was in front of me when he called out—leaning forward while attempting to direct his voice through the rubble. I heard a muffled response but could not make out the words. The team leader assured me that the voice I had heard was that of the SRSG. He looked at me... his eyes pleaded for me to do something, but there was nothing that could be done. If it was indeed the SRSG, he was buried under tons of debris. If it was him, it was a miracle that he was still alive.

The truth was, at that moment, we had no capability to remove tons of fallen concrete from over the heads of anyone that might be trapped. That would have taken engineer equipment, and we had none. If the SRSG was alive, might there be others trapped as he was? I felt a brief wave of helplessness that I quickly dismissed. There was no time for it.

There was nothing else for me to do. I called out in the direction of the muffled voice and into the tangled mass. "Hang on," I yelled, "Help is on the way." I lied. But it was a lie with genuine purpose. I knew that if the SRSG was still breathing, perhaps only hope could keep him alive. I meant to give him some. I squeezed the team leader's shoulder, and then left him in the rubble. I did not task him. His job was protecting his principal. While the SRSG was presumed alive, his job was there.

On my way back to the Triage Point I was met by a US Marine colonel. He was, he told me, then serving in the Office of the Coalition Provisional Authority and working for Ambassador Paul Bremer. We had never met. One of my staff had apparently pointed me out as the man in charge. He introduced himself, although I have regrettably forgotten his name. He informed me that he was under orders to assist me with any means at his disposal. I was not surprised to see him. I knew that the Americans would focus their considerable assets on assisting the UN.

The Marine was a few inches taller than me, perhaps six feet tall. He looked to be a model officer. He had an intelligent face and was clearly in excellent physical condition. His eyes were alert and caring. From my perspective, his arrival was more than timely.

I thought rapidly, what did we need? The colonel was awaiting an answer. I began, "We need engineer support ASAP. We have people trapped under the rubble. We also need standard life support. We need food and water for the survivors. Halal Meals Ready to Eat (MREs) should do. Your people are already doing an excellent job with our wounded. We need cell phones with international access for the survivors. We also require immediate communications connectivity between my office and the Coalition." The colonel was taking notes on a small notepad he had taken from his uniform pocket. He finished and then looked up. "Anything else," he said with concern in his voice. "Yes," I replied, "three things. If you approve, we can place one of your communications vans inside of our perimeter to enhance our ability to communicate with you and track the wounded. We also need additional armed security on our perimeter. Finally, we require help with the handling of the dead. We have no mortuary services unit." The Marine officer was as good as his word. All my requests were fulfilled within hours. I will be forever grateful for the assistance.

I thanked him with a heartfelt handshake that I hoped would convey my profound gratitude. I held his hand for a moment longer than usual and grasped his upper right arm with my left hand. I imagined that he knew how I felt. His eyes contained all the understanding in the world. He pulled out his cell phone, punched the speed dial and departed at a rapid but measured pace while holding the phone to his ear.

I was at that time unaware that there was a great tragedy unfolding inside the building, and under the rubble. Acting bravely on his own, a US Army Reserve senior sergeant, who was in civilian life a firefighter, found the SRSG and another victim with their lower extremities crushed by fallen debris, and therefore trapped. They both were alive and conscious but sandwiched into a very small space that allowed for extraordinarily limited movement. The firefighter attempted a one-man rescue without the equipment needed to do the job. Another US Army Reserve senior sergeant, and as luck would have it, a New York City paramedic, found them and offered his aid. The one-man rescue attempt, now doubled, was still insufficient to meet the need. To save both individuals, a half-dozen or more rescuers with proper equipment would have been required.

The two sergeants were acting out of the absolute best of intentions. They risked their lives to save others they did not know. Ultimately, and after strenuous effort, the two sergeants sawed off the horribly damaged legs of the second victim and managed to get him to safety. He is alive today because of their efforts. Tragically, the SRSG died of his wounds before they could get to him. I am not sure that the UN staff members attempting to save the SRSG from outside the building were aware of the soldiers' desperate rescue attempt transpiring inside. I was not.

Upon my return to the triage point, I saw one of my officers, Radies Rademeyer. He was helping what I hoped would be one of the last survivors out of the main entrance to the building. After he deposited his charge with the medics, I took him by the arm and led him to a point near the now shattered cafeteria. I needed to speak with him with no distractions. Although he had only recently arrived in Iraq, I intuitively knew him to be a good man. I was about to ask him to perform the most difficult of duties. I was not looking forward to it.

I spoke to Radies for perhaps a minute. I tried to make the task sound simple. "You are responsible for the dead," I said quietly. "Your task is to insure the positive identification, accurate reporting, and proper handling of the deceased. No information concerning the dead will depart this headquarters without your specific approval and through me." He looked back into my eyes and held my gaze. I did not look away. Neither did he.

Finally, he broke eye contact and gazed at the ground in front of him. I could see the pain in his face. He knew that this would be an extraordinarily tough and thankless job. Like me, he also knew that it had to be done. He nodded his assent. Words were unnecessary. Although I did not know it at that time, I had made the right choice. He performed superbly. I continued, "Let me know what you need. Select a work area and get organized. Now, get to it," I added gently. "I am counting on you." He gave me a weak smile. Radies bowed his head. He was all too conscious that his life had just gotten much tougher.

I drove the search teams hard, sending them back into the hotel's interior time and again. We had no idea how many people were in the building at the time of the attack. My single greatest fear was that we might miss someone in the debris that might just be still clinging to life. To their credit, nobody complained. All returned to the grisly work with resolute dedication.

I noted that the fire brigade arrived and successfully dealt with the blaze within the shipping container. I then directed that UN personnel return to the Tent City muster point.

The alternate operations center was shaping up. I held a quick meeting with all security personnel. I assigned various tasks. One of these was to establish a 24/7 security duty officer, so that there would always be an international security officer available and on duty in the operations tent.

The remainder of my day and night is a jumble of disjointed memories. Someone came to me for a decision, on average, every few minutes. My cell phone rang often, demanding attention. Calls came in from various UN headquarters in New York, Rome, Vienna, and Geneva. Many of these calls were personal in nature. Most wanted to know whether loved ones, friends, or colleagues were still alive. My phone number appeared to be the most popular on the globe at that time. I was in the habit of carrying an extra cell phone battery in my pocket. That propensity served me well.

In one rare free moment, I called my Dad's number in Melbourne, Florida. Nobody was home. I left the message on his answering machine, hoping that he would find out that I was alive and unharmed before seeing the news. He was old and frail. He did not need anything else to worry about.

Much later I discovered that my brother Mark, in Houston, called multiple UN phone numbers until he finally reached UNSECOORD in New York. They informed him that I was unharmed. Mark, in turn, notified the rest of our substantial family that I had survived. The suicide bombing attack on the UN in Baghdad led the news cycle that day and the next worldwide.

I also received calls from nearly every major news organization then operating in Iraq. I have no idea how they got my number. These included BBC, CNN, ABC, NBC, and more. They all wanted quotes for their upcoming broadcasts. I refused comment in every case. At times, I was none too polite. My previous experience with news people had not been altogether positive. Also, I had been informed previously in New York that the quickest way to be fired from a UN security post was to be quoted by journalists.

Senior UN security advisors are very credible sources. They know truths that are generally not shared with the public. I was certainly in that position now. I knew why the attack was so very successful, and why we were so utterly unprepared. The truth, as I would later discover, is a very dangerous commodity.

A captain from the 82nd Airborne Division reported to me shortly after dark. He was the Commander of a reinforced parachute rifle company and informed me that he had been tasked to secure our perimeter. I was grateful. I knew the 82nd from my many years at Fort Bragg, North Carolina. We were in good hands. Although I was nowhere in the captain's chain of command, he appeared willing to take some guidance from me. I made my suggestions and the captain went to work to establish his perimeter. I also introduced him to the security officer I had assigned responsibility for the inner perimeter. The two of them had instructions to get back to me later that evening with a status report.

The engineer unit arrived, commanded by a US Army colonel. He came to the operations tent and asked me to define his task for him. We stepped outside. There was too much noise inside for us to carry on a conversation. I began, "There are people alive and trapped under the rubble. One of these is the Special Representative of the Secretary General. Your unit must clear the debris quickly and carefully, in the hopes of finding anyone still living. Please also immediately notify me if you do." I had already arranged with US Army medical personnel to be standing by in the event any survivors were discovered.

The colonel looked me in the eye. There were a few moments of silence between us. He knew what I knew. Just how does one remove many tons of concrete and rebar carefully? Clearing the rubble too quickly with front-end loaders or cranes might also kill anyone trapped underneath. Being too careful and moving slowly could result in someone dying because of their wounds. It was a potential no-win scenario. We both knew it. He left to go to work. I did not envy him his painstaking task or what he would likely find under the tangled remains of the hotel. The SRSG's body was removed from the debris shortly thereafter.

Of all the calls I received that night, only one seemed thoughtful of my personal circumstances. The UNSECOORD Chief of Staff in New York called and asked what he could do for me. My response was immediate: "Please send me Marco Smoliner." Less than an hour later, Marco, who had only recently been returned to his original duty station, called me from Central America and asked, "Bob, what did you do?" Marco had been directed to immediately return to Iraq to assist me. He was glad of it, and I badly needed his help.

I assigned my administrative assistant, Fatin, the job of attempting to re-create the staff list. This was going to be tough. Our computer files in the main server had been badly damaged by the blast. The re-creation of the staff list would have to be accomplished from scratch. I also assigned her the task of interfacing with the American soldiers who were tracking our wounded. Her English language and administrative skills were impressive, making her the perfect person for the task. Injured staff members, national and international, were evacuated to multiple US Army mobile hospitals in the area around Baghdad.

Identification of the dead and wounded was more than problematic. Some of our staff members were so seriously wounded they were unconscious. Others were so badly carved up by the flying glass that they were unrecognizable. In contravention of security rules, many staff members did not like wearing identification badges. In addition, not all of those who had been hurt or killed were our staff. Visitors to the Canal Hotel were common. Our task was going to be extraordinarily difficult.

New York established an ad hoc Emergency Operations Center in response to the attack. I received numerous calls asking for updates on the dead and wounded throughout the evening. They were clearly receiving pressure from above. It was slow going. I had few answers for them. Not only did we not know who or how many UN staff were in Baghdad; we did not know who was in the building at the time of the explosion. We also did not know who had been evacuated or to what medical unit. Because of the condition of many of the bodies, the identification of the dead might take days.

Food and water were delivered, as were the cell phones I had requested. A US Army communications van also arrived. I placed it inside the perimeter not far from our operations tent. I directed that the international-access cell phones be distributed among the survivors so that they could speak with their relatives around the globe.

A US Army uniformed doctor sought me out to tell me that she had earlier seen Naima when she passed through her medical unit. Naima asked her to find me and to tell me that she was all right. I do not remember that officer's name or face. But at that moment I wanted to hug and kiss her for the welcome news. I settled for a handshake and a heartfelt thank you. Naima was never far from my thoughts, despite the circumstances.

I saw an agency security advisor, a highly valued member of the Security Cell, in the operations tent sometime after dark. He was sitting on a metal folding chair while staring straight ahead at nothing. I spoke to him quietly several times before he finally responded to me. He was hurt. I could not tell how badly... perhaps a concussion? The UN aircraft was coming the next day into Baghdad. I ordered him to be on it. He objected. I eventually won the argument.

I called New York at some point around 10:00 PM. I asked for the support of the UNSECOORD, through his deputy. Essentially, I knew that the following day I was going to recommend to my superiors in Baghdad that all our international staff members be immediately evacuated from Iraq. If I secured his support, the meeting might go easier. We simply could not protect ourselves from this sort of threat. The deputy told me that she would contact him to ask for that support. I remember receiving the return call from her around midnight. She told me that the UNSECOORD would take no position regarding the possible evacuation of our staff from Iraq. I could not imagine why. My disappointment was profound.

Once again, I was to receive little support from New York. After a moment's pause, she urged me to take care of myself and to try to get some sleep. Both of us remembered the nearly three days I had gone without rest while conducting the evacuation in Sierra Leone. I told her that I would soon attempt to do so.

An hour or so later, and just moments after I had lain down on a cot for a brief respite—I felt mentally and physically tapped out—I received another call from New York demanding an immediate response to a question of the SG through the duty officer. Reportedly, he wanted to know detailed information about the thirty-odd US soldiers who were providing additional security at the Canal Hotel.

It took me over an hour to respond in an e-mail. World Food Program technicians had set up a satellite Internet connection in a container office near the operations tent. I used one of these terminals to send the information via my personal e-mail account. All our UN e-mail accounts were down because of the bombing. There were no lights. Most of our power generation capabilities had been knocked out. Our radios and computers were operating on a small mobile generator that screamed in the distance. I typed in a large font and all caps because I only had the light of the screen to see by. It was very slow going, as I could barely see the keyboard. Also, I had flunked touch-typing in high school. Once I'd finished, I felt that there was one more task that needed my attention.

I was working now at my laptop computer in the operations tent by the half-light of the radio dials. My records show it was 3:00 AM when I finished writing up my recommendations. There should be little argument now. They must listen to reason... they must. Even without the UNSECOORD's support, the case for evacuation was self-evident. In addition to the recommendation for evacuation, I also wrote down that there would likely be a second attack at some point soon if we did not leave.

Throughout the evening hours I often checked on the progress of the engineers. It was hard work. Removing many tons of concrete and rebar carefully was an incredibly difficult and demanding task.

I relieved the duty officer in the operations tent and told him that I would remain there to answer any queries. He, like me, was exhausted; he trundled off to find some place to sleep. I finally lay down on a nearby cot. I thought that sleep would be impossible. I was wrong. The day caught up with me almost immediately. I used a Meal-Ready-to-Eat (MRE) packet as a field-expedient pillow. My sleep was dreamless.

17

An Angry Aftermath

The ultimate measure of a man is not where he stands in moments of comfort and convenience, but where he stands at times of challenge and controversy.
—Martin Luther King, Jr.

I awoke before dawn with an incredibly stiff neck. The radio operators had completed their tasks, so the VHF and HF radios were functional. Somehow, I had managed to sleep through all the noise they must have made. One of the radio operators handed me a very welcome cup of hot, strong, black coffee. I thanked him, laced up my boots, and stepped outside. I must have looked like hell. Except for the engineer equipment on the far side of the compound and the small generators that powered our radios, it was reasonably quiet.

It was my custom to accomplish a perimeter walk every day in Baghdad. There is simply no way to replace seeing something for yourself. After a piss-call, wetting and combing my hair, and splashing some water on my face, I was minimally ready for the day.

I went immediately outside of the compound proper to see how the captain from the 82nd Airborne Division had deployed his troops on the perimeter. The sun was rising, so I could see for some distance. The Commander had established sandbagged fighting positions and checkpoints at well over one hundred yards' distance from the compound on the high-speed avenues of approach: the roads. The Canal Road had been closed to all traffic. The troops were arrayed at intervals to create interlocking fire in the event of an assault. The soldiers on duty were all wearing helmets and flak vests. Their weapons, even at this early hour, were at the ready. It was good.

The young soldiers greeted me in friendly fashion. Apparently, they had been informed who I was. I felt out of place among the troops. I carried no weapon. I was wearing no flak vest. I had no helmet. My left sleeve was still caked with Naima's blood. I had nothing to change into. I carried only a radio on my left hip and a cell phone on my right. I thought while I walked. There was much to think about.

At various points after the attack, and perhaps understandably, I felt pangs of guilt. I wondered often what I might have done differently. I had not yet received a full accounting of the dead and wounded, but there were clearly as many as twenty or more dead and over one hundred injured, many seriously. The carnage was like nothing I had experienced previously, and I hoped never to again.

Finally, I went to the blast site. I might have unconsciously chosen to make this my last stop. The engineers had been working all night; much of the rubble had been cleared. The emergency lighting that they had set up last evening was still on. The over-bright lights were now dimmed by the quickly rising behemoth of the Iraqi sun. It would be another brutally hot day. A report from the senior officer present confirmed that they had found some bodies, none were alive.

The deceased in body bags were now stacked like cord wood near the front gate. The Americans had delivered the zippered bags the previous evening. A refrigerator van had also been promised and was supposed to arrive that day. I hoped that van would arrive soon; the sight of those body bags haunted me.

I ran into Radies, the officer I had appointed to care for the deceased. He was an early riser as well, or perhaps more correctly, neither of us could sleep for long. We spoke in low voices. I do not know why. Perhaps it was because we were standing so near the dead. Naima could have easily been an occupant of one of those anonymous black plastic prisons. I inwardly shuddered.

Radies told me that he had commandeered an office and computer from the World Food Program. He had established liaison with the Americans and tied in with Fatin. He also thanked me for assigning a local staff member to assist with the handling of the Iraqi families of the dead. I had forgotten that I had done that the previous day... so many decisions. The Iraqi staff member was proving to be very useful. He also confirmed to me that early identification of the deceased was going to be a huge problem.

By Islamic tradition, the dead should be buried as soon as possible after death, and no later than nightfall of the following day. Families of the deceased had already contacted us. They wanted the bodies of their loved ones immediately. We would have gladly complied, but we could not identify the corpses. Many were damaged beyond recognition. Falling concrete and flying glass had all but destroyed the usual markers of human identity. A mistake could not be permitted. We had to know absolutely that the right body went to the right family. We had no DNA capabilities. We had no dental or fingerprint records. Iraqi authorities were non-existent. By default, the job fell to the Americans. But the families came after us. It was a no-win scenario.

We had no capabilities to resolve the key issues regarding positive identification of the deceased. This problem would get much worse before it got better. We knew it. All we could do was to brace ourselves and plod along as best we could. I saw that Radies was already frustrated. I could provide him little comfort. I was frustrated as well. He went his way and I went mine... both, I felt, sympathetic to the other.

I walked by the former triage point. The grassy ground was tinted a rusty pink with dried blood and littered with gory bandages blowing in a light wind. Heroic life-saving efforts had taken place there only thirteen hours earlier. The images were still fresh in my mind. How many would survive their wounds? How was Naima?

I called for a meeting of all security personnel in the operations tent at 8:00 AM. I had not eaten in nearly twenty hours but was not hungry. For now, coffee was all I needed. The assembled group was very serious. They filled the tent. There was none of the usual joking. The Coalition was represented by the captain commanding our perimeter forces. I began speaking. They became immediately attentive.

I discussed with them my recommendations for our superiors that would be delivered at a Security Management Team meeting scheduled for later that morning. I read off the list that I had completed at 3:00 AM. All officers, with no dissenting opinions, concurred with my analysis. We must evacuate Iraq. We simply were not prepared to deal with the threat of suicide bombers. I added that, in my estimation, a second attack was likely. The group was unanimous in agreement.

The Security Management Team meeting was held later that morning. It was anticlimactic. No decision was taken on our collective Security Cell recommendation to evacuate. Although I was unaware of it at that time, the SG had gone on TV beforehand and announced that the UN was not going to depart Iraq. Apparently, most of the attendees were already aware of this fact. I only found out subsequently. The heads of all the UN agencies in Iraq were frozen to inaction by the SG announcement.

No decision of note came out of that meeting. I was enormously frustrated. My security colleagues shared that frustration. Once again, our concerns were ignored. Even my assessment that a second attack was likely got no traction. What the hell was going on?

This is not how things were supposed to be done. The mission was—by UN policy—to consider the matter at hand (possible evacuation) and then make a recommendation to the SG through the UNSECOORD. The SG short-circuited this well-worn and long-standing process by stating before cameras that the UN would not leave Iraq.

Several weeks earlier, I had received an informal proposal from the Americans. They offered us a large space within the Green Zone—the complex of Saddam Hussein's former palaces—taken over and now secured by thousands of US troops. I took that offer immediately to my boss, the HC. I thought moving into the Green Zone a terrific idea on security grounds. He refused, saying that it was politically a bad move for us to occupy a "palace." He also made the point that we in the UN needed to keep some distance from the occupying power. Once again, security concerns counted for less. It seemed that nearly every decision made in both Baghdad and New York by senior officials placed staff at ever-increasing risk. I did not understand why. Of course, much later, the UN did eventually move into the well-protected Green Zone.

Naima called me later that day to let me know that she was OK, although she could not tell me exactly where she was—except she said she was in an American field hospital somewhere outside of Baghdad in the desert. She could call me because I had given her a commercially available satellite phone for her birthday, three days prior to the attack. She clutched that satellite phone in her hand all throughout her medical evacuation.

She told me that she was waiting for surgery, and that there were many others wounded more seriously. It seems that eye surgeons were in very short supply in the area around Baghdad. The call was cut short. The connection failed. But no matter, it was just good to hear her voice and to know that her turn in the operating theater would soon come. I breathed a little easier after hearing her voice.

Before nightfall that day, a group of a few dozen Iraqis approached the Canal Hotel on foot. They carried a large wreath of flowers. Reportedly, they wanted to express their sympathy for the previous day's horror show. Once they were patted down, I permitted them into the perimeter so that they could make their expression of condolence. I assigned a native Arabic-speaking officer to the task of meeting with them briefly and thanking them in their native tongue on behalf of the UN.

A few hours later I received a phone call from the Deputy UNSECOORD in New York. She was angry. She wanted to know who the idiot was that had authorized a security officer to represent the UN. Apparently, my officer's performance made a news broadcast in the US. He did exactly what I had asked him to, and he did it well.

UN security officers, per internal policy, should never appear on TV speaking for the UN. Now it was time for me to get angry. There are no doubt good reasons for such a policy, but I was in no mood to hear about it. I told her the following in a voice that probably expressed my disdain. First, there were no senior Arabic-speaking UN management officers at the Canal Hotel to receive the group; only security personnel were present at that time. Second, I felt that it would have been both impolitic as well as discourteous not to greet them and receive their sympathetic offering.

Only the folks in New York could be so overly concerned with this sort of bullshit now. I hung up on the deputy. I suspect that she was none too pleased. That made two of us.

On the morning of the second day after the bombing, local staff reported to me the odor of decomposition in the area near the front entrance to the Canal Hotel. The immediate fear was that we had somehow missed finding one of the dead, and the remains had begun the inevitable process of decay in the stifling heat. Local staff members would not enter the building, afraid of what they might find. Rather than assign the task to a subordinate, I took it upon myself to discover the truth of the matter. I had no wish to task anyone else with such a potentially gruesome chore.

I proceeded to the entrance and literally followed my nose. It led me to the kitchen area adjacent the cafeteria on the first floor. Inside the kitchen was a large walk-in refrigeration unit. The odor seemed to emanate from that vicinity. I opened the door. The interior was very dark. I took a breath. A horrible odor assaulted me. I gagged and backed away, while trying to work up the courage to advance again to face the overwhelming stench of decay. When I did, I took out my flashlight and played the beam on the floor, looking for a human form. There was none. I next looked higher and found the reason for the powerful odor. There were several uncooked chickens that were rapidly decomposing on the shelves.

I sighed in relief, while backing hurriedly out of the unit. Dead chickens were manageable, even with the stench. I was not sure that I could stomach another human corpse. I asked the local staff to find some of the folks who worked in the kitchen, and to ask them to clean out the unit as quickly as possible. Once I had opened that door, the putrid odor of decomposition was much more pronounced. Fortunately, someone was found who was willing to scour the place clean.

Between her satellite phone and Mazzin's unflagging efforts, Naima was found. Following her surgery, she had been moved to the medical facility within the Green Zone that had formerly been Saddam Hussein's personal family clinic. They found the eye surgeon. His brilliant efforts saved her sight.

Naima later explained that she had used the satellite phone that I bought for her birthday to call both me and her son. Her son was then attending university in Cairo. She then offered the woman in the next bed over the use of the phone to contact her family. The woman thankfully accepted. She then made that call, only to find out that her relatives had already been informed by "someone" at UN Headquarters in New York that she was dead. Of course, her family was very glad of the good news of her resurrection, but also much angered, and who could blame them? With only a very few exceptions, I had not authorized the release of names of any of the dead to New York. Hers was not one of those few names.

A few days later, Naima and several other UN staff were medically evacuated from Baghdad to Amman via our UN aircraft. I drove her to the Baghdad International Airport myself. A large bandage covered the whole of her left eye. I was very glad to see her safely on her way to Jordan. The UN Oil-for-Food Executive Director left on the same flight. I remained in Baghdad with the security staff. There was still much work to be done.

I was very glad to see Marco Smoliner arrive shortly thereafter. His return to Baghdad was one of a very few positive moments I would enjoy for the next several months.

Many hundreds of UN staff members entered Iraq in June and July. Even though the SG had stated that the UN would not depart Iraq, individual staff members found a multitude of reasons to leave and did. The speed of the exodus was unprecedented in my experience. Fear of death is a powerful motivator.

A couple of weeks after the bombing, only a very few staff remained in Baghdad, and many of them were security personnel. Adding to the ever-climbing numbers of exiting staff, somebody in authority in New York had approved a mandatory, and nonchargeable as annual leave, two weeks off for all staff members present in Baghdad at the time of the attack. I would be the last staff member who was present at the bombing to avail myself of that policy largesse.

I found out later in a brief conversation with the Support Battalion Commander of the 2nd Armored Cavalry Regiment that the reason they were so quick in getting medical aid to us was a kind of fluke. His unit had used the UN Headquarters at the Canal Hotel as the site of a mass casualty event in one of their tabletop exercises. Therefore, every one of his command group, as well as medical personnel, was in a sense pre-prepared for a bombing of this magnitude at our head-quarters—a very fortunate coincidence.

I was subsequently informed by New York that the SG would appoint an investigative body led by the former President of Finland to examine the Baghdad bombing. Although I could not know it then, yet another investigative committee would be appointed in its wake. In any case, I knew that hard-copy evidence would be required. I thought it was clear that the UN security community in Iraq had done its job. The problem was documentation.

As mentioned earlier, the blast took down the server for the UN network. I sought out a woman who was an IT technician serving with the mission. I asked her to see what she could do to find my computer and e-mail records and download them to a thumb drive that I provided her. She warned me that those records might be irretrievable. I asked her to please try. She promised to give it her best efforts.

My life was soon to go from bad to worse, although I was at that time unaware of it. But Naima and I were alive. We were among the lucky survivors. Still, the events of the next year would teach me more about the true nature of humanity than anything else had in all my previous decades of existence. It was a learning process laden with anger, pain, and sadness.

It took her two days, but the IT technician handed me some of my work and e-mail files on the thumb drive. Although not one hundred percent complete, much of the security history of my time in Iraq was there.

It is the questions that drive us. I was filled with questions after the bombing. By now, everyone knew that this attack resulted in a greater loss of life than any previous violent event in the history of the United Nations. Why were twenty-two persons dead, and more than one hundred fifty more wounded? Why were our bosses unwilling to accept the security recommendations of their own people? What might I have done differently that could have changed the outcome? Unfortunately, the answers were long in coming.

In the aftermath of the suicide attack, two high-ranking UN officials visited the mission. They were the UNSECOORD and the SG's cabinet chief. Although there was a direct policy relationship between the UNSECOORD and the SG, the cabinet chief was the man to whom he generally reported. The latter visit was memorable.

We convened a Security Management Team meeting in Tent City especially for the cabinet chief. Each head of agency spoke to the recent tragedy. The cabinet chief kept notes. The most senior UN staff in Iraq were present, representing not only the mission, but the World Food Program, World Health Organization, UN High Commissioner for Refugees, UN Food and Agriculture Organization, and more. Many of the attendees had also been present in a multitude of such meetings previously, where a bevy of security recommendations made by me and the Security Cell had been ignored. I was scheduled to speak last.

Each head of agency spoke and gave their individual assessment on why we could never have anticipated an attack. The fact that their own security community had made such a prediction was conveniently never mentioned. I sat at the table with the heads of agency. By policy, I was senior to every other UN security officer in Iraq, regardless of actual rank. All the security officers sat along the tent wall. As each agency representative spoke, I grew more and more angry. Every excuse known to man was trotted out by the group. It all boiled down to a single point: that they could not have perceived the danger and therefore should not be held accountable. By the time it was my turn to speak, I could barely contain myself.

I stood up while moving behind my seat and grabbed hold of the chair back to steady myself. My knuckles were white. I was angry in a way I had never experienced. Everyone else had spoken while seated. I felt compelled to stand. I looked down at the table while attempting to compose myself. The tent went silent. Time passed. I finally looked up and began speaking. I required no notes. I tried to keep my voice rigidly calm. I had no idea what I was going to say until I began. I spoke with passion and surprising precision, given my level of emotion. To the best of my recollection, this is what I said:

You all took the position that anticipating the possibility of an attack on the UN in Iraq was all but impossible. I beg to differ.

IF IT WERE TRUE, then why was the possibility of an attack written up in our Threat Assessment?

IF IT WERE TRUE, why did my office twice make the recommendation to close access to the roadway used by the suicide bomber?

IF IT WERE TRUE, why did we say it was only a "matter of time" until we were attacked—an assessment agreed to by every senior UN security officer in Baghdad, and well prior to the bombing?

IF IT WERE TRUE, why did my office recommend the installation of shatter-resistant film on the windows in the Canal Hotel?

IF IT WERE TRUE, why did my office recommend the construction of a compound perimeter wall?

IF IT WERE TRUE, why did my office repetitively recommend a much more restrictive staff ceiling?

IF IT WERE TRUE, why was the Security Information and Operations Building at the front gate protected with thousands of sandbags, and its windows fitted with steel-plate blast shields?

There was more, of course. I went on, beginning each sentence with special emphasis on the same words, IF IT WERE TRUE. I spoke for only a few minutes. The frustration of many months poured forth in a torrent. In short, I highlighted the fact that most of the key security recommendations made by me and the Security Cell had been ignored by our collective superiors. My words could not have gone down well with them, even though I spoke the unvarnished truth.

I finished and retook my seat, suddenly feeling exhausted. My hands shook. I felt spent. The room remained eerily quiet. What I said, I had to say. It was the right thing to do. The dead and wounded, I felt, demanded of me as much. The silence was now thundering. Without realizing it, I had spoken for those now bereft of life. No one dared gainsay me. The truth is powerful, and for that reason threatening.

Finally, the meeting was declared over. Everyone left. No head of agency would look me in the eye. The security officers filed by last, some touching my shoulder as they passed. I was grateful for their support.

Although I was not aware of it at that time, I might have made an enemy that day. I made it crystal clear to one of the most powerful men in the UN that I had zero tolerance for whitewashing the obvious lack of UN preparedness prior to the bombing. The impact of my words would not become evident to me for some time. I eventually discovered that there are few things more dangerous than the truth.

It later became very clear to me that those most responsible for the deaths of our colleagues had one overriding mission; to survive the aftermath. I was either too mad or too stupid, perhaps both, to think of my own survival at that time. Moreover, I simply could not imagine that I might become a target. I was wrong.

I never or since experienced this level of frustration with my superiors in any job. The threat was clear-cut. We were extraordinarily vulnerable. The security situation had recently dramatically worsened with the bombing of the Jordanian Embassy. Droves of unprepared staff members entered Iraq in July and August—force-fed by New York. It became the "perfect storm." Many would die or have their lives shattered because our superiors in Manhattan refused to recognize the danger. I selected the word "refused" because in my estimation, Helen Keller could have seen the disaster coming.

A later investigative report conducted by the FBI discovered that the person who planned the attack on the Canal Hotel was none other than the Jordanian Abu Musab al-Zarqawi. This man eventually became the progenitor of the Islamic State of Iraq and the Levant (ISIS). He would die in 2006, the target of a US bombing raid on his safe house that was located just outside of Baghdad. But before his death, he would wreak havoc.

Roughly fourteen years later, and because of my research for this book, I came across a copy of the UNSECOORD's *Note to the Secretary General* that he wrote in the wake of his visit to Baghdad following the attack. The formal note was marked "Strictly Confidential." I found it fascinating that his recommendations to the SG following the attack mirrored those I had made well before the tragic event.

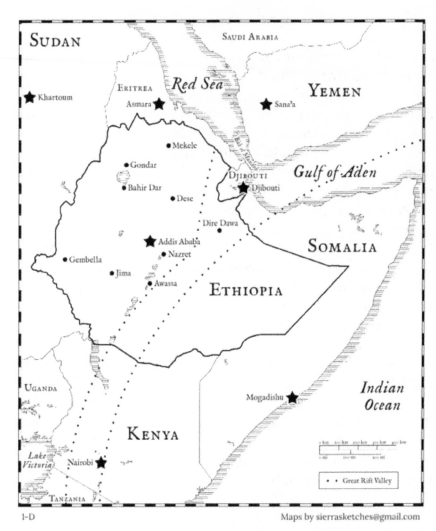

Maps by sierrasketches@gmail.com

Figure 4. Map of Ethiopia

18

The Aborted Road to Ethiopia

The past is prologue.
—William Shakespeare

On 11 September 2003, I left Baghdad in order take the mandatory two weeks off. I was directed by New York to make a pit stop in Switzerland to speak with the first UN investigative body led by the former President of Finland. I probably testified for a couple of hours in Geneva. I was exhausted. I remember being there, but I recall little of what I said. It was around this time that it began to dawn on me that my hearing might have been damaged by the bombing. I often found myself asking the members of the investigative body to repeat their questions.

My two-week respite began with a very necessary stop in New York City to re-unite with Naima. She had stitches removed from her inner eye. An extraordinarily expensive eye surgeon in Manhattan did the deed, while complimenting the fine work of his uniformed medical colleague in Baghdad. The surgeon assured us that her sight was in no danger, and that she would eventually enjoy a full recovery.

Much relieved, we subsequently visited Niagara Falls, New York; Gloucester, Massachusetts, for whale-watching; took a ferry ride to the beautiful Island of Nantucket; and finally, visited Stowe, Vermont, for the quiet and beautiful natural surroundings. After the horrors we had experienced in Baghdad, this trip seemed strangely unreal. We were safe in the US, but my mind was still filled with thoughts of the catastrophe in Iraq.

My deputy, Marco, called me in Vermont on 22 September to inform me that the second vehicular suicide attack that we had anticipated, and had warned the Baghdad Security Management Team about, had occurred. An Iraqi policeman was dead, and another badly mauled. Seven others were wounded. But the suicide bomber had failed to get close enough to injure any of the remaining UN staff near the Canal Hotel. The SG, later, finally relented and ordered that the remaining UN international staff in Baghdad be evacuated. Why hadn't anyone believed us?

After the two weeks mandatory time off, I was ordered to report to New York. There I was informed that I would be relieved of responsibility for Iraq following a turnover to be conducted with my desk officer on a temporary basis. The UNSECOORD told me that this was being done because I had "been through enough." I felt that this was in fact true. I had "been through enough," as he put it. I was disgusted and angry.

My desk officer later informed me that the UNSECOORD offered him my former job in Baghdad on a full-time basis. He declined. A short while later, the UN Children's Fund security officer who had pulled together the Security Information and Operations Center in Baghdad accepted my former post. I wished him well. However, I also handed him a draft copy of my expanded and updated Iraq Lessons Learned document that was highly critical of our leadership in New York. After reading about my history in the job, he quit even before deploying to Iraq. His total time served in my former position was about fourteen days. In my estimation, he made the right choice.

Literally, none of the senior officers in my department or UN agencies would take the position that I had so recently vacated. They would eventually have to go outside the UN to find someone willing to place his head in the noose. When an individual was finally selected and hired, he lasted less than a year on the job. He was not fired; his contract was simply permitted to lapse.

On 26 October 2003, I was placed on temporary duty at UN Headquarters in New York. There, I testified before the Security in Iraq Accountability Panel, hereafter referred to as the Panel. This was the second investigative body to be appointed by the SG, and the most important, or so I thought at the time. As the title suggests, "accountability" was the focus. I was very pleased to be of assistance. In my estimation, there might have been several people who should be held accountable, nearly all of whom were in New York.

The Panel called me to testify a total of nine times, more than any other individual. I provided them copies of my e-mail records and security files. I also provided them context and explained to them how the lack of budget and personnel had negatively impacted my office. I also explained how the repeated recommendations of the Security Cell had been ignored time and time again. On at least two occasions I was called to testify to provide clarification concerning key points regarding the UNSECOORD's and HC's testimony. I told the truth. I provided the investigators with plenty of hard-copy documentation. My hope was that justice would be done. I was wrong. Justice had nothing to do with this process. It was instead merely the appearance of justice.

It is worth noting that during one of my many appearances before the Panel, I was presented a copy of what appeared to be a US document stamped "SECRET." I quickly scanned the contents. If memory serves, the document stated that the UN Headquarters in Baghdad would be attacked. The person who handed me the document, then unexpectedly snatched it from my hand before I could note the precise date. I was then asked by a Panel member if I had ever before seen the document. I replied immediately, "no, of course not." The panel member followed up, "How can we know that to be true?" I shouted my response in anger, "Because I would have done something!" My face no doubt betrayed the upwelling of emotion that I felt at the question. My clenched fists likely punctuated the matter. In any case, the Panel asked me no more questions concerning that document. But the questions that query sparked in my mind went into overdrive.

It seems clear that the Panel had come into possession of a US Intelligence Community document confirming that the Canal Hotel was to be attacked. If that was the case, why hadn't we received a warning? This question kept me from sleep many subsequent nights.

In the very early morning hours of 26 December at the far western end of the Indonesian Archipelago and deep under the Indian Ocean, two huge tectonic plates violently shifted. This titanic shift created an undersea earthquake that measured over nine points on the Richter Scale. The resulting tsunami was nearly one hundred feet high. That giant wave eventually hit fourteen different countries, killing between 230,000 and 280,000 people. The devastation it created was unimaginable.

The Province of Banda Aceh on the Island of Sumatra took the brunt of the massive wave. Dozens of UNSECOORD security officers were immediately sent in a surge to the affected countries. Under normal circumstances, I might have been sent also. I was, after all, without an assignment. But I was instead held in New York because my testimony was considered critical to the Panel. Strangely, I felt left out... being left behind.

In February 2004, I was reassigned on temporary duty as the UN Security Advisor for Ethiopia. Naima came with me at her own expense. She expected to be able to secure employment there with one of the UN agencies. My temporary post was expected to become permanent, or so I was told in New York prior to my departure. There was no time for an area study. Therefore, what follows are only my impressions.

Addis Ababa was no tourist paradise. Unemployment was rampant. Poverty was ubiquitous. The war with Eritrea, a breakaway former province, had not ended well from an Addis perspective. The former brutal Mengistu rule had all but devastated the country—leading to the deaths of hundreds of thousands. The nation's disastrous flirtation with what passed for Socialist government had wrecked the economy. The once-proud nation of Ethiopia was all but destroyed by the ills of Marxism, dictatorial rule, and corruption.

I knew very little about Ethiopia, which I had visited only once before. I was vaguely aware of its proud history, and of Emperor Haile Selassie and his successful battle against Italian military forces during the Second World War. I was also aware that the Americans had used Ethiopia as a clandestine listening station during the Cold War.

Reality was worse than what I anticipated. Addis Ababa, the national capital, was an ugly ramshackle collection of Soviet-era architecture—essentially the worst of old East Berlin; consisting of dull gray concrete walls, too few windows, and early building decrepitude resulting from corruption. Nothing was built well. Nothing was built to last. It showed everywhere.

I had been in the country for barely a month and was performing a security assessment mission in support of UN humanitarian agencies in a region called Gembella, near the Sudanese border. On the morning work was to begin, I received a landline phone call at my dilapidated hotel from the Deputy UNSECOORD. She informed me that I had been relieved of duty by the SG, that effective immediately, I could no longer perform security-related functions; and that I had been recalled to UN Headquarters for reassignment to other duties. She even apologized. Clearly, she did not enjoy being the bearer of such news.

The ride back to Addis Ababa took several hours. I was at first stunned. Then, I became very angry. I was the most prominent person in Iraq who had consistently warned of the danger, both orally and in writing. I had been supported by every UN security professional in the country via the Security Cell. We had collectively made the appropriate security recommendations to our masters. How could it be that an advisor gives good solid advice—the decision makers ignore that advice—terrible things happen—then the decision makers blame the advisor? Moreover, this was, for all intents and purposes, the second time that the UN had fired me, and by no less than the Secretary General himself. That was the gist of it. I was pissed-off and spoiling for a fight. In the back of my mind, though, I knew that the SG held all the levers of power.

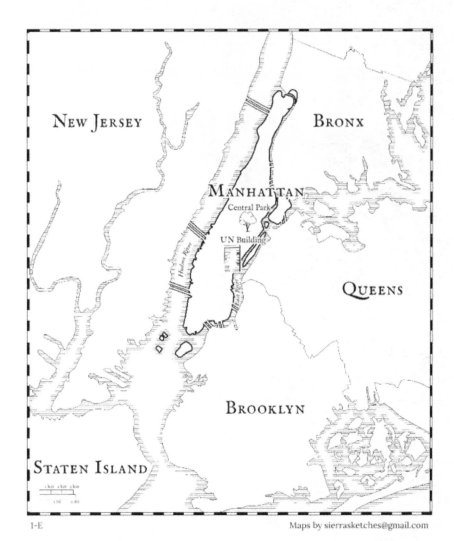

Maps by sierrasketches@gmail.com

Figure 5. Map of Manhattan

19

Falsely Accused

Thou shalt not bear false witness against thy neighbor.
—The Ten Commandments

It was a frigid day in early April 2004 when Naima and I returned to New York from Ethiopia to face an uncertain future. We checked into a hotel on Lexington Avenue. We later found a small studio apartment in a high-rise apartment building at First Avenue and Thirty-Eighth Street, very near the iconic UN building.

Had I been smarter, I would have accomplished an area study before reporting back to UN Headquarters. I had known at least in general terms what physical dangers I faced in Sierra Leone, Yemen, and Iraq because I'd either accumulated personal experience or completed research prior to these deployments. Unfortunately, I did not know what I would face in New York City.

I was about to step into the lion's den, unarmed and blindfolded. Essentially, I was entering a foreign country located in midtown Manhattan; a country with no real land mass; a country ruled by a man who exercised near-absolute control over internal judicial processes, the Secretary General of the United Nations.

The UNSECOORD was directed to submit his resignation. The HC was reduced in rank and returned to his parent agency. I was in legal limbo. The CAO and his subordinate were to face a formal disciplinary hearing. The SG, who made the major security decisions along with his cabinet chief, accepted no responsibility for the pile of corpses in Baghdad.

I was scheduled to meet with the Deputy UNSECOORD the following morning. I did not know what was ahead. My patience had reached its limits, or so I thought at the time. Once again, I was wrong. The meeting was an anticlimax. I was merely directed to see the UN Development Programs' administrative lawyers, who would handle the processing of my case. Based on those lawyers' availability, that meeting was delayed for a few days.

The SG also directed my department's deputy to report to the Under-Secretary General for Management, who was now the acting UNSECOORD. When I finally got to see the UN Development Program attorneys, they informed me that I was to receive legal due process at the hands of the administrator of their agency. Since his organization administered contracts for all UNSECOORD security officers worldwide, the ball was placed in his court.

I suspected that he was not pleased by this turn of events. Essentially, he would determine whether the action decided upon by his boss, the SG, was right and proper regarding my case. That could be no easy task under any circumstances.

The lawyers told me that a UN attorney would be appointed to advise me on the processes involved, and that I had two weeks to respond to the allegations made against me. I asked the obvious question, "What allegations?" The lawyer responded by handing me a copy of "The Extracts of the Security in Iraq Accountability Report." Apparently, the allegations were buried somewhere within its pages. I asked again, "What allegations?" They responded that I was to examine the extracts of the report and to answer any perceived criticisms.

I was momentarily stunned to silence. How could this be? I was expected to read through the extracts to make my own determination what might be interpreted as allegations. There were no charges. Of course, the lawyers had no answers for me. They were merely the messengers. Although clearly sympathetic, there was nothing they could do to rectify this absurd and otherwise-comical circumstance.

I then asked for a full copy of the Panel report. One of the lawyers responded, "The full report has been declared confidential. Only these extracts are provided to you. Per the SG's office, these extracts provided the rationale for the decision that was taken to remove you from security duties." I shook my head in disbelief. Once again, the UN system had managed to shock me. The lawyers could provide me no justification for making the full report confidential. That decision was well above their pay grade.

I must have looked as bad as I felt. The lawyers reassured me that I was in fact very lucky. They made the point that had I held a Secretariat contract, my options for the resolution of my case would have been substantially reduced. The fact that I held a UN Development Program employment contract meant that some basic legal and administrative rules would have to be followed.

I discovered much later that the SG has the authority to reassign any UN staff member anywhere, for any reason and at any time. He had used that unusual authority in my case.

I required time to prepare my defense. None of my superiors tasked me. I could not be tasked with any function that was security-related in any case, or I would be in violation of the edict that I was no longer permitted to work on "security related matters." The fact that there was no genuine case against me did not escape the administrative lawyers handling my case. Ultimately, it was my observation that literally everyone involved in the process appeared to be aware that we were all just going through the motions.

I was coming slowly to grips with something else. I was now a pariah. I had been identified publicly as one of those responsible for the twenty-two deaths in Baghdad. For many, that was good enough. I was judged in the court of UN public opinion as guilty. My name even appeared on the front page of the New York Times as one of those relieved from duty. I was devastated.

People I thought of as friends began to avoid me. Only a very few wanted to be in my presence. I was of course altogether innocent, but that did not matter. Many of my colleagues perceived me as guilty. From their perspective, why else would the SG have identified me for punishment?

I withdrew deep inside myself. The unfairness of it all was a leaden weight of monumental proportions that I carried with me from that time forward. I went from anger to sadness and back again on multiple occasions. I eventually wore out two pairs of shoes walking the streets of Manhattan in a vain attempt to mitigate the frustration and anger.

To be publicly and falsely accused of negligence in the deaths of others by your most senior leadership is a terrible burden, especially when there is absolutely nothing you can do about it!

My emotional state at that time is difficult to describe, even now, so many years later. I felt both hurt and betrayed. I also felt anger and bewilderment. What chance did I have for a positive outcome in a battle with the most powerful person within the UN? Still, it is in my nature to fight.

After calming myself, I read the report extracts in their entirety. Although those extracts suggested that I might have done my job better in a few areas, they also stated flat-out that my office did not have enough funds or personnel to accomplish the tasks at hand in Iraq. This meant I could draw from the extracts of the report that the SG had just used to condemn me to defend myself. It was odd that the very document that had been ostensibly used to come to the decision to remove me from security duties was also the document that might be used, in part, to clear me. The process fractured all conventional logic.

There was something else, too. The extracts appear to have been expertly cherry-picked: Only those portions of the report that supported the firing of the UNSECOORD, HC, me, the CAO, and his subordinate were there. All my testimony and documentation were missing from the extracts. In my estimation, that testimony and documentation, if made public, would have made my firing all but impossible.

I was also aware that nearly every single member of the Security Cell had been interviewed by the Panel. But since the report itself, minus the extracts, had been declared confidential, I was not permitted to review any of it in my defense. Therefore, I had no choice but to individually contact each person who might be knowledgeable of the events leading up to the bombing in Baghdad.

It took some time. Those officers had been spread worldwide by the UN winds. It was many days before I could track them all down. The eventual response, though, was overwhelmingly in my favor. Over the next few weeks, I received over a dozen supportive and signed sworn statements via e-mail saying what I knew they would, which I had no doubt these officers had also said to the Panel investigators. Most of the security officers in Baghdad provided written testimony saying that what the UN was doing to me was patently wrong. Some even suggested, correctly, that our superiors were at fault.

I consulted with the UN attorney who had been appointed to assist me. His advice fell well short of my expectations. He struck me as not terribly interested in my plight, and he told me that he would soon retire as well. This was the legal counsel assigned to me by the system. The word "frame" kept coming unbidden into my mind. No matter, I knew that a genuine advocate was required.

I thereafter sought out an attorney from outside the pool of UN lawyers at considerable personal expense. The old axiom is correct: you get what you pay for. My paid Manhattan attorney performed very well in helping me pull together my defense.

I ran into the former UNSECOORD on Second Avenue a few weeks following his forced resignation. We spoke briefly. The chance meeting felt awkward. He told me that he had "taken the bullet for the secretary-general." Whether that was merely his opinion, I cannot say. He also mentioned that he had been given a back-channel contract of some kind with the Secretariat immediately following his resignation. Why, I wondered?

Some weeks later, I also ran into the SG's cabinet chief, directly across the street from the UN building on First Avenue. He had not forgotten me. This chance meeting felt awkward too. He told me in a subsequent brief conversation that he had made the case to "them" that it would be wrong to include me with the HC and UNSECOORD for disciplinary action. The cabinet chief had, of course, been present at the meeting in Baghdad after the suicide bombing when I suggested that our senior managers were far from blameless. I later told Naima about the encounter. She suggested that he probably lied to me.

Another option for possible resolution was the secretariat ombudsman. I saw the ombudsman prior to tendering my request for administrative review. She provided no help whatsoever. She asked me if I felt any responsibility for the dead and wounded in Baghdad. My response was immediate. "No. I feel no responsibility," I said flat out. She told me that she was a negotiator, and that as such I had to give her something to work with. Since I was unwilling to admit to culpability, and I had refused to accept any other position within the UN, she felt that I was giving her nothing to work with.

The fact that I was wholly innocent of any wrongdoing or negligence did not matter. For her, being the ombudsman was a mechanical process. There was no right and no wrong... only some give on both sides and then a possible resolution. She no doubt considered me unreasonable. In any case, the visit to the ombudsman turned out to be a total waste of time.

On 11 May, I tendered my pro forma request under UN staff rules for the SG's office to conduct an administrative review of his decision. I felt dejected. I expected nothing from this action. Nevertheless, I would attempt to exhaust all legal options open to me.

Once I had tendered that request, I began work on the document required by the administrative lawyers. It was tough going without all my Iraq files in hand. I had sent multiple written requests for full access to the Security in Iraq Accountability Panel Report. None of these requests were ever answered. I also requested access to my department's Iraq files, which included much of my own correspondence. I was refused access by the under-secretary general for management, who was now the acting head of my department. How could she in good conscience deny me access to my own e-mail records for my own defense? Moreover, I requested copies of my files in writing. The acting UNSECOORD's response came via phone call—leaving no fingerprints on her refusal. I was feeling lonelier with every passing day. I am not a fan of conspiracy theories, but it felt like there really was somebody out to get me.

I made a conscious choice not to mention the secret document that I had been shown by the Panel. It was not part of the case against me, and perhaps more importantly, I did not wish to believe that the US or Coalition Intelligence community might have had pre-knowledge of the suicide attack, and then failed to provide warning.

I worked long and hard. On 21 May, I tendered my formal comments to the administrative lawyers. Unfortunately, my complete Iraq files still had not arrived from Ethiopia. The delays were maddening. That meant much of the supporting documentation was drawn from the extracts of the report, the various sworn statements from the senior security officers I had served with in Iraq, and my own records. I informed the administrative lawyers that there was more documentation, and that if needed, it could be provided at some point in the future.

I took a very hard line in my own defense:

1. No actual charges had been leveled against me.
2. I had been wrongly relieved of duty and based on information in a document (The Security in Iraq Accountability Panel Report) that I was not permitted to see.
3. I refused reassignment to a position "not involving security" (none was ever offered in any case).
4. I stated my desire "...to reverse the decision of the Secretary General to remove me from UN security functions; and to gain immediate, formal and public reinstatement without prejudice to my former duties..."

I also pointed out in several of my exhibits that the Panel made errors in both judgment and in fact. The documentation that I provided corrected those errors and provided either sworn testimony or hard-copy documentation as irrefutable evidence of factual mistakes.

The Mission Operations Coordinator in Baghdad, Robert Turner, who was present at the time of both attacks, sent a private letter to the SG that was later leaked to the public. A portion of that letter was included in my defense documents, and is quoted again below:

Sir, you will permit me to observe that it appears there exists a "shield" around the Secretariat building that protects those inside from being held accountable for their decisions and actions, a protection that does not exist once one crosses First Avenue.

...if it was not clear before, all authority for decision making related to mission— functions, budgets and re-sources—will be retained at headquarters, while those responsible for implementing those decisions will be held accountable for any failings.

First Avenue in Manhattan divides the UN building from many of the agencies, funds, and programs occupying offices to the west. Turner's letter spoke volumes to me. He summed up my feelings perfectly.

The administrative lawyers quickly reviewed my doc-umentation. They confessed to being astonished. They ex-pressed further shock that we security officers in Baghdad had taken money from our own pockets to purchase and in-stall the steel-plate blast shields in the Security Information and Operations Center. The substantial evidence that I pro-vided made it crystal clear that I was in no part to blame for the tragedy in Baghdad. In fact, their assessment confirmed what I already knew to be true; that had our recommenda-tions been followed, the death toll would have been much reduced. They now knew what I knew, that I was a wholly innocent man, who had been falsely accused. But would my now-proven innocence matter?

Until that point the two administrative lawyers felt that I might have been wrongly accused; that it was a mistake that I was selected by the SG for punishment. My evidence, sworn statements and hard-copy documentation made it abundant-ly clear that it was no mistake. In addition, much of that same evidence had been provided, by me, to the Panel, months earlier. Unfortunately, that evidence was now declared "UN Confidential." There seemed to be both bad intent and twisted purpose behind my firing. I remember wondering if the SG's diplomatic immunity equaled impunity. It certainly seemed so.

On 27 May, Naima and I were married in a civil ceremony in the Manhattan City Clerk's office. She had mentioned to me a few evenings prior that under no circumstances should I hire one of those gaudy stretch limousines for our wedding day. I subsequently hired a gaudy stretch limousine to pick us up outside of our apartment with my former Iraq desk officer and another close friend already aboard to act as witnesses. She can't tell me what to do!

We honeymooned on a cruise ship that took us to Bermuda and back the following week. For a short while, we left our troubles behind. Naima's support for me never wavered. Although I sometimes felt like quitting, she insisted that I never give up. We waited.

Shortly after our return to Manhattan, I heard through the office grapevine that the SG planned a visit to my department in the next few days in a sort of town meeting format. I was looking forward to hearing what my accuser might have to say. The topic was Baghdad and the future of security in the UN. I never got the opportunity. The Deputy UNSECOORD called me to her office and instructed me to stay out of the office that day. I was getting over being surprised by anything that happened inside the UN, but I was curious. I asked why I was singled out. Her response shocked me still. She said in a deadpan voice, "Per his office, your presence will make the Secretary General uncomfortable." I never asked the obvious question, why? Naima and I went on a picnic in Central Park.

A few days later I was summoned to the UNSECOORD front office to be informed that my former security assistant in Baghdad, Mazzin, had been shot dead. The sad news shook me to my core. At some time after my departure from the mission, Mazzin had left the UN and gone to work for the Americans. The report was sketchy, but it seemed that he had been singled out by former regime elements for his perceived betrayal of Iraq, and therefore murdered. His death hit me hard, as I had liked him so very much. Naima and I privately mourned his loss. There were tragedies piled upon ever more tragedies, with no end in sight.

It was 19 August 2004, the first anniversary of the suicide bombing attack on the Canal Hotel. The UN held memorial ceremonies worldwide. Two of the largest were in New York and Geneva. The SG went to the ceremony in Switzerland. I went to the one in Manhattan, and Naima stayed at home. I understood her reluctance to participate.

Appearances are important within the UN. There was an honor guard of uniformed security guards. There was also a candle lighting ceremony for family members. The SG gave a passionate speech concerning his personal loss. That speech was video linked to New York and presented on a huge screen near the General Assembly. Every seat was full. I was choking with repressed emotion. I left the ceremony halfway through for the streets of Manhattan. I walked for hours, lost in thought.

I no longer asked myself what I could have done differently. I knew that I had done my absolute best under the circumstances. But I was facing a huge dilemma. Nobody would likely hire someone like me while this false accusation continued to hang over my head. My professional life was at terrible risk. I have bills to pay, just like everyone else. Imagine for a moment: You are preparing your résumé for a move to your next possible job. If honest, would you feel compelled to inform your possible future employer that no less a personage than the UN Secretary General had personally fired you for negligence in the deaths of twenty-two and the wounding of over one hundred fifty? Make what excuses you will, but that accusation tends to stick.

Perhaps more importantly at the emotional level, the lifetime that I had spent building a reputation for integrity, hard work, and dedication was literally on the line. I had never felt so helpless.

As I returned to our apartment, which was very near the UN building, I saw that staff members were gathering to conduct a silent march. Some of them were holding placards. The UN Staff Association had called for a march to demand that the SG address their concerns about security. They apparently knew what I knew.

Their hand-outs mentioned the following:

> Deeply concerned that the United Nations has so far failed to adequately address the problem of a dysfunctional security management system and questions of accountability in a fully straightforward and transparent manner;

> Reaffirms the Council's position to completely reject the concept of "collective responsibility" that is used as a pretext to deny justice to the Baghdad bombing victims;

> Dismayed that the Organization is sending staff into insecure environments without having made the prerequisite security arrangements necessary to ensure their security and safety prior to deployment;

The UN Staff Association had a good bead on things. The UN security system was dysfunctional. The notion of "collective responsibility" at that time was all but meaningless. Finally, a year on, there had been no change in the system to provide "prerequisite security arrangements" for staff entering hazardous areas.

It was a year after the bombing in Baghdad, and nobody had been appointed to take over the duties of the UNSECO-ORD on a full-time basis. The post remained vacant.

Less than a week later, I testified once again. This time it was before the Disciplinary Board looking at the CAO. I had run into him a couple of times over the past months. At our first or second meeting, he told me confidentially that he had copies of everyone's e-mails from Baghdad, including the HC. Those e-mails could have potentially helped my case. I asked him to provide me any of the correspondence that might help. He never did.

The CAO was positioned to make few decisions relative to security matters. In my estimation, it was wrong to single him out for blame. He was fighting for his professional life. But he might attack me to deflect any perceived accountability. I had to be prepared for that eventuality.

The night before, Naima and I had attended a concert at Radio City Music Hall, a welcome respite. The never-ending pressure was a great leaden weight that was at times soul-crushing. We waited.

It was now late August. My testimony before the Disciplinary Panel was surreal. I spent nearly two and a half hours answering questions. The group was extraordinarily ill-informed because the full Panel Report was denied to it. How were they to make decisions concerning disciplinary actions when they were refused access to the most critically important evidence?

At their request, the following day, I provided copies of all my Security Management Team presentations and meeting minutes, Iraq Security Lessons Learned document, Threat Assessment, relevant copies of e-mail, and much more. They were most grateful for the assistance. But even they seemed to know that they were merely part of an absurd process.

In any case, both the CAO and his subordinate were eventually cleared of any serious wrong-doing, and as I was subsequently informed by a member of the Disciplinary Board, as a direct consequence of my testimony and the hard evidence that I provided. I was glad of this outcome. It seemed that facts and evidence counted for something. I only hoped that it would also count for me.

At this point, the Secretariat review of my defense documents, which was supposed to have been completed on 15 August, was ten days overdue. I heard that the UN Development Program Administrator, based on the recommendations of his administrative lawyers, had sent forward a draft decision that exonerated me. Weeks passed. I had heard nothing. I feared that further delay could mean nothing good. We waited.

I discovered a note on my desk from one of the UNDP administrative lawyers asking me to drop by. When I arrived at her office, she told me that my case, as well as the cases of the CAO and his subordinate, had been returned to the SG. "How," I asked with alarm, "can he any longer be involved in these actions? He kicked my case for adjudication to the UN Development Program Administrator." The lawyer merely shook her head.

She further explained that I had the right, because my legal action was already well beyond the extended deadline, to demand that my case be tendered to the UN Appeals Board. Of course, we both knew that if the case went there, it would be anywhere from two to four years to resolution. My UN employment contract would expire long before that.

She advised, as she had previously, that I be patient. Patience has always come hard for me. But she said that because their investigation had already determined that I should be exonerated and reinstated without prejudice, the favorable decision of the UNDP Administrator would likely be permitted to stand. However, although she informed me privately and confidentially that they had recommended that I be cleared, there was no documentation that I could hang my hat on.

I discussed these matters with Naima at lunch. I felt as if I were drowning in a barrel of molasses. Keeping hope alive was enormously difficult. The stress was never-ending and oppressive. I had never previously experienced the unique agony of prolonged personal uncertainty. There were times that I wanted to quit just to feel the relief of it all being over. Naima wouldn't hear of it. She provided me the necessary spinal support when I most needed it.

I later visited a UN attorney close to the action. She informed me conversationally that she wished that someone would take the UN to court on the issue of immunities. Her issue was simple. The UN received functional and diplomatic immunities in the United States based on the legal fiction that the UN had a parallel legal structure. That fiction was unsupportable. She pointed out that my case was proof of it. Under UN staff rules, the SG has all the advantages. All the facts supported my case, but the facts could be rendered irrelevant. I was getting a very expensive course in UN legal realities.

I then made an appointment to see Ambassador Patrick Kennedy at the US Mission to the UN. Now that the Secretariat had violated its own staff rules, I felt justified in doing so. He saw me on 31 August late in the morning. I have only rarely met a more sympathetic and understanding civil servant. Ambassador Kennedy listened attentively while I told my story. He stopped me at various points, asking probing and intelligent questions. At the end of my tale, he promised to immediately examine my case. He also asked for my relevant supporting documentation and promised to read it himself. I agreed to provide him my formal comments (defense documents) that very afternoon.

The ambassador also told me that he would gladly contact the acting UNSECOORD as well as the UN Development Program Administrator to put both on notice that he was interested in the disposition of my case. I left his office in far better spirits. Ambassador Kennedy was the first person I had spoken to who gave me the sense that there was somebody in my corner. Until this point, except for Naima and a few close friends, I had felt distinctly alone and almost entirely isolated.

After a quick lunch with Naima in our studio apartment, and after I informed her of all that had transpired, I returned to the ambassador's office and provided his secretary with the requested data. My mood improved.

The following day, I attempted to gain an appointment with the UN Development Programs Administrator. Frankly, I did not know if he knew that his authority to adjudicate my case had been potentially hijacked. It was tough going. I spoke with various subordinates, none of whom seemed to have the authority to grant me five minutes of his time. I told my story more than once. I knew that I was getting the runaround. That suggested something all by itself, and nothing good.

At this point I was convinced that there was literally nothing that I could do to hurt my case. In my estimation, it looked like a stacked deck. I feared that a loss was the most logical outcome. All I could do was proceed on my current course and hope for the best. "Hope," one of my generals told me years earlier, "is not a viable course of action." He was right, but I had no other options open to me. Hope was all I had.

The day after the Labor Day weekend, I found a voice message on my work phone. It was from one of the subordinates of the UN Development Program Administrator. The message was clear. The administrator wanted me to know that his agency merely administered my contract, and that in his estimation the authority to adjudicate my case was "shared." All my hopes now rested with Ambassador Kennedy and the US mission. We waited.

One early evening in our apartment, I received a phone call from a senior officer of the Secretariat. The woman asked me what I considered to be at that time an odd question: what I planned to do if I was cleared by the UN. My response was straightforward. I remember saying, "I just want my life back."

The following morning, shortly after arriving at the office, I received a four-page letter exonerating me of culpability in the deaths that resulted from the bombing in Baghdad. The letter was signed by the UN Development Program Administrator. I was ecstatic.

I notified Naima first by phone. She too was beside herself with joy. She had stuck by me. She had never faltered. Her steadfast refusal to permit me to even consider the option of quitting was critically important. This was her victory every bit as much as it was mine.

In part, I credit Ambassador Pat Kennedy with the positive outcome. He let senior UN Secretariat officials know that they were being watched. In my estimation, this may have tipped the scales in my favor; wrongdoing cannot easily endure a spotlight.

The UNSECOORD staff threw us a going-away party in our offices on Forty-Fifth Street that was in part a victory celebration as well. I reveled for a time. Nothing tastes quite so sweet as a long-sought and hard-fought victory. I was subsequently reassigned as the UN Security Advisor for Egypt, Naima's country of birth—a gift from the Deputy UNSECOORD—for which I was very thankful.

The never-ending stress and pressure, the rank unfairness of the situation, the resulting negative impact on my recent marriage, my months-long status as a pariah—all of this and more added up to a huge emotional release. I could breathe again. I could plan again. I had, in a sense, reclaimed my honor. I could also look forward to a future that did not involve lawyers! It was a wonderful moment.

I was also reminded of the pep-talk given me by "Mitch" Mitchelson in Freetown right after I was removed from the senior staff by the HOM. I was essentially fired from two of my initial three assignments with the UN. I hoped that this would not become a recurring theme. It was more than a little worrisome.

I received over one hundred congratulatory e-mails from around the globe, and in many cases from UN security officers I never met. I came to realize only subsequently that I had won a battle for the entire UN security community. Had my relief from duty been made permanent, it would have established the absurd precedent that a security advisor could be removed from service for advice given, but not taken.

The larger lesson that I took away from my relief and subsequent legal-administrative battle with the SG is, "never quit!" In truth, it is a lesson that was reinforced multiple times over my many years of military service too, and of course I added it to *Bob's Laws*.

Still, and despite my undeniable joy at being exonerated, there remained nagging questions.

20

The Final Road

*In the depth of winter, I finally learned that there was within
me an invincible summer.*
—Albert Camus

Beyond my many suspicions, the intensely personal question went unanswered for more than a decade. Why was I singled out for punishment by the SG? I did not fail in my duty.

In 2017, a member of the Security in Iraq Accountability Panel, Stuart Groves, provided me a copy of the summary of their report. In so doing, he broke his sworn oath to remain silent. He did so because, he said, "I want to do the right thing." In other words, he broke his word in the service of a higher cause, the truth. I appreciate that sentiment more than he could possibly know. Moreover, his well-meaning action is clearly against self-interest. He knows, as I do, that he will probably never be called upon again by the UN. This is the very definition of honorable behavior and became another of Bob's Laws.

I was fascinated to read the summary after so many years. Two quotes from that still UN confidential document are especially illuminating and provided below.

The panel was of the view that the UN security officers on the ground in Baghdad can not (sic) be held responsible for the failure to recognize the clear warning signs that the situation was deteriorating and that there was a possibility that the UN could become a target.

It is probable that if the security measures that were recommended by the security staff had been implemented in a full and urgent manner, the number of casualties sustained in the attack on 19 August would have been considerably reduced.

I am in full agreement with both quotes. The Panel investigators felt strongly that we in the UN security community in Baghdad had done our jobs. Why, then, were these two sentences declared "UN Confidential" by the SG?

Had I merely kept silent at that fateful meeting in Baghdad after the suicide attack, I might never have been singled out for punishment. My stating the truth out loud made me a potential whistleblower. Whistleblowers in the UN, as elsewhere, are sometimes brutally sanctioned for speaking the truth.

Was I foolish? My twenty-five years of military service had resulted in my internalizing a "mission focus" which made me tend to place mission requirements first, and my personal interests second. I had unconsciously brought this focus with me into UN service. American soldiers place their trust in one another and their superiors, knowing that somebody will always have their back. However, I wasn't in the US Army's Special Forces anymore. Several years ago, my wife unkindly dubbed me, "one of the very few Boy Scouts serving in UN." I feel compelled to concede her point.

From my entrance into the UN Civil Service in Sierra Leone until the time I was exonerated in Manhattan, I had spent four years under the UN flag. I was much maligned, badly bruised, and battered. But I was still standing, and in no small part because of the love and loyal support of a remarkable woman, my wife, Naima. Although it was clearly a very near thing, we were successful in *Surviving the United Nations*.

We proceeded to our new home in Cairo in October 2004. One of the first phone calls we received was unexpected. The future US Ambassador to the UN, Samantha Power, then teaching at Harvard University, asked to interview me concerning my knowledge of the Canal Hotel bombing. She was writing a book about the deceased SRSG in Iraq. I knew better than to speak with her on the record, but my not-yet-fully-dissipated anger got the better of me. I gave her several quotes that she used in the book. Fortunately, nobody in New York thought that my *faux pas* demanded disciplinary action.

My only gripe concerning her book is that she misidentified me as a former US Marine instead of a Green Beret. I got over that quickly, though. The fact is that the Marines are some of the finest warriors on the globe. Being mistakenly called a Marine is a long way from the worst thing that could have happened to me. I only hope they don't mind.

I served as UN Security Advisor in Egypt for four years, and then accepted a new post as Head of Safety and Security for the UN Relief and Works Agency for Palestinian Refugees (UNRWA). That critically important agency supports the Palestinian refugee population in Jordan, Lebanon, and Syria, as well as the West Bank and Gaza Strip. I was in that job for less than two years when selected to become Chief of the Middle East and North Africa in the Department of Safety and Security at UN headquarters in New York, just prior to the "Arab Awakening."

During the following twenty-four months, my staff and I facilitated the evacuations of five countries, supported political and humanitarian operations during the war in Libya that included the now-famous NATO bombings, conducted security training in pre-conflict Syria, and much more. After two years of burning the candle at both ends, in 2012, I was re-assigned—at my own request—as UN Chief Security Advisor for Indonesia, a position from which I retired in 2014.

Since that time, Naima and I have lived in Bangkok, Thailand; Arlington, Virginia; and Rome, Italy. I began writing this book in the US while recovering from shoulder replacement surgery and completed the effort while living in Europe.

It is important to state clearly that I was lucky. First, my wife recovered fully from her wounds. Second, I survived the suicide bombing with barely a scratch. Third, I was ultimately successful in defending myself against false accusations and winning full exoneration and reinstatement to my former UN position—but perhaps only when a US Ambassador made it known to the powerful that someone was looking over their shoulders. Finally, and surprisingly, I was later promoted and entrusted with the most difficult and demanding security region on the planet.

I discovered in the years following my UN retirement that many of those who stand up for what is just, trying to do the right thing by speaking truth to power, are destroyed personally and professionally by the institutions they once loyally served. Given this understanding, I was fortunate indeed.

After all that occurred—and this came as a surprise to me too—I am very proud of my UN service. At the personal level, I received some badly needed lessons in humility. More importantly, I admire the aspirations found in the UN Charter and Universal Declaration of Human Rights. Both documents reflect principles first laid down in the American Declaration of Independence and Constitution.

On reflection, the organization stretched me in ways I find impossible to describe. Nearly two hundred nationalities are represented. It is wildly diverse. The number of languages spoken is mind-boggling. The variety of cultures is astounding. The opportunities therefore for learning and individual growth are simply without equal. The personal and professional challenges of working within the UN, despite its highlighted deficiencies, forced me to attempt to understand extraordinarily differing perspectives. I am hopefully a far better person for my experiences while in international service.

I am also grateful that the UN provided me a rare opportunity for a second act, following my retirement from active military service. My life within the US Special Operations Community, my first act, is best characterized by service to the nation. The UN gave me a chance to remain in service, in this case, to humanity. The US Army and UN provided my life with both meaning and purpose.

In and out of uniform, I accumulated almost twenty years with the UN, living and working daily with people from other nations. Although humanity is clearly diverse, my observation is that our similarities far outweigh our differences. Recent genetic studies seem to back up my conclusion. Homo sapiens worldwide are ninety-nine point five percent the same. The point five percent difference predominantly relates to how we look, the least significant difference of all.

I spent well over two decades of my life learning the soldier's trade—the taking of life. The UN Security Advisor's mission is the mirror opposite—the preservation of life. It is interesting to note that the skill sets for both are much the same.

Learning to live with what I have seen and experienced has been challenging. Sometimes the memories intrude and cascade into my present life, leaving me breathless for a time. Years of stress have taken a toll. I unconsciously created compartments in my mind. I stashed away those images that were too terrible to contemplate in those hidey-holes—so that I could continue to function. Predictably, though, there has been occasional leakage. Still, and this is a very important point, I remain alive to face that challenge. Some of my friends and colleagues are not.

Tragically, the terrible events in Baghdad were followed later by an attack on the UN in Algiers, Algeria, on 11 December 2007; another attack occurred in Islamabad, Pakistan, on 5 October 2009; and then in Mazar-i-Sharif, Afghanistan, on 1 April 2011; and again, in Abuja, Nigeria, on 26 August 2011; and again, on 8 December 2017 in the Democratic Republic of Congo; and more recently, on 10 August 2019 in Benghazi, Libya. There will no doubt be more. The death toll continues to rise year by bloody year. Deadly assaults on the UN have become all-too common.

Over time, the UN realized that it had to expand its key security service. The replacement of UNSECOORD with the UN Department of Safety and Security (UNDSS) while I was serving as the UN Security Advisor in Egypt was a great step in the right direction. The appointment of an under-secretary general to head that department was also a welcome change. In addition, the UN provided more money to the security budget, while significantly increasing the number of personnel. Unlike when I was hired, the department now formally trains and certifies its staff. We have come a very long way.

The UN humanitarian agencies that we supported, like the World Food Program, UN Children's Fund and UN High Commissioner for Refugees, perform tasks that nobody else on the globe can. They feed the starving, care for children in dire need, and assist families who have lost their homes and villages to the ravages of war. They often endanger themselves to help those who have nowhere else to turn. There is nobility in their calling. I am honored to have played even a small part in helping them accomplish their many missions of mercy.

The best of all things is that I know that some people are still alive today because of my actions, whether they are aware of it or not. There is no better feeling than possessing the knowledge that you are responsible for saving lives. No medal for bravery, no certificate of achievement, no promotion—in fact, no formal acknowledgement of any kind—can compete. I know that my life counted for something for this key reason. I will take that feeling with me to my grave. Although, I confess, I would have preferred not being fired for it.

There are several hundred professional level UN security advisors performing this job worldwide as you read these words. They work behind the curtain. They respond to tsunamis, earthquakes, landslides, volcanic eruptions, typhoons/hurricanes, and epidemics; as well as wars of all sizes, description, and intensities in support of UN humanitarian, peacekeeping, and political goals and aspirations. Some are armed. Most are not. They negotiate for the release of hostages, seek passage through armed checkpoints, accompany humanitarian convoys, advise senior managers on mitigation measures, manage violence in refugee camps, train staff, and very much more. In my opinion, they are some of the least known yet most intrepid people on this planet.

It is a privilege to count myself among their number.

Epilogue

The measure of a man is what he does with power.
—Plato

I included this Epilogue to provide startling information that only came to light following the completion of the writing of my story. What comes now is my attempt to shed more light on what might have occurred in Baghdad and New York.

When working on the final chapters of this opus, I contacted a very senior former UN staff member for the purpose of conducting background research. I was shocked when this person offered to send me a mailing envelope containing a hard copy of the still "UN Confidential" Security in Iraq Accountability Panel Report. He told me that it had years ago "fallen off the back of a truck." I immediately accepted the offer. The long wait for the mail to arrive was hard, though. I had been wanting to read this document for well over a decade. Patience never came easy for me. Weeks passed. Finally, it arrived. The report was one hundred fifty-three pages long, divided into twelve sections. I read it twice over three days. Why did it take so long? I had to put it down several times and walk away. I was overcome with both disgust and anger.

The SG in my story died when this book was nearly finished. However, I reached out to him in e-mail 2 years prior to his passing via his foundation in Geneva, Switzerland. I wanted to be fair and give him a chance to explain his actions regarding Iraq. He never responded to my queries.

I was unable to find contact information for his former cabinet chief. I subsequently attempted to reach out to the former Deputy-Secretary General and the Under-Secretary General for Management (acting UNSECOORD). They too did not respond. My former boss, the HC, and his some-time deputy have also chosen silence. The Deputy UNSECOORD declined all comment as well. So much silence... so many unanswered questions... why?

The only senior knowledgeable person that agreed to speak to me was the former UNSECOORD. He was an assistant-secretary general in rank at the time of the attack. You may recall that he was asked to tender his resignation by the SG in the wake of the publication of the cherry-picked "Extracts" of the Panel Report. In a telephonic interview he told me the following:

1. He was the first full-time UNSECOORD. His predecessors all held additional portfolios. Perhaps because he was the first, he was not provided a Terms of Reference for the job by the SG. If true, this is a significant oversight concerning a person who was held responsible for global UN security matters.

2. Just like his predecessors, he possessed no formal security background—all were generic UN senior managers.

3. He had a direct line of communication with the SG, but continued the precedent established by his predecessors of reporting through the cabinet chief.

4. He also mentioned that he forwarded several of my warning messages up the chain to the Iraq Steering Committee. If true, members of the Iraq Steering Committee could have been considered culpable.

5. When I began asking the UNSECOORD some tough questions, he ceased communication with me for a time. Later, he contacted me again using threatening language. I had previously asked him if he ever took my many security concerns, detailed in my reports, sufficiently to heart to take them forward to either the SG or cabinet chief. In a nutshell, he responded that none of my messages to New York would qualify as "ac-

tionable intelligence." He seems to forget that the institution of UNSECOORD was not an intelligence gathering organization. Moreover, formal intelligence gathering, per UN policy, is the sole province of its nation-state membership. Assuming he understands what "actionable intelligence" means, such was never going to be acquired by my office. It would have been an impossible standard for us to meet.

Why was the bulk of the Panel report declared "UN Confidential?" Some thoughts based on known facts follow:

1. The Panel was directed by the SG to focus their primary attentions between 1 May and 19 August 2003. Assuming his direction was followed, his questionable decision to enter Iraq without the conduct of a security assessment was made prior to 1 May, as well as his flawed decision to remain in Iraq following the 19 August suicide attack, would both be placed outside the Panel's window of consideration. The second attack that we anticipated occurred a little over a month later, 22 September. Two Iraqis died and several others were wounded.

2. Twenty-two people were killed on 19 August. Over 150 were wounded. Blame had to be assessed and heads had to roll, but clearly only so long as the SG and those others at the rank of under-secretary general (those closest to him) were carefully protected from any possibility of actual accountability. The very powerful all kept their jobs.

3. I was clearly identified as a potential whistleblower at that fateful meeting with the cabinet chief in Baghdad following the attack. I spoke the truth. I therefore had to be dealt with. Since there was overwhelming evidence in the full Panel Report that I honestly attempted to do my job, that report had to be made "UN Confidential." There are perhaps other reasons as well, but I dare not speculate without hard evidence that is currently lacking. However, the truth was intentionally buried!

4. Per the Panel Report, someone within the UN in Baghdad made the decision to refuse US Military protection at the Ca-

nal Hotel prior to the attack. Who made that fatal decision remains a continuing mystery to this day, despite my many continuing efforts to discover the answer. All seemingly knowledgeable persons are silent.

5. A senior UN insider, who wishes to remain anonymous, confirmed that the SG did not permit the Panel to conduct a review of the emails of the SRSG, HC, and UNSECOORD. In so doing, he ensured that the final Panel Report would never reflect the whole truth, which of course, was likely the idea.

6. Something else, too, and some readers may recall that while I was still in Yemen, and prior to my reassignment to Iraq, I attended an UNSECOORD work shop in Vienna, Austria 29-31 October 2002 that focused on planning for the UN's re-entry into Iraq in the wake of the US invasion that occurred the following March. The group was composed of some very senior and experienced security officers. The planning sessions were professionally conducted, and the scenarios we used as a baseline accurately captured many of the challenges we ultimately faced in Baghdad. To my knowledge nobody ever saw that planning data again. Curious.

7. Finally, there is the issue of liability. The SG approved the HC's plan to re-enter Iraq on 1 May that was supported by the UNSECOORD as well as the Iraq Steering Group chaired by Deputy-Secretary General. In contravention of UN security policy and normal practice, we were not permitted to conduct a security assessment prior to the re-introduction of staff back into Iraq. I have often wondered if there might be an issue of legal liability on the part of the UN because of such cavalier decision-making. While he lived, the SG could not claim security policy ignorance. He was a former UNSECOORD himself.

Even though all roads seemed to lead back to the SG, the Panel ultimately gave him a pass—taking the position that because his Deputy-Secretary General and UNSECOORD both approved the HC's plan for the re-entry of UN staff into Iraq, he was therefore blameless. I could easily take issue with their assessment.

As previously mentioned, the SG ignored UN security policy when he directed that we enter Iraq without the conduct of a security assessment. He also ignored UN security policy when he pressured the HC to permit more staff in Baghdad. The SG additionally ignored UN security policy when he directed staff to remain in Iraq following the suicide attack, short-circuiting the formal and long-standing security decision-making mechanism of the Designated Official for Security advised by the Security Management Team.

In my reading of the full Panel Report, I found mention of one of the SRSG's close protection officers coming into possession of a US secret document outlining a planned attack on "United Nations interests" in mid-June. Reportedly, the document came from an unidentified, "contact he had in the American military." This document reportedly also mentioned, "targets of these attacks included the UN building in Baghdad." How did a close protection officer on the detail come by such a document? Who gave it to him? If there was a known and credible threat to the Canal Hotel ("the UN building in Baghdad") within the document, why wasn't it shared with me? As a former US Army Military Intelligence Officer, I could have certainly verified its authenticity and then subsequently recommended appropriate and immediate preventive action. I never got the chance. Regrettably, a copy of that secret document is not included with the Panel Report in my possession. I only have the text portion, and not the many exhibits. More troubling unanswered questions...

Then there is the matter of the representatives from the 2nd Armored Cavalry Regiment that came to my office to inform me on 21 June that they were going to secure the Canal Hotel more than two months prior to the attack. Per the Panel Report, the unit later attempted to do what they said they would do and "secure the compound." However, they were turned away. I know that I didn't, and so informed the Panel in testimony in 2004. I was later able to produce documentary evidence to that effect in my own defense following my relief. In his testimony before the Panel, the HC denied making this decision. If not him, then who? He was, by policy, the only UN senior official in Baghdad who possessed the authority to do so.

I also contacted the former head of the Coalition Provisional Authority, Ambassador Paul Bremer. He admitted to hearing the same thing stated by the Panel—somebody within the UN refused the US offer of protection. However, Ambassador Bremer did not know who made the refusal. Bremer subsequently suggested that I contact his former Chief of Staff, Ambassador Pat Kennedy. He implied that Kennedy might hold my answers. This of course was the same Pat Kennedy who assisted me in New York with my extraordinarily unusual legal case. Small world...

Through a mutual friend, I was able to reach out to Ambassador Kennedy in email. Unfortunately, he too had no answers. I will continue to pull on this thread, and others, in the hope of one day finding an answer. American citizens working for the UN were among the dead and wounded in the Canal Hotel. If there was an allied intelligence service, or entity within the US Intelligence Community that knew of the coming attack, and no warning was given the UN, are there potential legal liability issues from a US Government perspective?

With the kind assistance of Lieutenant General (retired) Terry Wolff, then a colonel, who as Commander of the 2nd Armored Calvary Regiment greeted the HC and I at the front gate of the Canal Hotel on 1 May, I was able to contact Major General (retired) Brad May. May assumed command of the unit on 18 June 2003. One of his first duties was to conduct a walkthrough of the UN Compound. Interestingly, the vulnerabilities subsequently identified by his operations officer, that he shared with me, mirrored my own security assessment, including the desire to close the road that was later used by the suicide bomber. May ordered that road closed. His troops immediately complied. Then, someone in perceived authority within the Canal Hotel demanded that the road be re-opened, and the additional troops be removed. The 2nd Armored Calvary Regiment Commander reluctantly complied. This action occurred without my knowledge.

Once again, the people who might know who made that decision aren't talking. There were only four UN staff members in the Canal Hotel that might have been perceived by the officers of the 2nd Armored Calvary Regiment as possessing the authority to refuse their protection; me, HC, the HC's occasional deputy, and SRSG. I did not, and the HC denies it. His deputy has not responded to several email queries. Who, then, is left... the SRSG who died in the attack? The US Army never responded to multiple requests from the Panel in 2004 for statements to clarify this matter with knowledgeable senior soldiers in Baghdad. I cannot say why. When I reached out to them in 2019 they gladly spoke with me.

Per a former senior US State Department official, and unknown to me in 2003, America's diplomats have a policy in place often referred to as a "duty to warn." This means that US State Department officers are required to downgrade classified materials to warn organizations like the UN that they are under immediate threat of harm. However, I am not familiar with any corollary to that policy within the US Department of Defense.

It was apparently clear to the Panel that the US Intelligence Community had hard intelligence that the Canal Hotel would be attacked. If that information was shared formally with the UN, I am not aware of it. In way of explanation, intelligence officers are required to protect (keep secret) both their sources and methods of gathering sensitive information. If adversaries, say in this case jihadists, discovered that they were compromised, they might immediately change their communications methods or kill a suspected traitor in their midst, and future valuable intelligence will be lost. Was this the case in Baghdad? Was an entity who was either allied with or inside the US Intelligence Community protecting sources and methods?

In the continuing search for answers, I sent e-mail queries to the former senior US Army intelligence officer in Iraq, my classmate, Major General (retired) Barbara Fast. She informed me that a mechanism to warn, not unlike that of the State Department's, was implemented, but she could not remember if it came into force before or after the attack. The result speaks volumes. The policy was likely implemented after the attack on the Canal Hotel. Major General Fast denies having knowledge of intelligence of a possible attack on the Canal Hotel.

It is perhaps necessary to review just a few of the relevant conclusions relating to my office in the full Panel Report that were all declared "UN Confidential" by SG (two you have already seen):

> To a large degree, the warnings and some of the more urgent recommendations regarding security went unheeded, or else they were dealt with in a manner so lethargic that it defeated the purpose of the exercise.

> ...the UN security officers on the ground in Baghdad can not (sic) be held responsible for the clear failure to recognize the clear warning signs...

> A genuine team spirit developed in the security community, which was fostered by an increasing exasperation with what the group perceived as a lack of response to their warnings...

> The danger was recognized by the UN security community in Iraq and there are signs that some of the security officers suffered extreme frustration when their warnings were unheeded.

> It is probable that if the security measures that were recommended by the security staff were implemented in a full and urgent manner, the number of casualties on 19 August would have been considerably reduced.

It is my belief, and the belief of many of my reviewers as well, that had these above Panel Report conclusions been made public, I could not have been relieved of duty by the SG. It is therefore clear, at least to some, that I was callously designated a scapegoat and fired for the literal mortal sins of my most senior superiors.

A couple of my reviewers asked me if there was any relationship between the outrageous corruption within the Iraq Oil-for-Food Program and the repetitive security failures of the UN leadership in Baghdad and New York? I cannot say for sure. However, the UN Executive Director of the Iraq Oil-for-Food Program was later indicted by an American prosecutor for wire fraud tied to the program. He subsequently fled to his home country of Cyprus where he cannot be extradited for financial crimes. There is a standing Interpol arrest warrant with his name on it if he ever steps foot off his small Mediterranean island. This individual is yet another former UNSECOORD.

Events involving the Executive Director of the Iraq Oil-for-Food Program are highlighted in the book *Backstabbing for Beginners: My Crash Course in International Diplomacy* written by former UN Oil-for-Food program staffer, Michael Soussan. This book was later made into a movie starring Sir Ben Kingsley that has only a limited relationship with objective truth.

It was reported that the SG felt pressure to resign his post because of the early findings of the Independent Inquiry Committee led by former American Federal Reserve Chairman, Paul Volcker. It came to light during the investigation that the SG's son was given a job with a Swiss-based Iraq Oil-for-Food contracting company. Volcker's lead investigator wanted to know if that job was given the young man because of who his father was, and to curry favor in return for lucrative UN contracts? This is a good question. In my opinion, it was never satisfactorily answered. As the name of Volcker's committee suggested, his report was supposed to be "independent." It wasn't independent at all.

The SG's cabinet chief was fired during the conduct of this investigation. He was reportedly terminated because he destroyed thousands of documents relating to the Oil-for-Food Program before they could be examined by Mr. Volcker. Was the cabinet chief fired for shredding documents, or for getting caught shredding documents? This is yet another good question, among many, that deserves an answer. I don't have one, although I have suspicions galore.

Because of my continuing research, I found a more up-to-date reference online concerning the cabinet chief. Per that reference, this individual was still listed as a UN under-secretary general and special advisor to Secretary General Ban Ki Moon. If true, why? Hadn't he been fired? Attempting to discover the answer to the above pressing question, I reached out to the current SG's spokesman by e-mail. Although I sent my message twice, I never received a response. Of course, by now, I am accustomed to the thundering silence emanating from the UN Headquarters relating to all matters concerning the subject matter of this book.

Based on Paul Volcker's report, the Iraq Oil-for-Food Program was later declared by the American Heritage Foundation as "the biggest financial scandal in modern history." The 60 billion-dollar program was beset with kickbacks, bribery, and fraud on a truly global scale. My reviewers asking if there was a relationship between that massive corruption and subsequent egregious security lapses leading up to the Canal Hotel bombing may have a legitimate query that is regrettably beyond the scope of my story.

Some of my reviewers interpreted this book as an assault on the UN. It was never meant to be that. In my estimation, and as earlier mentioned, the UN reflects both the best and, sometimes, regrettably, worst, of humanity. It could not be otherwise. To borrow some religious verbiage from my youth, there are clearly "saints and sinners" within the organization. I think it is far more important to focus on the accomplishments of the saints—those who repeatedly risk their lives in pursuit of peace and human rights that are fundamental to the world's best known yet least understood international body. The sinners will always be us, and despite all valiant efforts to curb their self-interested and sometimes nefarious activities. However, I believe we can do better.

The lesson for me is a very old one. The person selected to lead the UN must be of good character and high integrity. Many of my reviewers felt that the SG during the period of my story missed this mark by a wide margin.

Shortly after resigning his senior position with the UN, former Assistant-Secretary General Anthony Banbury on 18 March 2016 published a brilliant commentary in the New York Times entitled, "I Love the U.N., but It Is Failing," Banbury correctly identifies many of the worst characteristics of the organization. In his closing paragraph he speaks for me and many others:

...the United Nations is filled with smart, brave, and selfless people. Unfortunately, far too many lack the moral aptitude and professional abilities to serve. We need a United Nations led by people for whom "doing the right thing" is normal and expected.

I agree! Tragically, such is not currently the case. Banbury hopes that reform measures might transform the UN into an organization capable of hiring, supporting, and promoting persons capable of "doing the right thing." The problem might be culture. Banbury's values are clearly not shared by all. How does one go about transforming the UN when at the most basic human element, values, are not shared?

While conducting research for this book, a former UN staff member sent me a link to the Security in Iraq Accountability Panel Report on a UN website. I noted a troubling change in the title, though. When first released in 2004, the front of the 47-page document included the word "Extracts." For reasons unknown, the critical word "Extracts" has now been removed. The staff member sending me the link wrongly assumed that the report she was reading was the whole document. Why the change? The word "cover-up" popped unbidden into my mind.

A quick and final review of the punishments doled out by the SG follow:

1. The UNSECOORD was directed to submit his resignation. However, he was immediately given a back-channel contract by the Secretariat that permitted him to achieve some additional months of service to maximize his UN retirement pension. He confirmed this fact to me in a telephonic interview conducted in late 2018.

2. The HC was reduced one grade and returned to his parent agency. He was later promoted again to the higher rank and retired with full pay and benefits. I attempted to speak with him several times from 2017 to 2019. He consistently refused all communication on this subject.

3. Although relieved of duty, I was exonerated, later promoted, and went on to retire with full pay and benefits as a UN Chief Security Advisor.

4. The CAO and his assistant were reportedly cleared of any serious wrong-doing, and in large measure due to my testimony.

5. The remainder of the Security Management Team (heads of UN agencies in Iraq) all received letters of censure. Such letters reportedly had little if any impact on their careers.

Who was held accountable? It would be fair, I believe, to call this result a travesty of justice.

What about Sierra Leone? Was the HOM engaged in the illegal blood diamond trade? We will never know. The allegations that I reported to UN Headquarters in New York were never investigated. Did a sub-Saharan African military inflate their force numbers with "ghost soldiers?" Again, we will never know. To my knowledge, they were never independently verified.

However, in fairness to all concerned, it may be important to highlight a possible cultural component of corruption in the sub-Saharan African context as I experienced it. As explained to me by one of my observation post mates when serving with the UN peacekeeping mission in Iraq in 1996-97, "corruption is not corruption." I confess, his assertion required greater explanation. Although he used different words, his explanation as I understood it, and in my verbiage, follows. Life in sub-Saharan is very hard and has been for several millennia. Tribes formed from family groupings for self-protection and as shield against the many vicissitudes of life. First loyalties were then, and are now, in large measure, to self and family, followed closely by village and tribe. If one member of a family becomes successful, then he or she is fully expected to share their bounty with the whole extended family, and perhaps even village and tribal members as well.

It struck me that the nation-state is nowhere in this equation. Note also that the individual's primary sense of worth is derived from the collective--family/village/tribal connection, which is quite different from the American focus on the primacy on the individual. My observation post mate was from the West African country of Ghana.

Further, the nation-state is a Western concept that was imposed on a thoroughly tribal context in colonial sub-Saharan Africa. But tribalism never died. Successful family members are still expected to bring home the bacon to their families. This explanation is perhaps far too simplistic, but I hope adequate to make the necessary point. For many in sub-Saharan Africa, "corruption is not corruption." I am no cultural anthropologist, but my personal observations, as well as some of those of my reviewers, tend to verify the truth of these assertions. The circumstances in Yemen appear similar based in tribal realites.

Please note that skin color (what some people call race) is not a determinant here; culture, on the other hand, might be. Anyone who judges another based on the color of their skin is simply a fool.

It is perhaps necessary to make the point that corruption is hardly unique to the African Continent. Corruption has a long-storied history in the United States and across the globe as well. Individual greed, which is often a key motivating factor in corruption, is a common and very human failing.

As example, the multiple Oscar award-winning movie, The Godfather, had a memorable scene where James Caan in the role of Sonny chides his younger brother after hearing that 30,000 men enlisted to fight the Japanese in the wake of the attack on Pearl Harbor. The younger brother is played by Al Pacino, who states, "...they risk their lives for their country." Sonny replies in a didactic voice, "...They're saps because they risk their lives for strangers..." and "...Your country is not your blood—you remember that." Sonny was paraphrasing his dad, played by Marlon Brando, the Godfather. Sicilian Mafioso culture of that era and previous illuminates. Moreover, and to hammer home the point even further, the Mafia named their criminal organizations "Families."

What of Yemen? The UN seemed to work well in Yemen. Despite the corruption that I identified within the refugee camp the humanitarian aid workers did great work in my opinion. My boss in Sana'a, James, was assiduously honest and forthright. He demonstrated both care and concern for UN staff, as well as the suffering millions in that sad country. In my later experience with the UN, I noted that this appeared to be the global norm.

As always, the first step in correcting a problem, such a corruption, no matter how you define it, is to know of its existence. Once it is identified and in the light, it can be appropriately addressed, as we did in the refugee camp in Yemen over the issue of thousands of excess rations. The solutions are sometimes dangerous, which is why so many senior UN managers tend to let sleeping dogs lie. On the other side of the coin, unscrupulous senior UN staff might perceive the honest and honorable with hostility. For this reason, the best and brightest, the most capable, and those possessing deep reservoirs of integrity could be perceived as menacing.

The UN is a microcosm of the world at large, possessed of both positive and negative attributes. It is the world's greatest human learning laboratory. Hidden from outsiders, though, there is a little discussed and seldom acknowledged values-driven clash of cultures on-going within every day. According to former colleagues of mine still serving in the UN, nothing much in this regard has changed in the ensuing years since the attack.

My friends were concerned that the UN might attempt to retaliate against me when this book is published. Once this work is in print, I am in technical violation of my UN oath. Violating my oath was never my intent. However, like Stuart Groves, who violated his oath as a former member of the Security in Iraq Accountability Panel, "to do the right thing," I feel a responsibility to a higher power too, the truth. I considered publishing the entire Panel Report with this book. However, I ultimately decided against it. That report is still considered "UN Confidential." I extracted and shared only those few passages that were directly relevant to my unfair relief. I have no standing to release to public scrutiny the whole document, despite the powerful human impulse to do so. So at least by my lights, I am attempting to remain true to my UN oath. Which certainly cannot be said of my most senior UN leadership of that time.

For those interested in how the UN has treated whistleblowers in the past, I suggest an examination of the book, *Unsilenced: Unmasking the United Nations Culture of cover-ups, corruption and impunity*, by Rasna Warah. It is a genuine eye-opener.

In the US Army there is an institution called the Inspector General. Although perhaps not a perfect remedy, any soldier may go to the Inspector General to report perceived wrong-doing, particularly when that wrongdoing may involve the soldier's chain of command. In all instances the soldier is protected from potential retaliation. Essentially, this system guards the identity and military careers of whistle blowers. There is no corollary to the Inspector General system within the UN, and there should be. Moreover, such a system must be independent in order to function properly without undue political interference. I am concerned that there are elements of this story that I might have gotten wrong, especially about Iraq. However, since the very senior persons who are knowledgeable of these events refuse to speak, I can only hope my readers will forgive me any resulting errors.

The suicide bombing of the Canal Hotel was an extraordinarily traumatic emotional event for everyone directly concerned. Some of my friends and colleagues felt that this book was long overdue. Others wanted nothing to do with it. A few still blame me, not knowing the whole truth. Several simply did not want to revisit what had been the most gut-wrenchingly horrible day of their lives. For me, I had to write this book, and tell the truth, no matter the consequences.

It is regrettable that I am suggesting bad acts on the part of a dead man who can no longer defend himself. However, I gave the former SG advance notice that I was writing this book and its subject matter a full two years prior to his passing. He chose to remain silent, as have so many others. Following his death, he was much lionized by the media. I am acutely aware that he was a heroic figure to many around the globe. It is clear, though, that he possessed another and far darker side.

The word that keeps coming to my mind is "betrayal." It appears that the UN Secretary General, aided and abetted by others, betrayed their oaths of office; played fast and loose with the lives of staff in Iraq; ignored well established security policy followed by consistent warnings; and then, when the corpses were counted, chose to cover it up by blaming subordinates for their clear negligence. In many jurisdictions around the world such negligence is considered criminal.

The dead and wounded deserve far better, as do their families. Based on long experience, the SG's former subordinates and admirers will prefer to attack me rather than admit to the possibility that he was capable of such perfidy. It is a very sad commentary. Accepting the hard truth is sometimes just too difficult to contemplate.

This story is in great measure about the UN, which is considered necessary by some and unnecessary by others, in the country of my birth. Place me on the "necessary" side of the fence. Although I recognize fully, and perhaps more than most, that the organization is flawed, those imperfections mirror the world at large, and a badly polarized Security Council. For good or ill, the people working in the UN reflect the nearly two hundred countries from which they are drawn. Moreover, and as previously mentioned, the UN is not monolithic, but many organizations under one umbrella. I am a life-long supporter of the UN's humanitarian and development objectives, and peacekeeping if the mission is well-defined, and when the forces selected are up to the challenge.

Unsurprisingly, one of my reviewers commented that I seem to have a "flexible moral compass." Sometimes I complied with UN policy and on other occasions I chose not to. He wanted to know what guided my actions. First and foremost, my job was to preserve life. That was always *the* priority. Second, I worked in a UN that seemed to me, at best, morally ambiguous. Not enough staff members seemed genuinely concerned with the UN Ethics Office mantra of:

> ...promoting an organizational culture based on the shared values of integrity, accountability, transparency and respect.

At least based on my experience, there appeared to be few such "shared values" within the UN. The goal, although laudable, is clearly aspirational. Accordingly, I leaned heavily on my US military training. That meant that I would assiduously avoid engaging in any activity that I considered to be either "illegal or immoral." This was tough on both counts. Illegality differs from country to country. Morality may even be more slippery. Morality is largely a matter of perspective based in culture. However, I was an American soldier for over twenty-five years. I trusted in the moral compass that the culture of US Army provided me. In my estimation, that compass never failed me.

While serving in the US Special Operations Forces, I supported counterterrorism (offensive measures). While serving in the UN, I worked in antiterrorism (defensive measures). While in Baghdad, my wife and I became actual victims of terrorism. This is a trifecta I could have lived without. However, these varied experiences did force me to think more critically about the phenomenon we perhaps erroneously call terrorism.

It strikes me that we are collectively using the wrong word to describe an all-too-human phenomenon. To my way of thinking, terrorism is a tactic used by extremists who embrace either fanatical religious or secular ideologies. Extremism has a blood-soaked modern history involving those who would kill thousands, and in a few cases millions, in the vain attempt to create a perfect society that can exist only in the mind. Humans are incapable of such perfection. The reason why terrorism has so many different definitions is because it is the wrong word that came into common usage. Everyone seems to have a different take on the meaning. The UN alone has identified over 100 wildly differing definitions.

A better descriptor, therefore, may be simply "extremism." Extremism, though, is in my opinion, part and parcel of the human condition. Extremists of various stripes have always been with humankind. If true, this creates a conundrum. For if terrorism is a tactic, and extremism is part of the human condition, then the American Global War on Terror is a conflict that can be fought but never won. How do we define victory over our fanatical enemies when they can never be defeated in the military sense? Yes, we can kill extremists by the many thousands, and have. Tragically, and if my musings reflect reality, there will always be many more waiting in the wings. The word "causality" comes to mind. These troubling thoughts continue to this day. I can't shake them. Could we really be so wrong?

Afterword

The mistake you make… is in thinking one can live in a corrupt society without being corrupt oneself.
—George Orwell

It took nearly three years to complete this work. I spent thousands of dollars and invested many hundreds of hours conducting research in the attempt to ensure that this book is as factually based as possible. It was a conscious choice to select reviewers who were often participants in the events that I have chronicled. I wanted to ensure that their perceptions aligned with my own, particularly when I make assertions that suggest bad acts. Except in those few cases where I was the only other person present as witness, my reviewers have thus far confirmed nearly all my interpretations.

One of the toughest things to do was to accurately capture the moment. When you're working through fear and confusion, this can seem an almost impossible task. Hindsight is sometimes not a reliable marker of veracity. Unconscious bias tends to creep into the text. In every instance, I fought hard to be scrupulously fair, especially to those I characterized within the narrative in negative ways. This story reflects my perspective of these events. There are no doubt others. Only a fool could believe that he has captured the only truth. As example, and in 2019, I contacted the former Force Commander in Sierra Leone, now a retired lieutenant general, for the purposes of this book. I wanted to know if my perceptions of what happened in this war-torn country were, in his estimation, reality based. He responded with, "Your description of the situation in Sierra Leone is quite accurate...". The Force Commander read my book in its entirety and kindly provided a formal book review as well.

This book was written predominantly for an American audience. Hence, distances are described in yards as opposed to meters. The ground floors and first floors of buildings are synonymous, unlike in Europe, where the first floor is the second floor and so on. I ask my international readers, if any, to please forgive me. The metric system seems to be lost on my fellow citizens.

I also wrote this work with academics in mind. There is a gulf between what some describe as the "real world" and those from the realm of Academe, where some scholars may perceive the globe through a tinted lens defined by their no doubt well-intended philosophies—reflecting humanity as they might wish it to be, as opposed to the way we really are. Too often many write about the UN from an idealistic perspective where it can do no wrong. Others write from an ideologically hostile perspective where the organization can do no right. The truth is far more complex and nuanced. Reality is the graveyard of scholarly theories dealing with our kind. It may be that the human equation is far more complex than any of Einstein's theories in Physics. It is my hope that in some small way this work will help bridge that gap. In my estimation, knowledge derived from books represents only the beginning of wisdom. There remains a stark difference between knowing the path and walking the path.

Other potential target audiences for this book, and beyond the general population, are the UN staff, soldiers, intelligence professionals, diplomats, international security officers and advisors, humanitarians, peacekeepers, and perhaps my own

Special Operations brethren as well. There is of course one other critically important group that must be mentioned here: the families of the dead and wounded. This effort is my attempt to answer some of the questions that may have plagued them too.

Unlike purely academic works, this book has no footnotes. The reason why is that the preponderance of my quotes were derived directly from personal records and legal defense documents. These are the same records and documents that were declared "UN Confidential" by the SG along with the Security in Iraq Accountability Report.

Also, my experiences were those of a practitioner. Life in the field is messy and disordered. I did not try to provide answers to all questions raised in this book, nor could I. There is much I simply do not know. This reflects the reality of my years with the UN. Many times, I felt compelled nonetheless to act on insufficient available information. I could not know the minds of the jihadists planning to attack the Canal Hotel. I could not know when the RUF would invade Freetown. I never knew when or where a kidnap victim might be snatched off the streets of Sana'a. But I had to attempt to select and implement mitigation measures against all these threats to UN staff, and much more. I lived in a world best characterized by profound uncertainty.

The UN possesses a dizzying array of acronyms relating to titles, agencies and missions. Readers of my early chapters—friends and family—all screamed that I must somehow simplify these for the reader. I have attempted to do so by limiting the use of acronyms to only those that are often used and essential to the narrative.

I have used capitalization in places where the style manual says I should not. I did so for special reason. In both the US Army and UN we often capitalize formal ranks and unit designations, so it is what I am accustomed to. Also, I capitalized both Somali "Elders" and "Security Cell" because they were extraordinarily important to the story, and I felt that they deserved the honor. Finally, I capitalized the word "Commander." I had the privilege of commanding four times in my military career, twice in Special Forces and twice in Military Intelligence. Command is both an honor and great privilege. Commanders at all levels deserve the respect conferred through the capitalization of this hard-earned title. I just wish that I had done a better job of it.

Early drafts of this book included many of the names of people who worked with me. There were several well-meaning and dedicated individuals. Based on a recommendation from an author whom I trust, several of those names were removed from subsequent drafts. It was my desire to recognize them in a public forum—this book—for the superb work they did. It was pointed out to me, though, that introducing a multitude of characters by name to the reader who were not central to the story line was counterproductive. I therefore removed their names from the narrative but added an "In Recognition" section at the end of this book that identifies each person by name. Please note that I cannot possibly name every deserving individual, but only those whom I knew.

Despite being, for all intents and purposes, twice fired by the organization, I am often asked what was the secret of whatever success I later enjoyed with the UN. The answer beyond the obvious—hard work and dedication—is always the same. The late great Queen of Soul, Aretha Franklin said it best in song, "R-E-S-P-E-C-T." I always attempted to treat my multi-national, multi-ethnic, and multi-religious subordinates, colleagues, and superiors with respect. This was especially true when dealing with the local population anywhere in Africa, the Middle East, and Asia. In fact, and in my experience, everyone everywhere is deserving of the presumption of their own dignity. And if you want respect, first start by giving it. This may be the most important principle of successful cross-cultural communications.

Except for the chapters on Sierra Leone, I chose to remove mentions of nationalities from my earlier drafts. I kept such mention in my chapters on West Africa only because nationality was central to the story. My wife pointed out to me that people everywhere very often have pre-conceived notions of the characteristics of persons—for good or ill—based in their identified country of origin. Sometimes these characterizations are true, and sometimes they are not. I have no wish to perpetuate the latter case.

This book does not pretend to be an academic and detailed examination of the Revolutionary United Front invasion of Freetown, Sierra Leone, that occurred in early May 2000, nor the subsequent hurried evacuation, of which I was largely in charge; kidnappings and gunfights in Sana'a, Yemen; the Canal Hotel suicide bombing in Baghdad, Iraq; or corruption within the UN, although I have spent substantial time writing about these matters. This book is instead one person's story.

I have not written "the whole truth." But I have attempted to write "the essential truth." There are people whom I wish to protect. My belief is that others should not be made to suffer because I feel the need to write and publish. Some others simply wish to remain anonymous. I will respect that desire.

Also, I have been advised by people I trust not to share all my stories. This is good advice. I will only offer the following thought in explanation—those who work repetitively in the borderlands, where there is little in the way of justice, may feel the compulsion to seek out some of their own.

I consciously attempted to avoid turning this book into an exercise in self-aggrandizement, which I understand is an all-too-common failing of many books of this type. Anyone familiar with me knows that I am far from perfect. Where I made mistakes… when I was wrong… I admitted it clearly in the text.

I was never able to convince an agent to represent me. Therefore, none of the Big Five publishing houses would ever consider my work. Therefore, I sent multiple query letters to dozens of smaller publishing companies in the US and abroad. Three reputable businesses eventually responded with offers. Two were commercial entities, and one was academic. After much consideration, I chose the academic house because I felt that they would best maintain the integrity of my book, and they were the only publisher that demanded that my work be peer-reviewed for accuracy.

I am told that first-time authors are great risks to publishing houses because only a very few fledgling scribblers ever actually make money. However, my writing this story was never about the cash. It was instead about bringing the truth to light.

Both before and after my UN retirement in 2014, I was asked by senior colleagues within the UN Department of Safety and Security to make presentations to security officers concerning what happened in Baghdad—before, during, and after the bombing—with a special emphasis on my relief by the SG and my unexpectedly successful defense and ultimate exoneration and reinstatement. It seems that the story still resonates within the community. I made the latest such presentation in 2018 in Beirut, Lebanon.

On a few of these occasions I was asked how I dealt with fear. Those questions compelled me to examine a corner of myself not previously explored. The answer can perhaps be best expressed through a brief story.

When I was a staff sergeant in the 10th Special Forces Group, I volunteered to attend the extraordinarily difficult and demanding Parachute Jump Master Course. The washout rate at this course was over fifty percent. It was a major risk. Nobody enjoys failing. I took this step for a very specific reason: I was terrified of jumping out of airplanes. Every time we went up, I was genuinely afraid that it might be my last. Of course, I never let on. So I placed myself in a position where I could not focus on my fears.

Jump Masters are one hundred percent in charge of all parachutists aboard an aircraft. It is a very great responsibility. By becoming a Jump Master, I compelled my attentions elsewhere. In so doing, I was forced to set my own fear aside. Essentially, I distracted myself by placing a bulls-eye one hundred percent on the well-being of fellow soldiers. While paying close attention to all things related to the safety of parachutists, I had no time to wallow in my personal anxiety about exiting a perfectly serviceable aircraft in flight. This is how I dealt with my fears in the UN context. I focused all my attentions on the safety of others.

I have also been asked often why I chose to remain with the UN after having been treated so shamefully by the organization's most senior leaders. A full answer may be complex, but the short version is that I loved the idea that underpinned the job: to protect the lives of those who seek to assist the most vulnerable of humanity.

The decision not to discuss matters closely surrounding the kidnappings in my book is wholly intentional. Our Scotland Yard instructors in the Hostage Incident Management Course were adamant in training that these matters should never be revealed. If they were to be revealed, such information could someday benefit bad actors.

Please note that I wrote about matters that occurred several years ago. I lived inside these events. That does not mean that my memory is one hundred percent perfect, or that my insider's perspective was the best perch from which to accurately tell the story. In fact, while researching for this book, I discovered that several of my remembrances were faulty. Therefore, I contacted many of my former friends and colleagues from Iraq, Sierra Leone, and Yemen, as well as some senior UN staff members in New York, to attempt greater accuracy.

Some have asked me why I waited so long to write this book. After all, the suicide bombing in Baghdad occurred approximately sixteen years ago. That attack, followed by my relief and ultimate hard-won exoneration, were traumatic both personally and professionally. Frankly, in the immediate aftermath I was physically and emotionally wrung out. These events were followed by some even more personal tragedies that kicked the wind out of me for several years. I could not have contemplated writing this book until well after my UN retirement. In many ways the writing process was therapeutic.

Finally, it may be important to point out that I was unable to answer some of the questions that have haunted me for nearly two decades. The reason is clear. Much of the UN's most senior leadership made a conscious choice to remain silent. Their continuing silence speaks volumes to me. However, and despite all the dead air, in the end, all mistakes, errors, and/or omissions in this book are mine and mine alone.

In Recognition

(Some of those not mentioned by name in the narrative)

The following named individuals performed admirably in sometimes-difficult conditions. I owe each a debt of gratitude. Some others whom I wanted to mention here requested anonymity. Their wishes will be respected.

Sierra Leone

Connor O'Hara-Military Liaison to my office, Vladimir Plecko and David McIver (UNMO)
Deborah Burke (Human Resources Officer)
Phil Harris (Chief of Air Operations)
Miki Kraljevic (Air Operations Officer)

Yemen

Robert Newman, Vic DeWint, Bob Innes, and John Dagostino (US Embassy)

Iraq

Mick Lorentzen, Nicoline Landman, Aliverti Tuimavana, Matt Hollingworth, John Williams, and Robert Kasca (WFP)
Andries Dreyer and Jim Abelee (UNICEF)
Tom Metcalf (IOM)
Heinrich Kolstrup and Kim Bolduc (UNDP)
Nurse Monica (Swedish Rescue Committee)
Leo Powell (SRSG Close Protection Team)
Doctor David Nabarro (WHO)
Major/Doctor Tony Johnson (Naima's military eye surgeon in Baghdad)

Fady El Murr, Jean-Luc Massart, Charles Hock, and Mohammed Haque (UNSECOORD)

New York

Mary Dorman (my paid Manhattan attorney)
Mark Malloch Brown, James Provenzano, and Francois No-
quet (UNDP)
John Ahlstrom, Annette Leijenaar, Alan Brimelow, Leslie
Fair-Page, and Terry Burke (UNSECOORD)

Appendix

Bob's Laws

First

People generally believe what they are taught to believe in their youth. In later life, they tend to embrace whatever is most convenient for them to believe. Essentially, people believe what they wish to believe. Facts hold little sway against often strongly held emotional positions based in those beliefs, which are wholly emotionally satisfying, but often devoid of reason.

Second

Those with the highest-sounding motives have often been responsible for some of the world's greatest human tragedies.

Third

Self-interest, or the individual perception of self-image, which can be in direct opposition to the former, nearly always provides the bedrock rationale for individual decisions and postures.

Fourth

People often develop logical excuses to justify irrational behavior based on their emotions.

Fifth

One's ego is frequently an impediment to learning the truth.

Sixth

Humankind is defined by its mortality and fallibility. The best of us accept that we are short-lived and imperfect vessels striving to be better than the sum of our parts.

Seventh

Doing "the right thing" invariably means doing "the hard thing." This is the true meaning of the word "honor" within a Western cultural context.

Eighth

Hope is the only illusion consistently worthy of embrace. Still, hope is not a replacement for intelligence, hard work, and perseverance.

Ninth

Knowledge becomes wisdom only when it is tempered in the crucible of human experience.

Tenth

In human affairs, consistently good judgment can be found only in the middle ground between cold logic and a keen understanding of emotions.

Eleventh

Absolute honesty is practically a myth. Nearly everyone lies. Discerning why a person lies is the key to discovering the basic goodness or venality of their character.

Twelfth

Reason tempered by kindness is humanity's best chance for a more peaceful future. Fanaticism of any sort is the enemy of reason, and kindness is the antithesis of cruelty and indifference.

Thirteenth

The greatest battle faced by each of us is the struggle to overcome our own internal demons—prejudices and biases. Most of us fail, even if we are aware enough to attempt it. Essentially, this is a life-long effort that is well worth the expenditure in time and effort. The struggle itself makes us better.

Fourteenth

Peace is not the absence of war; it is instead the presence of justice.

Fifteenth

Failure, now and always, remains the best teacher. Why? Because we remember.

Sixteenth

Money may be necessary, but it can never be important. Only people are important.

Seventeenth

Happiness cannot be pursued and captured as many believe. It is far better to seek meaning and purpose in life. If you succeed, contentment, which is far more resilient than happiness, can follow. Be forewarned, though: Attaining meaning always demands sacrifice.

Eighteenth

Never quit!

Nineteenth

LIVE until you die.

Twentieth

There is only one race: The human race. Issues we think we know and understand as "racial" are non sequiturs. Skin color is not now, nor has it ever been, a behavioral determinant, but culture often is. Never confuse the one with the other.

Twenty-First

To truly love another, while permitting them to love you, may provide the most durable form of fulfillment in life.